RACE, CRIME, AND POLICING
IN THE JIM CROW SOUTH

MAKING THE MODERN SOUTH

David Goldfield, *Series Editor*

RACE CRIME
AND
POLICING
IN THE
JIM CROW
SOUTH

African Americans and Law Enforcement in
Birmingham, Memphis, and New Orleans, 1920–1945

BRANDON T. JETT

LOUISIANA STATE UNIVERSITY PRESS

BATON ROUGE

Published by Louisiana State University Press
www.lsupress.org

Designer: Mandy McDonald Scallan
Typeface: Sentinel

A portion of chapter 3 first appeared, in somewhat different form, in *Crime and Punishment in the Jim Crow South,* edited by Amy Louise Wood and Natalie J. Ring (Urbana: University of Illinois Press, 2019).

Library of Congress Cataloging-in-Publication Data

Names: Jett, Brandon T., author.
Title: Race, crime, and policing in the Jim Crow South : African Americans
  and law enforcement in Birmingham, Memphis, and New Orleans, 1920–1945 /
  Brandon T. Jett.
Other titles: Making the modern South.
Description: Baton Rouge : Louisiana State University Press, [2021] |
  Series: Making the modern South | Includes bibliographical references
  and index.
Identifiers: LCCN 2020042743 (print) | LCCN 2020042744 (ebook) | ISBN
  978-0-8071-7507-1 (cloth) | ISBN 978-0-8071-7554-5 (pdf) | ISBN 978-0-8071-7555-2
  (epub)
Subjects: LCSH: African Americans—Southern States—Government
  relations—History—20th century. | Police-community relations—Southern
  States—History—20th century. | Discrimination in law
  enforcement—Southern States—History—20th century. | Law
  enforcement—Southern States—History—20th century. | African
  Americans—Segregation. | Southern States—Race relations—History—20th
  century.
Classification: LCC E185.61 .J467 2021 (print) | LCC E185.61 (ebook) |
  DDC 305.800975/0904—dc23
LC record available at https://lccn.loc.gov/2020042743
LC ebook record available at https://lccn.loc.gov/2020042744

To Dori,

whose support of me and this project never wavered.

CONTENTS

ACKNOWLEDGMENTS

As anyone who has ever written a book knows, it is not an individual process. I am delighted to thank the many people and institutions that contributed to the completion of this project over the course of nearly a decade. I am sincerely appreciative of the support, encouragement, and assistance that you all provided. Thank you all for the multitude of ways you have made my life and this project significantly better.

First and foremost, dozens of archivists and librarians assisted me throughout the research phase. Irene Wainwright and Christina Bryant of the Louisiana Division/City Archives and Special Collections at the New Orleans Public Library, Jim Baggett at the Department of Archives and Manuscripts at the Birmingham Public Library, Vincent Clark of the Shelby County Archives, and G. Wayne Dowdy and Scott Lillard at the Memphis and Shelby County Room at the Memphis Public Library directed me to primary sources, answered questions, and provided professional support in person and via email and phone conversations. The interlibrary loan staffs at the Smathers Library at the University of Florida, Rollins College, and Florida SouthWestern State College fielded requests for obscure articles, books, and newspapers with incredible efficiency.

Many students assisted in the larger research in several ways. Melissa Dunham, Sami Manausa, and Desmond Nichols assisted me in creating a database of thousands of stolen-property cases from New Orleans, and Martez Files found and scanned several grand jury indictment records at the Birmingham Public Library. I am appreciative of their individual efforts to assist in the project and their willingness to help me at critical junctures throughout the research process.

I am indebted to numerous institutions and organizations that provided support for this book. I received funding from multiple organizations throughout the course of my time at the University of Florida. The History Graduate Society and the University Women's Club provided funding that supported my early forays into the archives in Birmingham that fundamentally shaped the larger project. The Department of History and the Graduate School provided substantial monetary support that contributed to an intensive and grueling three-month-long research trip that included stops in Birmingham, Memphis, New Orleans, and Washington, D.C. The Center for Humanities in the Public Sphere at the University of Florida and the Tedder Family Fellowship contributed additional funding and a forum to present my research at an early stage. The College of Arts and Sciences provided me with funding to complete an early stage of this book. Finally, I am incredibly thankful to the William Nelson Cromwell Foundation and the American Society for Legal History for awarding me the Early Career Scholar Fellowship in 2017. The Cromwell Fellowship allowed me to pursue additional research in the archives that ultimately led to the final version of this book.

I was very fortunate to work with some of the most dedicated and patient faculty members at the University of Florida. Elizabeth Dale, Sean Adams, Jack Davis, and Jodi Lane provided great guidance and insight. Steve Noll and Ben Wise served in largely informal, but significant ways in terms of support for my project. They also shaped me as an instructor and, over the span of several years on the basketball court, demonstrated that there is more to being a professor and academic mentor than scholarship. Finally, Jeff Adler did more to shape me as a scholar and my scholarship than any other individual. He read drafts of each and every chapter multiple times, provided timely and insightful feedback, pushed me in new directions, exposed me to larger ideas from a variety of fields, and was patient and kind enough to do so in ways that did not discourage me. I owe him more than I could possibly ever hope to repay, but hope this small token will be a step in that direction.

I owe a debt of gratitude to several friends and colleagues. Johanna Mellis, Greg Mason, Nick Foreman, Alex Tepperman, John Hames, Mike Gennaro, Michael Blum, Dwight Watson, Amy Wood, Melissa Milewski, Hannah Ewing, Ángela Pérez-Villa, Shan-Estelle Brown, Claire Strom, and Leslie Poole read drafts of chapters, conference papers, or the entire manuscript, or just listened to my ideas. Their insight and suggestions introduced me to new ideas, helped me clarify my larger points, and made this book significantly better. Their contributions were multiplied by their constant and continued friendship and support of me in ways far outside this particular project. Whether it be over dinner and drinks, emails, phone calls, or web chats, their friendship helped me maintain balance while working on this project.

I would also like to thank all of the people associated with LSU Press who helped throughout the publication process. Rand Dotson and series editor David Goldfield guided me throughout the progression of this book from the initial contract, to review and revision of the manuscript, to its publication. Their feedback proved critical in the early stages of this work. I would also like to thank the reviewers who took the time to read the manuscript and provided insightful and constructive feedback that sharpened my analysis and improved the book's readability. There were also several people in the editorial and art departments that I never met, but that took time to work with me and did most of the legwork during the final year of the publication process. I appreciate all of your time and effort.

Most importantly, my family's unwavering support over the last decade far surpassed anything I could have hoped for. My parents and brother, although they did not always understand why it took me so long to "finish that paper I was writing," were always there when I needed support and encouragement. More than any other person, though, my wife, Dori, is the reason this project came to fruition. She endured multiple moves to cities she had not heard of before, maintained our apartment and later house when I went on research trips and traveled for conferences, and had more faith and belief in my abilities than I did. I am truly inspired by her commitment, grace, and love. Finally, my daughter, Poppy. While she at times distracted me from sitting down for hours on end to craft the perfect sentence or revise another chapter so we could play tag, ride bikes, or color with markers, she was the reason I pushed myself to finish this book. I hope that this work, in some small way, demonstrates my dedication to supporting her in any and everything she wishes to pursue in the future.

Finally, to you, the reader. Thank you.

RACE, CRIME, AND POLICING
IN THE JIM CROW SOUTH

Introduction

At 2:30 p.m. on Saturday, January 15, 1938, William Glover, a fifty-six-year-old black porter working in Memphis, Tennessee, awoke to the sound of police officers banging on his door. One of the officers informed Glover that the chief of police needed to speak with him, and without further information they placed Glover in their car and drove him to the police station. Once at the station, three officers put Glover in an interrogation room and berated him for allegedly having an affair with a white woman, Miss Duke. Glover roundly denied the accusations, but with each denial the officers only became more vehement. One officer declared, "You remember that nigger George Brooks that was killed, you may join him before the day is over." Police then moved Glover to a cell, where he stayed for several hours. Later in the evening, officers brought Glover to Chief William D. Lee's office, where he interrogated Glover himself. Lee struck Glover several times with his fists, pulled out his blackjack, and, as Glover attempted to protect himself from the blows, said, "Take your God damn black hand down I want to beat your head!" Lee beat his victim so ferociously that he knocked a hole in his forehead. Glover received no medical attention while in custody and was not allowed to contact his family for forty-eight hours. The police held him until Monday morning, when officers took him to the Pullman office and made him resign his job. They then brought him back to the station, where they held him until his wife came and paid the police twenty-five dollars. Officers then took Glover to the train station, where he joined his wife and relatives, and they boarded a train and left Memphis.[1]

Unfortunately, William Glover's treatment at the hands of police was part of a decades-long effort by southern law enforcement to maintain the Jim Crow racial hierarchy through violence and intimidation of African Americans.[2] In his seminal study of the Jim Crow South, Gunnar Myrdal stated, "The Negro's most important public contact is with the policeman.

He is the personification of white authority in the Negro community."[3] Since the publication of Myrdal's study in 1944, scholars of the Jim Crow South and African American history have reiterated this theme, especially the role of southern police officers as enforcers of Jim Crow laws and customs among the black community.[4] In this role, law enforcement officers engaged with African American communities in racially discriminatory, abusive, and often violent ways. How police officers enforced Jim Crow ranged from writing a ticket or arresting an African American for violating segregation ordinances to acting as judge, jury, and executioner when killing black southerners who violated the many social mores and customs of Jim Crow. As historian Leonard N. Moore stated, as African Americans "tested the limits of segregation . . . conflict with police was inevitable."[5] As the case of William Glover demonstrated, African Americans often found themselves at the mercy of brutal police treatment.

Yet, despite the obvious importance of the police to the experience of African Americans in the Jim Crow South, there is a surprising lack of scholarship exploring the development of southern police forces that served such a vital function in southern society.[6] The role of the police officer as the agent of white supremacy in the black community, as described by Myrdal and as experienced by William Glover, was the result of a series of developments that occurred throughout the late nineteenth- and early twentieth-century South. The end of Reconstruction brought about a period of vast economic and demographic change throughout the region, and—although the southern economy remained tied to agriculture and the production of cash crops, such as cotton—extractive industries and manufacturing expanded at a rapid pace. Railroads spread across the former Confederacy, and the region became more interconnected than ever before. Economic expansion and improved transportation ushered in an era of unprecedented urban growth.[7] Southern boosters coined the phrase "New South" to describe these changes, and state politicians and businessmen sought to develop an economy more aligned with that of the industrialized North.[8]

As the economy of the urban South expanded and more job opportunities became available, the southern demographic landscape became more urbanized. By 1950, twenty-five of the one hundred most populous American cities were in the former Confederacy, with a combined population of 5,936,259.[9] The movement and concentration of hundreds of thousands of black and white southerners into urban spaces provided new opportunities in terms of employment, leisure activities, and experiences, but also presented many new challenges to residents and city officials alike. Old, traditional ways of social control seemed inadequate in these growing urban spaces. During the first half of the twentieth century, local officials and the wider public became increasingly focused on problems of crime and violence in southern cities.

Race, Crime, and Policing in the Jim Crow South explores the ways in which southern city officials responded to these demographic and economic changes through a sustained investment in and a significant expansion of the criminal justice apparatus. In the late nineteenth century, formal criminal justice institutions remained relatively weak in the region. Yet, as part of a larger effort to reestablish white supremacy and black subordination in the wake of emancipation, southerners attempted a multipronged approach. Southern states introduced debt peonage and convict leasing during the late nineteenth century as one method of controlling African Americans. These "legal" practices coexisted with such extralegal methods of enforcing black subordination as lynching.[10] Yet, as increasing numbers of black southerners migrated to cities below the Mason-Dixon line beginning in the early twentieth century, and especially during the late 1920s and 1930s, white southerners turned to the formal institutions with greater enthusiasm as informal methods of social control became seemingly ineffective or damaging to the reputation and economic viability of southern cities and towns.[11] In response, formal criminal justice institutions, such as the police, became more robust, violent toward African Americans, and they largely assumed the responsibility of enforcing Jim Crow laws and customs on the swelling urban black populations. Thus, what Myrdal described in 1944 represented the culmination of several decades of work by southern city officials to develop criminal justice institutions as efficient and effective tools in the fight to maintain black subservience in the expanding and increasingly complex urban environments. The growth and modernization of southern police departments occurred largely as a response to the surge in black urban residents and growing fears of black criminality during the 1920s and 1930s.

But this is more than a study of institutional developments or an examination of the role of police officers in maintenance of white supremacy in Jim Crow South. *Race, Crime, and Policing in the Jim Crow South* traces the way African Americans in the urban South responded to the development of police departments between 1920 and 1945. Keenly aware of the racially discriminatory and violent nature of southern police departments, African Americans worked to reform policing in ways that would benefit black communities. In response to attacks on black residents, as in the case of William Glover, African Americans often expressed their disdain with violent policing strategies and seeming lack of interest on the part of law enforcement in crimes committed against them. These criticisms notwithstanding, black residents also voiced a desire for the police to become more involved in their communities. In response to several killings in the late 1920s, an editorial published on April 14, 1928, in the *Louisiana Weekly* articulated many African Americans' views on the relationship between law enforcement, or lack thereof, and crime. "Negroes continue to kill one another and get away with it in this city while the police wink at the crime because only the colored man in involved," the writer stated. The editorialist bemoaned the unwillingness of the local criminal justice institutions to appropriately punish African Americans accused of committing crimes against black residents. The writer concluded, "The good citizens of New Orleans must form a committee to combat the rising menace of lawlessness within our group and seek to have those guilty punished, thereby checking crime and making our homes safer. We have the laws, but need them enforced."[12]

Much of this desire stemmed from the seemingly intractable problem of crime in black neighborhoods. During the Jim Crow era, African American communities often faced much higher rates of crime and violence than white communities experienced. Crime rates are in many ways social constructs and often reflect simply who the police and other law enforcement agencies decide to arrest or prosecute. As a result, higher arrest rates for African Americans for vagrancy or disorderly conduct did not indicate that African Americans were more likely to engage in this kind of behavior, but merely that law enforcement was likely to arrest black citizens for these issues at higher rates.[13] In addition to the criminalizing of certain behaviors and the racially discriminatory way that police officers enforced public safety violations, a variety of institutional barriers, such as inadequate housing, a lack of employment opportunities, and few city services, created conditions that also contributed to high rates of crime in black communities.[14] In response to these issues, black urban dwellers, largely from the black middle class, expressed concerns over criminal activity or delinquency in their communities and believed that law enforcement could play a role in reducing those occurrences. These concerns peaked in the late 1920s and 1930s as a crime panic swept the nation. In response to this panic, black writers and activists repeatedly demanded, among other things, better and more equitable policing in black neighborhoods.

For many black residents in southern cities, law enforcement offered one potential remedy to the problem of crime in black neighborhoods.

Emphasizing the attempts by black residents to reform the police, a force created, funded, and utilized to maintain black subordination, in an effort to try to improve black communities, is only part of the story. In the Jim Crow South, African American demands placed on civic institutions often met with little official response. Lack of political power and the racist zeitgeist of the Jim Crow era almost ensured that encouraging law enforcement officers to do more to combat crime in black neighborhoods or requesting that they make arrests in cases with black victims only went so far. Thus, African American victims and witnesses to criminal activity were forced to work through and at times with racist police departments. Yet, through processes of adaptation and negotiation with law enforcement officers, African Americans capitalized on the growing presence of police in black neighborhoods to promote the interests of those communities.[15] During the late 1920s and 1930s, as Jim Crow police forces modernized and became more focused on controlling swelling black populations, black crime victims and witnesses deployed several strategies designed to manipulate the police into serving their interests by enforcing laws in black neighborhoods. These strategies are not evident in the pages of the black press or in the official pronouncements or publications of black organizations. Instead, they appear in the street-level interactions that occurred between African Americans and the police.

These interactions included moments when individual officers and African Americans engaged each other during investigations of crimes in black neighborhoods. This is largely how the black working class engaged with the police. While middle-class activists and writers often bemoaned the inequitable treatment black communities suffered at the hands of the police and called for improved and equal treatment for African Americans in the criminal justice system, working-class African Americans attempted to extract more equitable treatment through the police differently. Throughout investigations, African American victims and witnesses influenced the way officers conducted their investigations in myriad ways that often increased the likelihood that an arrest would be made. Because of their centrality to police investigations of crimes in black communities, African Americans proved capable of using the police for their own benefit. More so than written critiques or organizational activism, street-level interactions also provide insight into the strategies utilized by working-class African Americans, who did not *primarily* voice their opinions through the black press or in largely middle-class organizations, but instead demonstrated their views through actions that are recorded in police and court records.

The expansion and modernization of southern police departments and the efforts of African Americans to use those forces to ameliorate problems of crime in black communities led to interesting moments of interaction. Take, for instance, the case of George Gordon. On May 30, 1937, forty-eight-year-old Gordon, a black porter, left his job at an auditorium just before midnight and walked down North Main Street in Memphis. He eventually crossed paths with forty-four-year-old black male Sherman Miles, and minutes later Gordon stabbed Miles in the stomach. By 12:45 a.m., witnesses transported Miles to the John Gaston Hospital, where he spent the last hours of his life. Shortly after his arrival, hospital officials called and reported the stabbing to the Memphis Police Department (MPD). Officers Bauer and McReight proceeded to the scene and arrested Gordon at the auditorium, where he sat awaiting their arrival. Following the arrest, police interrogated Gordon, who claimed, "Miles came on him with a knife and that he knocked the knife from his hand and then picked it up and stabbed Miles in the stomach." In addition to Gordon's testimony, at least five other African American witnesses recorded statements with police. Abe Moore insisted that he "was talking with Gordon and that Miles came walking south on Main Street and walked up to them and without a word, Gordon stabbed Miles in the stomach." Other black witnesses, however, informed police that "Miles had been picking at Gordon at the corner of Market and Main just prior to the trouble" and suggested that Gordon stabbed Miles in response to these insults. To supplement the witness testimony, MPD detectives later consulted their own records and discovered that Miles had an extensive rap sheet and "had been arrested several times on charges ranging from assault to murder to vagrancy." Several black witnesses further corroborated this history, and MPD reported that "many people 'colored' have come to the homicide office and report[ed] that Miles never worked and made his living by strong arming both negro men and women of their earnings."[16]

On the surface, this case seems like an anomaly for several reasons. First, the fact that the police made an arrest in a black intraracial crime case is surprising. Throughout the Jim Crow era, black residents faced the dual problem of being both over- and underpoliced: overpoliced in terms of high rates of black arrests for nonviolent offenses such as vagrancy; underpoliced in the sense that law enforcement officers typically showed little concern for crimes involving black victims, including homicide.[17] Second, given the history of law enforcement's use of violence and brutality as a means of maintaining African American subordination, the willingness of black residents to interact with the police throughout the investigation, and even go to police headquarters to make statements, is unexpected.[18]

However, George Gordon's case was also an example of a much larger, decades-long trend regarding the relationship between the police and African Americans in the early twentieth-century South. Nonviolent interactions occurred between African Americans and law enforcement officers with surprising frequency in the Jim Crow era. Between 1920 and 1945, 8,438 African American witnesses to homicides provided testimony to police officers in Birmingham, Memphis, and New Orleans. Due largely to the effort of these witnesses, police arrested suspects in black intraracial cases relatively frequently. From 1920 to 1945, for example, the MPD and the New Orleans Police Department (NOPD) arrested a suspect in 76 and 73 percent of black intraracial homicide cases, respectively. Moreover, the NOPD arrested a suspect in 39 percent of thefts and burglaries committed against African Americans, and only 16 percent of cases with white victims.[19] Thus, police arrests of suspects in black intraracial criminal cases occurred more regularly than previously thought or acknowledged. Benevolence and notions of racial equality were not the impetus for southern police officers to make these arrests. Instead, the clearance rates in black intraracial criminal cases largely resulted from the efforts of African Americans themselves. Well aware of the racial discrimination that shaped the Jim Crow criminal justice system, black crime victims and witnesses took it upon themselves to improve the likelihood that an officer secured an arrest in cases involving African American victims. While scholars have typically focused on African American resistance to police violence and discrimination or argued that African Americans avoided interactions with police, *Race, Crime, and Policing in the Jim Crow South* emphasizes another aspect of African American interactions with law enforcement: cooperation.[20] The modernization and expansion of police departments allowed the police to assume the role of enforcers of Jim Crow. This role led to thousands of instances of violence and abuse of African Americans like William Glover, but also provided a space for African Americans concerned with crime and violence in black communities to attempt to use the police to try to address crime and violence there.

This book explores black communities' reactions to the expansion of police forces and encounters with law enforcement largely in response to black intraracial crime cases (instances where black people victimized other

African Americans). Its focus is in no way meant to downplay the ferocity and significance of interracial crimes and acts of violence (instances where whites victimized African Americans) in black communities. Interracial assaults, killings, rapes, sexual assaults, and thefts, among other crimes, represented an omnipresent threat to black lives and livelihoods throughout the Jim Crow era.[21] These forms of violence and intimidation contributed to the injury and death of black people and the destruction of their communities and also played an important role in maintaining white supremacy and black subordination. I chose to focus on black intraracial cases for two reasons. First, most crimes, regardless of racial community, are intraracial. White people are more likely to victimize other white people, black people are more likely to victimize other black people, and Latinx people are more likely to victimize other Latinx people. In a larger critique of the phrase "black-on-black crime," legal scholar Michelle Alexander has argued that "due to hypersegregation ... crime is inevitably intraracial. Most crime is intraracial. When white people murder someone they typically murder someone of their own race. When they steal, they typically steal from someone of their own race. Because of the segregated nature of our society, the overwhelmingly majority of crime is intraracial."[22] Although she discussed American society in the twenty-first century, her explanation is equally applicable to the Jim Crow era. Segregation, disenfranchisement, lack of employment opportunities, limited access to education, and other structural impediments placed on African Americans by Jim Crow regimes led to higher rates of crime in black communities. Thus, the dataset of intraracial cases was significantly larger than that of interracial cases.[23] Second, by focusing on black intraracial crimes, this book emphasizes black reactions to criminal acts that were not *as* tainted by potential appeals to racial solidarity by the white police officers and detectives investigating the cases. While race certainly affected every interaction between police officers and African Americans, the way in which white police officers investigated a crime committed by a white person against an African American or a crime committed by an African American against a white person would be bound up in larger notions of race in ways that intraracial crimes would not. The emphasis in this book is on how African Americans attempted to use law enforcement to improve their communities and curtail incidents of black intraracial crime. This is done largely for practical reasons and is not meant to detract from the issue of interracial violence and criminal activity that white southerners used against African Americans during the Jim Crow era.[24]

African Americans responded to Jim Crow in many different ways. Some avoided interacting with whites as much as possible; others violently resisted their subordinated status, formed organizations designed to combat white supremacy, and deployed hidden strategies to undermine the racial caste system; while still others accepted the dictates of Jim Crow and worked within the system to improve their lives.[25] In many ways, black interactions with police followed a similar trajectory. Many southern African Americans avoided the police as much as possible because of the potential for violence and abuse. Some responded with hostility, attacked officers, or challenged the authority of law enforcement via black institutions such as the National Association for the Advancement of Colored People (NAACP). As this book illustrates, however, an increasing number of black residents also turned to law enforcement to help ameliorate problems of crime and violence in their neighborhoods. Like all interracial interactions, African Americans relied on signals and rituals that demonstrated to the police, at least on the surface, that they accepted the officers' authority. Notifying law enforcement of a crime and assisting them throughout their investigations represented the two most powerful ways black southerners acknowledged their acceptance of police authority. However, the outward appearance of legitimization often represented a subtle and more subversive strategy designed by African Americans to manipulate law enforcement into serving black interests. By lodging complaints with law enforcement, providing evidence, and identifying suspects, African Americans presented the police with signals indicating their cooperation. In so doing, they also used the police to try and reduce crime in black communities or get stolen property returned. In other words, black victims and witnesses used the police, the institution designed to maintain black subordination, in ways that aided black individuals and their larger communities. This book traces the growth of the police in the South, the role of law enforcement in maintaining control over urban African American populations, the ways black southerners responded to these developments, and most importantly, how African Americans proved capable of shaping their interactions with and exerting influence over the police.[26]

The emphasis on African American interactions with the police demands that *Race, Crime, and Policing in the Jim Crow South* focus on the urban South. Of course, formal law enforcement institutions, particularly the county sheriff, existed in the rural South, but formal civic police departments typically developed in major urban centers. While the focus is on urban centers, the emphasis is on three major southern metropolises: Birmingham,

Alabama; Memphis, Tennessee; and New Orleans, Louisiana. Of course each of these cities is undoubtedly unique, but the similarities between them, and between almost any other southern cities at the time, are more important for the purposes of this book. First, in each city, officials and boosters all embraced the mantra of the "New South" in ways that mirrored the diversification of the southern economy in other twentieth-century cities in the region. Although Memphis suffered serious setbacks throughout the late nineteenth century, most notably the Yellow Fever epidemic of 1878 that decimated the population and caused the city to lose its charter, by the early twentieth century, Memphis had rebounded and emerged as a regional hub of manufacturing and commerce. Throughout most of the nineteenth century, commerce in Memphis had centered on cotton, and this trend continued into the early twentieth century. New businesses developed around the grading, compressing, trading, and storing of cotton produced from the surrounding rural areas of Mississippi, Arkansas, Tennessee, and Louisiana.[27] "Cotton Row" on Front Street became the center of Memphis's economy, and by the twentieth century the city ranked as one of the largest inland cotton markets in the world.[28] Many of Memphis's other economic activities also remained tied to agriculture. Grain merchants and retailers sold a wide variety of agricultural products to the growing urban population or traded them for transport to other regions of the country. Dozens of sawmills, lumberyards, and companies making hardwood flooring, barrels, boxes, building supplies, paper, furniture, and any number of wood products flourished, and the city became one of the largest hardwood-producing cities in the country.[29] The manufacturing sector grew too, albeit more slowly than the agricultural sector. By 1921, 311 manufacturing establishments existed in Memphis, most notably the Ford Motor and Fisher Body plants.[30] The economic success of Memphis was closely linked with the growth of railroads. Memphis's location along the Mississippi River had long made the city a transportation hub, but the introduction of railroads cemented the Tennessee metropolis's role as a major transportation center.[31] By the 1930s, Memphis reigned supreme over the mid-South region and became the focal point of, in the words of historian Michael K. Honey, an "interlocking and resource-based regional economy that to a large measure determined the nature of its industrialization."[32]

Similar trends also occurred in Birmingham, Alabama, but at amplified rates, making it one of the most exaggerated examples of a city that embraced the New South creed.[33] Industrialization and coal mining undergirded much of this growth after developers discovered large deposits of limestone, coal, and iron ore under the hills of central Alabama. Capitalists from the American Northeast and England invested heavily in the area and, along with companies such as the Tennessee Coal, Iron and Railroad Company, the Sloss-Sheffield Steel and Iron Company, the Woodward Iron Company, and the Republic Iron and Steel Company, transformed Birmingham into the "Pittsburgh of the South."[34] By the turn of the century, Birmingham had become a hub of coal production, railroads, manufacturing, real estate, and banking and finance.[35] This astounding level of growth and economic modernization far outpaced that of other southern cities and prompted many people to proclaim Birmingham "the Magic City."[36] Historian Blaine A. Brownell described Birmingham in the 1920s as "the most striking example of urbanization in the South and one of the most impressive in the nation."[37]

But it was New Orleans that ranked as possibly the most important southern city throughout the nineteenth and into the twentieth century.[38] Throughout the antebellum period, New Orleans's importance stemmed from its location near the mouth of the Mississippi River, and the city became a trading hub largely driven by importing foreign goods and exporting cotton to American and European markets. New Orleans also emerged as the largest slave market in the United States, thus becoming the "dominant metropolis of the antebellum South." [39] Between 1830 and 1860, the city's population exploded and due to a flood of European immigrants its population grew by 366 percent.[40] Following the Civil War, however, immigration to the city slowed, and, although the population expanded, it did so at much lower rates than in the antebellum era. During the last half of the nineteenth century, New Orleans fell from the fifth most populous city in the country to the twelfth. Nonetheless, the Crescent City remained an important southern metropolis, and its economy continued to grow.[41] In 1900, it was one of the busiest ports in the country, and city officials invested money in improving the ability of the Louisiana metropolis to remain a center of commerce.[42] Between 1900 and 1920, city officials modernized the port facilities and constructed riverside warehouses, grain elevators, built canals, and added more dock space. Port improvements allowed agriculture-related business to thrive, including cotton oil factories, rice cleaning mills, sugar refineries, and firms serving the molasses and sugar trades. Following World War I, the oil industry came to dominate much of the New Orleans economy.[43]

The second determining factor in the selection of these three cities is that each one experienced massive population growth in the first half of the twentieth century, mirroring the trends in most major southern metropolises (see table).[44] By 1900, Memphis's population had reached 102,320. This represented a 59 percent increase over the population in 1890, and the city became the third most populous urban center in the South.[45] People continued to flood into Memphis over the next thirty years, and the population reached 253,143 by 1930. Birmingham's population grew at even more dramatic rates. The availability of jobs in coal mines and iron foundries produced one of the most impressive rates of population growth of the late nineteenth and early twentieth centuries, and Birmingham grew as fast as or faster than any other city in the South. Between 1880 and 1930, the population exploded from 3,086 to 259,678: an increase of roughly 8,300 percent.[46] While the growth and economic development of cities such as Houston, Atlanta, Birmingham, and Memphis challenged the Crescent City's regional dominance economically, New Orleans still housed more people than any other southern metropolis except St. Louis, Missouri.[47] From 1880 to 1930, the population of New Orleans more than doubled as the city grew from 216,090 to 458,762.[48]

Much of this demographic growth resulted from the movement of African Americans from the countryside to cities. Throughout the late nineteenth and especially in the early twentieth century, millions of rural African Americans migrated to urban areas in the North, South, and West.[49] As with the desires of rural whites, African Americans had several reasons for migrating to urban spaces, but better employment opportunities remained the driving force.[50] The black population in Memphis climbed from 14,896 in 1880 to 96,550 by 1930. The census records did not count Birmingham's black population in 1880, but in 1890 there were 11,254 African Americans residing in the city. By 1930, the city had one of the highest percentage of African Americans in the country, and the black population reached 99,077.[51] In New Orleans, the decline of the city in terms of overall regional importance did not stymie the migration of African Americans to the city. The black population nearly tripled, from 60,937 to 124,783 between 1880 and 1930.[52]

These economic and demographic changes prompted similar reactions from local officials. Their reactions will be documented in detail in the subsequent chapters, but are important here for understanding the logic behind focusing on Birmingham, Memphis, and New Orleans. Local governments in each of these cities embraced racial segregation and Jim Crow laws and customs similar to those of most other southern cities; police departments expanded, incorporated new technologies, emphasized control of African Americans throughout the early twentieth century, and although other southern cities employed African Americans as police officers, these three

Proportion of Black Population to Entire Population in
Three Southern Cities, 1880–1950

	Birmingham Population: Black Population	Memphis Population: Black Population	New Orleans Population: Black Population
1880	3,086 : N/A	33,592 : 14,896	216,090 : 60,937
1890	26,178 : 11,254	64,495 : 28,706	242,039 : 57,605
1900	38,415 : 16,575	102,320 : 49,910	287,104 : 74,072
1910	132,685 : 52,305	131,105 : 52,441	339,075 : 75,952
1920	178,806 : 70,230	162,351 : 61,181	387,219 : 99,128
1930	259,678 : 99,077	253,143 : 96,550	458,762 : 124,783
1940	267,583 : 108,938	292,942 : 121,498	494,537 : 141,932
1950	326,037 : 130,025	396,000 : 147,141	570,445 : 175,126

Source: Historical Census Statistics on Population Total by Race, 1790–1990, and by Hispanic Origin, 1970–1990, for Large Cities and Other Urban Places in the United States, by Campbell Gibson and Kay Jung, U.S. Bureau of the Census, Washington, DC: U.S. Government Printing Office, 1996.

cities did not do so until after World War II.[53] This is significant because *Race, Crime, and Policing in the Jim Crow South* highlights the ways black residents interacted with white police officers, who seemingly had less interest in protecting and serving black communities than black officers would have had. Finally, and most important, the interactions between African Americans and the police were remarkably similar in each of these cities. By emphasizing the core similarities between the cities, this book reveals a wider, regional pattern in the development of police departments and police by depicting African American interactions throughout the South in the Jim Crow era.

A pragmatic factor also makes these three cities ideal for an exploration into African American interactions with the police.[54] Each city is well represented in the Papers of the National Association for the Advancement of Colored People and had an African American newspaper. Most crucial, however, are the more than 21,000 police homicide reports, police offense reports, and grand jury indictment records.[55] These police and court records include demographic information of people involved in homicides, robberies, and assaults, the location of the incidents, the date and time of investigations, and arrests. Perhaps most important, these documents also include lengthy narratives of what occurred and how police investigated the crime. These sources provided data to establish trends in the types of crimes reported to the police by African Americans, the number of arrests made in black intraracial crimes, and how often black witnesses gave statements to the police. Equally important, the qualitative evidence from these sources allows for the words of African American victims, suspects, and witnesses to come through as they explained to law enforcement officers what happened in each case and why they decided to call the police.[56]

While I focus on the urban South, the trends identified are not unique to the region. The question of southern exceptionalism, especially regarding racial practices, has been challenged in recent years by several scholars.[57] Undoubtedly, there were economic, social, and political distinctions between the development of law enforcement institutions in the North and the South. Major northern cities in the mid-nineteenth century adopted professional, uniformed police, organized as quasi-military units meant to prevent crime and disorder. That these shifts in the criminal justice apparatus occurred earliest in northern cities is related to the market and the later industrial revolution, growth of urban spaces, shift to wage labor, and the influx of immigrants that occurred during the nineteenth century. Although southern states relied on slave patrols to monitor and control the behavior of enslaved blacks, most southern cities did not adopt formal police departments until after the Civil War when urban populations expanded more drastically and the economy diversified.[58]

Despite the differences in timing, the changes in southern policing documented in this book mirrored that of cities across the nation. The expansion of the state apparatus, including police forces, and utilization of law enforcement agencies as methods of controlling "others" occurred across the country's urban landscape in the late nineteenth and early twentieth centuries. Even in seemingly more racially progressive cities in the North, officials and police departments adopted more aggressive strategies targeting black communities as the number of African Americans living in those cities exploded during the Great Migration. During this time, many Americans, largely from the urban middle and upper classes, rejected notions of extralegal justice because of the threats to social order and economic development that it entailed (although instances of lynching and rioting did not disappear from the urban landscape). Proponents of law and order or due process encouraged the development of formal institutions of criminal justice, such as police departments, prosecutors, and prisons, to replace informal methods of social control, such as lynching.[59] By the 1920s and 1930s, police practices against African Americans in the North, South, and West were remarkably similar. As police forces modernized, police violence against African Americans became a mainstay of American law enforcement agencies.[60] While the development of police departments and other criminal justice institutions occurred at slightly different times, from Philadelphia, New York, and Boston, to Chicago and Milwaukee, to Los Angeles and Houston, the developments identified in this study reflected a larger change occurring on a national scale.[61]

Across the country, African Americans responded to these institutional developments in similar ways. Black urban dwellers tried to utilize the growing state apparatus to alleviate concerns over criminality and deviance throughout the early twentieth century.[62] However, largely barred from full participation in the political process or at least lacking the political clout to affect it in any substantial way, these black residents often enveloped their demands on city officials and institutions in ways that, on the surface, demonstrated subservience, but, nonetheless, as historian Cheryl D. Hicks argued, articulated their "belief in their entitlement to state services."[63]

The efforts that I document of African Americans acting to utilize law enforcement agencies to help combat crime in black communities focus on the early twentieth century, yet these trends continued well into the twentieth and twenty-first centuries. Black struggles against police brutality remained a priority of activism throughout the postwar era.[64] Efforts to reform policing coincided with demands for an increased law enforcement presence in black neighborhoods and more effective law enforcement responses to crime in black communities. Black residents in New York City and Washington, D.C., implored criminal justice institutions to do something to help combat crime in black neighborhoods, including supporting harsher penalties for drug possession and mandatory prison sentences, from the 1960s through the 1990s.[65] More recently, black residents in Baltimore, Maryland, blamed the lack of effective policing in their neighborhoods for the spike in black homicides that occurred in 2015, and they called for more officers on the ground in the largely black sections of the city.[66] I trace the roots of more recent black demands for better and more equitable law enforcement practices in their communities anchored in concerns over crime and inadequate policing in the early twentieth century. The fact that black Americans' demands on policing remain incredibly consistent over the last century is indicative of just how resistant American police departments have been to the larger, structural changes that would work to reduce instances of violence and racial bias in policing and indeed how resistant other governmental institutions have been to enact policies that would work to actually reduce crime and inequality in black communities.

As the problems between law enforcement and African Americans appear especially strained today, *Race, Crime, and Policing in the Jim Crow South* analyzes the historical trends that contributed to this relationship. Without a doubt, by the late 1920s and 1930s the police had established themselves as the enforcers of white supremacy and racial inequality, and relied on violence and intimidation to monitor and control African Americans. Despite the dangers that police forces posed for African Americans, however, black residents demanded better policing and more law enforcement in their communities as one way to help combat crime. Whether in the pages of the black press, through black organizations, or in the actions of individual black crime victims and witnesses, African Americans demonstrated their willingness to avail themselves of the services that law enforcement was *supposed* to provide. *Race, Crime, and Policing in the Jim Crow South* points to ways that African Americans in the Jim Crow South were critical and suspicious of the police, and of the criminal justice system more broadly, but also to how African Americans developed and deployed strategies to work within and through that same corrupted system in ways that benefited black communities. If the case of William Glover illustrated the vulnerability of African Americans when interacting with the police, the street-level interactions emphasized in this book demonstrate the subtle ways African American crime victims and witnesses used, managed, and even exploited Jim Crow policing.

CHAPTER 1

Crime, Race, and the Development of Police Departments in the Urban South

"The average citizen holds the policeman in contempt or fear or does not consider him at all," stated Jack Carley, a reporter for the *Memphis Commercial-Appeal,* in 1924.[1] In fact, throughout much of the early twentieth century, police departments across the nation dealt with a crisis of legitimacy as urban dwellers viewed them as ineffective, inept, dangerous, and corrupt.[2] In the South, these critiques emerged at the same time that southern civic boosters embraced the mantra of the "New South," promoted economic diversification, and encouraged urban expansion. As more and more people flooded into southern cities, fears about crime, race relations, economic changes, and corruption consistently rose to the fore as city officials championed the benefits of the New South ideology but also struggled to combat the problems that accompanied it. Through the police, these officials attempted to assuage local concerns of problems associated with rapid urban growth. This proved especially difficult in southern cities as many recent migrants from the countryside were traditionally distrustful of formal legal institutions and instead preferred extralegal methods of social control.[3]

To overcome the popular perceptions of police as corrupt and ineffective, the police departments in Memphis, Birmingham, and New Orleans underwent incredible transformations in the first half of the twentieth century. As in so many other cities across the United States, the departments in these three cities began to professionalize.[4] Beginning in some of the country's larger urban centers, such as New York and Chicago, in the late nineteenth century, reformers worked to disassociate police departments from politics, attempted to limit corruption within city government and the police, and pushed for increased efficiency through the centralization and specialization of police forces and integration of technology.[5] By the 1920s, then, many police departments fundamentally differed from their nineteenth-century predecessors. Promoters of the police departments worked to change the popular conception of police as corrupt and ineffective and instead implored citizens to understand "the force and what it represents—safety for your homes and those you love."[6]

Safety for white southerners, however, was largely defined in racialized terms as crime and blackness became interlinked in the minds of urban whites.[7] Southern whites viewed African Americans as inherently violent and criminally inclined, and during the 1920s and 1930s, those fears heightened as more African Americans migrated to urban areas and challenged the Jim Crow racial hierarchy with greater success. A spike in crime in the mid-1920s only exacerbated white concerns over urban African Americans.[8] Extralegal justice proved incapable of assuaging white fears and, as a result, city officials turned to the enhanced criminal justice institutions to control urban African Americans. These officials attempted to instill institutions such as the police with legitimacy in the eyes of the white public. Criminologist Tom R. Tyler argues that police officers gain legitimacy by "acting in ways that will be viewed as fair."[9] In the Jim Crow South, police departments sought legitimacy from white southerners by appealing to their racist instincts and demonstrating their capacity to monitor and control large urban black populations. What appeared as "fair" to white southerners focused on more effective and intrusive policing of urban blacks. Policing strategies incorporated aggressive and abusive treatment of African Americans as officers' crime-fighting strategies largely focused on solidifying the Jim Crow racial hierarchy by enforcing segregation, arresting more black residents, and monitoring and harassing black political and labor organizations.[10]

Crime in the Urban South

As a result of southerners' embrace of the New South ideology, economic diversification across the region, and urbanization, myriad issues confronted city officials and residents in southern cities.[11] While southern urban dwellers grappled with issues related to overcrowding, urban development and expansion, housing, diseases, healthcare, and political corruption, crime and violence proved to be one of the biggest concerns. Gambling, prostitution, and other illicit activities seemingly overran several New South cities. In Memphis, for example, a police report from 1900 declared, "the sale of cocaine has reached such an alarming extent that the department is unable to cope with its ravages."[12] As a river city and transportation hub, Memphis traditionally attracted a transient population that often partook in heavy drinking, gambling, and prostitution near the city's port. Throughout the late nineteenth and early twentieth centuries, this trend continued, prompting one contemporary to claim that the city "attracts numerous conventions and is the mecca of thousands of pleasure-seekers, some harmless and some harmful to the good name and the welfare of the community."[13] Similarly, New Orleans's historic reputation as a city of brothels, saloons, and violence continued into the early twentieth century. In 1907, reformer Carrie Nation described New Orleans as "too tough a place for me to tackle." She concluded, "It is a very, very bad place."[14] Although the legendary bordellos of Storyville were shut down in 1917, prostitution and other illicit activities continued to thrive as part of an underground economy throughout the city.[15] In Birmingham, one commentator noted that in 1920 "hold-ups and other crimes in Birmingham have become so prevalent that people may well ask themselves if it is safe to leave their homes after dark."[16]

Homicide proved a particularly troubling problem, and southern cities routinely ranked among the most homicidal cities in the country.[17] Although northern cities such as New York faced pressures similar to those of cities in the South, the homicide rates remained well below that of southern cities. Scholars suggest this regional distinction grew out of the honor culture of the South, the use of violence in maintaining white supremacy, and the weakness of southern legal institutions.[18] The homicide rate in New York City, for example, remained under 6 per 100,000 throughout the first half of the twentieth century.[19] On the other hand, Birmingham had some of the highest rates of violence in the country, and homicide rates in the city peaked at 89.6 homicides per 100,000 people in 1913. Although the homicide rate fell in the subsequent two decades, by 1930 Birmingham ranked as the fourth most homicidal city in the United States, with 128 total homicides and an overall homicide rate of 52.6 per 100,000. The homicide rate in New Orleans, although lower than in Birmingham, followed similar trends. During the first two decades of the twentieth century, the city's homicide rate hovered between 20 and 25 per 100,000. However, in the early 1920s the rate spiked, and by 1924 reached 32.5. Rates declined in the city throughout the 1930s and 1940s, but, as in Birmingham, remained much higher than the national average.[20] Perhaps more than in any of its southern counterparts, crime and violence in Memphis reached alarming numbers. Despite all the efforts to modernize the city, in the first three decades of the twentieth century it ranked as *the* most homicidal city in the country. From 1882 to 1911, the average homicide rate was 47.1. Over the next five years, the average rate totaled 74.9.[21] By 1923 the homicide rate in Memphis declined a bit, but remained highest in the country at 65 homicides per 100,000 residents.[22] Statistician Frederick Hoffman found that "during the fourteen years ending with 1923, 1,274 persons have died as a result of homicide in the city of Memphis alone."[23] Homicide rates fluctuated throughout the first half of the twentieth century, peaked in the mid-to-late 1920s, then underwent sustained decline through the 1940s. Yet, in any given year, Birmingham, New Orleans, and Memphis consistently ranked among the most homicidal cities in the country.

Although the problems of crime and violence plagued southern cities in general, in the black community the problems were amplified. The economic, political, and social restrictions with which Jim Crow laws and customs saddled African American communities drove the higher rates. Black southerners faced higher rates of poverty than white southerners, they lacked access to many civic and social services, including health care, that were available to whites, and the criminal justice system often ignored black residents' concerns and complaints.[24] In Memphis, Birmingham, and New Orleans, the rates of homicide in the black community outnumbered the rates in the white community by a large margin. In 1922, for example, the homicide rate among the black community in Memphis was 145, compared to 24.5 in the white community. In Birmingham, the rates were 108 for African Americans and 26.7 for whites. Finally, New Orleans's homicide rate was 57.5 in the black community and 9.8 in the white community.[25] The migration of thousands of African Americans into cities such as New Orleans, Birmingham, and Memphis coincided with what seemed to be ever-increasing homicide rates, particularly among black residents.[26] Across the country, blackness became tied to criminality as social scientists, criminologists, and social critics began to use high rates of crime, arrests, and incarceration for African Americans as proof of the inherent criminality of black Americans. As a result, southern whites grew more and more fearful of African Americans.[27] In an article examining violent deaths in Atlanta, Birmingham, New Orleans, and Memphis from 1921 to 1922, authors J. J. Durrett and W. G. Stromquist stated, "It thus appears that our real problem, insofar as homicides are concerned, arises in the killing of negroes by negroes."[28]

Commentators and scholars on crime in the early twentieth century typically described the high rates of violence in the black community in disparaging ways. Discourses of crime and blackness became commonplace beginning in the 1890s as scholars and social critics began using statistics regarding imprisonment rates to discuss crime in racialized ways. As historian Khalil Gibran Muhammad has argued, by the late nineteenth and early twentieth centuries "the statistical rhetoric of the 'Negro criminal' became a proxy for a national discourse on black inferiority."[29] In his seminal work *Race Traits and Characteristics* (1896), statistician Frederick L. Hoffman declared definitively, "Without exception . . . the criminality of the negro exceeds that of any other race of any numerical importance in this country." Moreover, he did not see the problem abating any time soon. Hoffman wrote, that until "the negro learns to respect life, property, and chastity, until he learns to believe in the value of a personal morality operating in his daily life, the criminal tendencies . . . will increase." He concluded, "the race as a whole has gone backwards rather than forwards."[30] These sentiments continued throughout the twentieth century and were echoed across the South, especially in cities. In the 1920s, legal scholars Andrew A. Bruce and Thomas S. Fitzgerald declared that "crime among the colored population [in Memphis] is fairly rampant and the race shows a high degree of criminality." The causes, according to Bruce and Fitzgerald, were African Americans' "shiftlessness, lack of industry and thrift, and the poor and sordid, and oftentimes vicious, nature of their surroundings."[31] In fact, African American criminality was beyond the control of criminal justice institutions. The study concluded, "the most effective police system in the world could not prevent the murders which are committed in the heat of sudden passion and fury among the negro population."[32] Proclamations such as these painted African Americans as impulsive, emotionally unstable, and inherently criminal—decidedly placing them outside the mainstream culture of white upper and middle classes.

Across the South, city officials enacted segregation laws in an effort to protect white communities from the influx of black—supposedly criminally minded—migrants.[33] These laws, officials suggested, solved the problem of large numbers of transient and unknown black men and women by maintaining the racial caste system of the South and providing rules and customs that managed interracial interactions. Beginning largely in the 1890s, states such as Louisiana passed bills requiring segregated rail cars, and the U.S. Supreme Court upheld the legality of segregated facilities in the *Plessy v. Ferguson* decision in 1896. A cavalcade of segregation laws followed as southern states mandated segregated housing, schools, public transportation, and employment.[34] City and state legislatures further divided the races by enacting miscegenation laws prohibiting interracial marriage and by curbing African Americans' right to vote.[35] These laws, in addition to voting restrictions, ensured the political, economic, and social subordination of the black population.[36] Many white southerners championed segregation as a panacea for crime and violence, as captured by Mayor George B. Ward's 1906 annual message to Birmingham when he stated that segregation "has done more to prevent thievery, debauchery and murder; more to prevent insidious temptation; more to reduce licentiousness, incipient and chronic, than can ever be known by the public or the authorities."[37] In their study of crime in Memphis, Bruce and Fitzgerald concluded, "Segregation is the policy and, perhaps, the only possible policy" that could adequately address the problems facing the city.[38]

In addition to the legal aspects of Jim Crow, many southerners relied on "rough justice" to control the behavior of African Americans.[39] As historian Michael J. Pfeifer argued, rough justice supporters "demanded the harsh, personal, informal, and communally supervised punishment of what was perceived as serious criminal behavior."[40] Rough justice centered on communal and at times ritualistic punishment for crimes that was often performed by members of the community, such as lynchings. While most lynchings occurred outside of the major southern cities, at times lynch mobs arose in urban spaces.[41] One of the most infamous lynchings in a major southern city in the first decades of the twentieth century occurred in Memphis in 1917, when a mob of several thousand whites lynched Ell Persons for the alleged rape and murder of a sixteen-year-old white woman named Antionette Rappel. On May 22, a mob tied Persons to a stake, doused him in ten gallons of gasoline, and burned him alive. Later in the day, a group of white Memphians threw Persons's head from a car onto Beale Avenue, in the heart of Memphis's black community, to intimidate the city's black population.[42] Although lynching was a rare and certainly declining occurrence throughout the early twentieth century, white southerners utilized it and lesser forms of extralegal social control to maintain black subordination.[43]

Rough justice resonated with many southerners, but instances of extralegal violence like the Persons lynching threatened the progressive images many city officials and middle-class boosters sought to cultivate.[44] In a resolution published in the *Memphis Commercial-Appeal,* several local clergymen decried the Persons lynching. The resolution stated, "It should be brought home also to the consciences of other representatives, men and leaders of this community, that they, too, had failed to do their duty: that it appears also that the constituted servants of the law had failed, by subservience to the will of the mob." The writer further lamented the apparent inadequacy of local authorities to uphold the law and prevent lynching, especially law enforcement's "inadequate preparations to resist their anarchic designs, to take the proper measures to defend the dignity and majesty of the law and or civilization."[45] In other words, middle-class city boosters believed that strong law enforcement would preclude the willingness of white residents to resort to extralegal violence and help promote Memphis as a stable place for economic development.

While lynchings continued throughout the first five decades of the twentieth century, the Persons lynching proved to be the last recorded one in Memphis, New Orleans, or Birmingham. For the most part, officials and boosters across the South promoted the tenets of due process and the rule of law as a preferred alternative to rough justice.[46] As southern cities grew and economic bases diversified, middle- and upper-class whites eschewed chaos, such as widespread crime and violence, which threatened social order and stability and which could curtail the flow of capital.[47] Concerns with order and economic stability pushed many middle- and upper-class southerners to support the development of stronger police forces in southern cities.[48] An editorial responding to the Persons lynching stated, "We are face to face with the old question of whether society disorganized can better accomplish results than the organized forces of law." The writer continued, "When a sheriff, constable or policeman, or any other officer sworn to uphold the law is engaged in the discharge of his sworn duty he should be supported."[49] The belief that justice, social control, and punishment needed to be removed from the hands of the community and entrusted to formal criminal justice institutions—police, prosecutors, and prisons—prompted city and state officials to invest in those institutions.[50] While many rural migrants viewed formal institutions of criminal justice with suspicion and urban dwellers across the nation viewed the criminal justice system as inept, southern city officials worked to promote the legitimacy of institutions such as the police.[51]

The Development of Police Departments in the Early Twentieth-Century South

To combat crime and extralegal justice, early twentieth-century city officials worked to enhance their respective police departments.[52] Criminal justice historian Samuel Walker defined nineteenth-century policing as "a form of casual labor, not a lifelong career."[53] Officers had little to no training and typically gained employment as a result of their political affiliations. Departments ran rife with corruption and lacked the respect of many residents. City officials and police departments began to confront these problems and embraced the idea of "professionalization" in policing. The professionalization movement of the early twentieth century represented a drastic change in policing away from its nineteenth-century antecedents. Police professionalization lacked a clear definition, but it stressed several ideas: restructuring police departments to make them more efficient, depoliticizing the police, and giving police a role in promoting social reform. Over time, the social reform goals of police professionalization, which focused on the rehabilitation of offenders and the prevention of crime, faded, and city officials worked instead to limit the amount of political influence over the operation of police departments and stressed structural changes that centralized police authority within the department. By embracing professionalization, police departments across the country attempted to cement their legitimacy as effective crime fighters. Although problems with crime and violence persisted, most police departments worked to make their forces more professional and more effective in at least some ways well into the 1930s.[54]

In the first two decades of the twentieth century, southern police forces often seemed incapable of maintaining control over the urban black population. The most infamous example of the inability of the police to maintain order, particularly black subservience and subordination, occurred in New Orleans in 1900. Around 11:00 p.m. on July 23, 1900, Robert Charles, a black man living in New Orleans, refused to placate two white police officers, who, without provocation, attempted to arrest him. The altercation began when Charles and a friend named Lenard Pierce sat on the steps leading to the front door at 2815 Dryades, waiting to meet two women named Virginia Banks and Ernestine Goldstein. While making his nightly rounds in the neighborhood, NOPD Sergeant Jules C. Aucoin noticed Charles and Pierce sitting in front of the white residence, and together with Patrolmen Joseph D. Cantrelle and August T. Mora, approached the black men. When the officers asked them several questions, Charles and Pierce did not answer in a way that satisfied the police officers. As Charles stood up, Officer Mora grabbed him, a minor scuffle ensued, and shots were fired. It is unclear who fired first, Mora or Charles, but one of the officers' bullets struck Charles, who fled, and one of Charles's bullets struck an officer. According to historian William Ivy Hair, "At this seemingly trivial encounter, commenced one of the bloodiest, most anarchic weeks in New Orleans' history."[55] Over the next several days, Charles hid in various locations, evaded arrest, and shot twenty-seven whites, including seven policemen, before being killed while barricaded in a house at 1208 Saratoga Street. The inability of the NOPD to maintain control over Charles initially, his successful evasion of police for several days, and the seeming chaos that engulfed New Orleans as a result personified the larger white public's lack of faith in the early twentieth-century police departments.[56]

City officials across the South bemoaned the seeming ineptitude of their police departments at that time. Birmingham's mayor, George B. Ward, captured the feeling of many southern city officials when he declared in the city's 1906 annual report, "This department needs a drastic reorganization, and then more discipline." He continued, "It needs such a weeding out of 'undesirables,' that the change in its personnel will give an average so high, both in efficiency and in looks, that the conscientious officers we now have will be saved from the criticisms caused by the work and habits of others."[57] In Birmingham, Memphis, and New Orleans, prostitution, gambling, and other illicit activities operated with seeming impunity because of the close relationship between police and criminal bosses in the underworld. As other metropolises across the country did in the early 1900s, municipal officials in these cities sought to make their police forces more professional and enacted several structural changes.

In response to myriad critiques, officials pushed to reform urban police as part of the larger changes to government during the Progressive Era. From roughly 1900 to 1920, Progressive Era reformers sought to ameliorate many of the problems associated with industrialization and urbanization by, according to historian Robert H. Wiebe, creating local, state, and federal bureaucracies of "trained, professional servants [to] staff a government broadly and continuously involved in society's operations."[58] They promoted new regulatory agencies, expanded government services, and introduced the commission style of local government. Through bureaucracies of trained professionals, reformers sought to curb corruption and promote efficiency in government. These same tenets guided some of the main proponents of police professionalization, who stressed improved education and training, centralized and specialized organizational structures, and the integration of technology into policing in an effort to make policing more efficient.[59]

As cities grew and crime seemingly spiraled out of control, police departments transformed as well. In 1900, the MPD's annual budget was $100,000, and the force consisted of eighty-five men.[60] By 1907, the budget expanded to $149,886, and the department consisted of a chief of police, a chief of detectives, three captains, fourteen detectives, eight sergeants, and 102 patrolmen.[61] In 1911, MPD added a new substation in Barksdale with fifteen mounted patrolmen, and two sergeants (see chart).[62] The department continued to grow throughout the 1920s and even during the Great Depression. By 1935, the police department included a 201-man force, complete with a chief, two inspectors, two deputy inspectors, three captains, two lieutenants, ten sergeants, twenty-nine detectives, and 137 patrolmen.[63] NOPD underwent similar expansion. In 1900, the police force consisted of 325 men and twelve total precincts.[64] When John Journee became superintendent in 1901, he stressed the fact that NOPD did not have enough manpower to police a city the size of New Orleans and he pushed for more officers. City officials seemed to agree and throughout the 1910s the force continued to grow, such that by 1915 NOPD totaled 520 people.[65] By 1933, the city's police force had grown to 817, including thirty-nine clerical workers, seven radiomen, and nine telephone operators.[66] While information on BPD for the early twen-

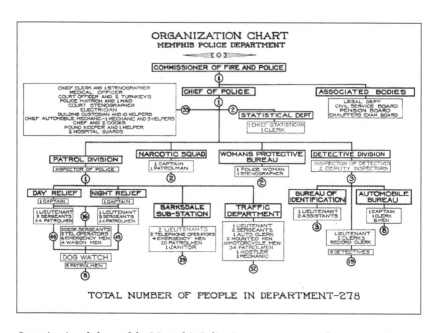

Organizational chart of the Memphis Police Department, 1924, from *Memphis Police Department Year Book for 1924* (Memphis, TN: Memphis Police Relief Association, 1924), 13. Image provided courtesy of the Memphis and Shelby County Room, Memphis Public Library.

tieth century is sparse, by 1921 BPD consisted of 167 men and by 1935 it had expanded somewhat to 231 people, including 165 working as patrolmen.[67]

As departments grew in size, they embraced structural changes to promote efficiency and specialization.[68] The structure of the MPD is representative of the alterations most departments in the United States underwent in the early twentieth century.[69] The most drastic organizational transformations to the Memphis Police Department occurred in the 1910s and 1920s. Beginning on January 1, 1910, the city changed to a commission style of government, and the police department embraced the principles of efficient management with clear lines of authority and specialized units each devoted to different aspects of policing. The organizational chart for the MPD reproduced here provides a general understanding of what these new organizational structures looked like. A commissioner of fire and police oversaw the entire operation of public safety, while the chief of police managed the police department. Beneath the chief, the MPD force consisted of a series of specialized units, ranging from basic patrol units, to narcotics and detective squads, to a women's protective bureau. Within those specialized units, the officers were organized into even more specialized subunits, all with clear lines of authority leading up to the commissioner. By embracing these types of organizational reforms, city officials tried to promote a business-like efficiency while also allowing the development of specialized officers within the department.

Despite the growth in manpower of each department and increased visibility, these police forces remained consistently undermanned as the populations grew at astounding rates. In New Orleans, for example, Police Superintendent John Journee despaired that in 1901, "only 325 men were responsible for maintenance of law and order in a city of 300,000 persons, spread out over 194¼ square miles."[70] BPD Chief of Police lamented in 1924 that his police force remained "admittedly undermanned."[71] These types of critiques continued across the region as cities grew faster than their police forces. In 1935, Dr. Carleton Simon, a criminologist of the International Association of Chiefs of Police, stated in a report compiled for BPD that "to render the service necessary in the protection of your community, with nine railroads entering your city, numerous express companies and numerous banks which depend on your department for protection, you should have at least 600 patrolmen as a minimum for a city of this size."[72] The population of cities grew at rates that far outpaced police personnel, and critics often linked the lack of personnel with the lack of police effectiveness.

To make up for a lack of personnel on the ground, police departments invested heavily in technological improvements.[73] One of the most visible changes came as southern police departments increasingly integrated automobiles. City officials and police believed automobiles "represented the new age" and would make policing urban areas more efficient, and by the 1920s they became essential for modern police departments.[74] The implementation of automobiles in Memphis occurred over several decades. In 1910, the department purchased the first two automobiles, one as an ambulance and the other as a patrol wagon.[75] The biggest advance came in 1915 when the department introduced the emergency car system. This system consisted of six officers and "operated out of headquarters, where they waited with the car parked at the rear of the station. When the telephone operator received an emergency call, he contacted the captain and advised him of the nature of the crime and the address. He then rang a gong and the two emergency patrolmen responded and were on their way in a matter of seconds."[76] The use of automobiles by police departments therefore allowed officers to respond to complaints more quickly and helped make up for the lack of manpower. In August 1921, for instance, MPD purchased a black four-door, eight-passenger Packard, complete with a folding top, running boards, and electrical sirens on both the running boards and the windshield. The car could seat eight officers, but perhaps most important, it came with a bulletproof steel windshield to protect officers.[77] The introduction of cars increased the visibility of police in quickly expanded urban areas.[78] Automobiles also allowed police departments to make up for their lack of personnel by making it possible for officers to move throughout the cities quickly.

The NOPD also incorporated automobiles in its force in the early 1910s. In New Orleans, "mechanization began" between 1911 and 1914 under Inspector James W. Reynolds. The department purchased two automobiles and four motorcycles to assist with patrolling the city. By 1922, the department drastically increased the number of automobiles in operation to thirty-three total cars and twenty-one motorcycles. Four years later, with the introduction of five armored motorcycles capable of speeds up to 100 miles per hour, the department boasted that the new vehicles "would be used in 'striking relentless blows' against a wave of 'petty hold-ups and burglaries in the outlying precincts.'" Automobiles proved so effective in the city that by 1936 the mounted division (which consisted of officers mounted on horseback) nearly ceased to exist.[79]

While it is unclear when BPD first introduced automobiles for its force, the department recognized their importance and by the 1930s had fully incorporated cars into its policing strategies. In a jovial article tracing the career of Patrolman Jim Ellard, the *Birmingham News* reported, "The final touch towards modernizing Birmingham's Police Department has been achieved—Jim Ellard, a veteran patrol driver in the days of two horsepower patrol wagons has now learned to drive a 75 horsepower call car." Ellard, who joined the force in 1908, began his career by manning the horse-drawn patrol wagon for the department. "As the horse drawn patrol became passé in Birmingham," Ellard worked the telephones and accompanied other officers as they went out on calls. He did not learn to operate an automobile until 1929, when the ability to drive a car proved essential to policing in the city. According to the *Birmingham News,* "Within the past two weeks Jim has been sitting under the wheel of the fast touring car that is used by the call officers to speed to the scene of bank robberies, drunken brawls and the thousand and one places the 'call officers' are asked to go."[80] Between the years Ellard joined the force in 1908 and when he finally learned to drive in 1929, the automobile and policing became inextricably linked as patrol vehicles embodied the "visible manifestation of the police."[81] With the incorporation of automobiles into regular policing practices, departments appeared more modern, efficient, and more capable of combatting crime in southern metropolises.[82]

The implementation of advanced communication devices allowed the police to respond to problems more quickly and helped police chiefs and other officials monitor the activities of officers on their beat. The NOPD used eleven phone boxes scattered throughout the city by 1900 and also relied on telephones in homes and businesses to request assistance.[83] While it is unclear exactly when BPD introduced telephones, by 1907 the department spent $1,200 a year to rent the phone system.[84] The most complete description of a telephone system is found in Memphis. In the early 1900s, city officials installed the Gamewell Police Telephone System, which consisted of eighteen receivers or "signal boxes" on the streets for patrolmen to contact police headquarters. In addition to these eighteen signal boxes, there were another thirty-seven telephones located in public buildings and private businesses that were made available to MPD officers. According to one historian of the MPD, "officers were required to find a call box or business telephone and contact the station once every hour."[85] By 1907 the city had expanded the system to forty units because it proved so effective.[86] Police departments relied on telephones to regulate officers, report crimes, and respond to problems throughout their growing cities with greater speed.

Radio systems, however, soon eclipsed telephone systems. In 1928, MPD's chief, William D. Lee, attended a convention in Atlanta for police chiefs. While there, Chief Lee heard the commissioner of Detroit talk about the effectiveness of radios in police cars. Lee was intrigued and added an additional $12,500 to the next year's budget to offset the costs of buying new radios for police cars. The Delco receivers cost around $144 per unit, and the department originally equipped twelve cars with radios. Radio-equipped cars began patrolling on July 29, 1931, and, according to one history of the MPD, "put every citizen just a telephone call away from the police."[87] They proved so effective that by 1934 the department had installed several police motorcycles with radios as well. On December 25, 1932, the *Memphis Commercial-Appeal* declared, "Only a few seconds or minutes are required for [an officer] to answer your call for protection. The police radio is responsible."[88] The most important advance in radio technology in Memphis arrived in 1937 when the MPD installed two-way radios in patrol cars and built a 225-foot radio tower to foster better communication between cars and headquarters.[89] NOPD began constructing a radio transmitter in 1931, and it became operational in 1932. The transmitter was located at the Detective's Office, and several patrol cars had receivers in them. According to the department, "the system proved so effective in that it eliminated minutes and considerable time in having at least one automobile proceed to the scene of a serious offense."[90] City officials in Birmingham called for a radio system as early as 1932. According to one news report, "A modern police radio system may be installed here to rid Birmingham of the stigma it carries as one of the most criminally inclined cities in the world and at the same time bring about a reduction in the cost of operating the police department."[91] Birmingham implemented its radio system by 1933, and just five years later the chief of police declared the radio system "crime's greatest enemy" because "the results obtained by the service have been so marked that the city's comparatively small police force has been enabled to accomplish much in the way of law enforcement that otherwise would have been impossible."[92]

By introducing new technologies, police departments tried to increase their presence in the growing urban environs and make policing more discernable and efficient.[93] Distinctive uniforms and automobiles made officers and detectives easily identifiable and provided a distinguishability in the city that their nineteenth-century predecessors had lacked. Improved visibility also signified a shift toward the notion of preventative policing in an effort to curtail crime in urban areas.[94] Instead of criminals being apprehended after they committed a crime, supporters of preventive policing believed, making police more discernable throughout the city would mean that criminals would be less inclined to commit crimes. As we've seen, police departments also incorporated automobiles, telephones, and radios, which allowed the police to move and communicate throughout the city at incredible speeds. Those departments that integrated these technologies hoped that quicker response times to calls would increase the likelihood of an arrest and help curtail criminal activity. By improving their visibility and decreasing response time, departments *hoped* technology would improve their ability to monitor the massive urban populations.

Technology changed policing in very obvious ways, though enhanced training focused on refining the ability of individual officers to solve crimes and track down criminals.[95] The BPD introduced an officer training school on November 13, 1928, when the first class of twenty-eight recruits entered the program. New recruits were paired with older officers for field instruction and attended ten weeks of daily classroom sessions for an hour each day. In addition to new recruits, all existing members of the BPD attended fifty hours of training. The courses ranged from "Criminal Law and Procedure," "Rules and Regulations of the Department," and "First Aid to the Injured," to "Marksmanship." In all, city officials hoped the school would "initiate and prepare for efficiency new men who [were] being constantly added to the force."[96]

In perhaps the most impressive example of these training programs, in 1937 the MPD opened its "crime detection school," with the intention of making detectives and police officers "super sleuths."[97] This school inculcated MPD officers and detectives in the "scientific methods of crime detection evolved by J. Edgar Hoover," focusing on "how to deal with burglary, housebreaking and larceny, the use of the pistol and homicide detection."[98] MPD also showcased its new technologies in the newspapers, during parades, and on at least one occasion, at a local theater.[99] City officials ferreted out some corrupt cops and publicized the accomplishments of officers as part of their larger effort to regain public trust.[100] Despite their efforts, however, these officials never completely eradicated corruption and inefficiency within their departments.[101]

Despite these professionalization efforts that many southern police departments engaged in, sensationalized news reports of murders, a spike in crime in the mid-1920s, and a continued concern with crime and violence throughout the 1930s and 1940s prompted police departments to go even further.[102] When Prohibition became the law of the land in 1920, organized criminal enterprises spanning several major urban areas capitalized on the demand for alcohol and the illicit sale and distribution of liquor made the exploits of criminals, such as Al Capone, incredibly visible.[103] Historian Robert Lane stated that salacious media reports of murders, such as the Leopold and Loeb killing in 1924, unsettled many Americans, who felt "fearful and embarrassed about murderous violence and what it seemed to imply about 'the national character.'"[104] High-profile criminals and murders coincided with a surge in robberies and robbery-homicides in the mid-1920s that further terrified city dwellers.[105] Americans in the 1920s and 1930s, argued historian Jeffrey S. Adler, grew fearful of "a new breed of criminal that seemed more calculating and more predatory, as holdup men and bank robbers, armed with Thompson submachine guns and fast getaway cars, invaded business districts, targeted respectable citizens, and evaded law enforcers."[106] While structural changes, increased visibility, new technologies, and better training were all part-and-parcel of the goals of professionalization, by the mid-1920s these reforms seemed inadequate to the challenges police departments faced. As a result, departments became much more militarized in their fight against crime. Even when the crime wave of the mid-1920s subsided, the crime panic continued, and city officials across the country launched a "war on crime" that spanned the 1930s.[107] As part of the "war" effort, police adopted more aggressive tactics and "reinvent[ed] themselves as crime fighters."[108]

Nationwide, police departments described their policing tactics in militaristic terms, often painting themselves as defenders of the public at large in a war against crime.[109] In 1928, a report published by the American Institute of Criminal Law and Criminology congratulated the MPD for its "warfare against dope selling."[110] Memphis police periodically engaged in raids aimed at ferreting out various forms of vice. On June 17, 1935, for example, the *Memphis Press-Scimitar* touted that "police raiding squads are harassing bootleggers, gamblers and prostitutes and vice has retreated to the shadows of the underworld."[111] These raids typically made headlines and demonstrated to the public that the police could be effective in their fight against crime and vice.[112] Again in 1942, Memphis officials declared a "war on prostitution" to thwart "prostitutes reported drifting toward Memphis from 27 Middle Tennessee Counties."[113] Officials even framed efforts to combat nonviolent and non-morals-related issues in militaristic terms. In an attempt to regain the title of the "Nation's Safest City," in terms of traffic accidents, "the entire Memphis Police Department, led by a large staff of well trained, seasoned traffic officers, girded itself yesterday for the fight which they hope will regain Memphis its title."[114]

The militarization of the police was about more than terminology. While police had utilized guns since the mid-nineteenth century, departments across the country incorporated advanced weapons in their arsenals.[115] Throughout the late 1920s and 1930s, these weapons seemed more appropriate for a battlefield than for a city in the United States. The NOPD introduced tear gas, which was "successfully tested in the first World War."[116] By the 1940s, the MPD possessed dozens of submachine guns, gas masks, and high-explosive grenades.[117] As police weaponry became more advanced, officers' tactics also became more aggressive. On January 14, 1938, the *Birmingham News* reported that the BPD had issued a "shoot to kill" order against "breakers of windows." Police Commissioner Eugene "Bull" Connor and Police Chief T. A. Riley issued "orders to 'shoot to kill' anyone found perpetrating this particular act of vandalism."[118] Throughout the interwar period, police became heavily armed and aggressive crime fighters as a result of military-grade weapons and military-style tactics. By publicizing the use of new weapons and tactics, police departments suggested to the populace that officers would utilize them to combat crime and maintain law and order in their respective cities.

Race and Policing in the Urban South

By the late 1920s and 1930s, maintaining law and order in the Jim Crow South largely aimed at controlling the swelling urban black populations in order to assuage white perceptions of black criminality.[119] Enforcement of segregation laws remained part of the police officers' duties, but from the late 1920s to the 1940s, police monitoring and patrolling of the black community became more vehement as white urban dwellers came to rely on the police to protect them from African Americans. By targeting African Americans, police in southern cities demonstrated their commitment to white supremacy and crime fighting at little political cost, as most nonwhites in southern cities remained disenfranchised.[120] The connections between blackness and crime compounded with new challenges to white supremacy produced a more aggressive policing that targeted the black community as part of a larger effort to calm white fears regarding potential breaches to the Jim Crow racial caste system.[121] Although crime and violence fell precipitously during the 1930s, white southerners' concerns over crime, especially those committed by African Americans, did not abate. In fact, police and other law enforcement agencies arrested more African Americans during the 1930s and simultaneously cracked down on any perceived challenges to white supremacy.[122]

Following the end of World War I, African Americans' renewed fight against white supremacy frightened many white southerners. The "New Negro" of the 1920s demanded full inclusion into American society.[123] In New Orleans, a brief article in the *Louisiana Weekly* summed up the feeling among black southerners. The writer excoriated African Americans who acquiesced to Jim Crow laws and customs and championed those African Americans who defied their subordinate status. Black Americans, the writer stated, "want good homes, clothes, education, jobs, businesses and all the other things their hard-earned cash enable them to buy. These same Negroes have enough courage, manhood and bravery to fight in defense of their homes and ideals. This is a sign that the Negro is rising." The author finally urged black New Orleanians to do the same, claiming, "examples of militant, ambitious and progressive Negroes have recently appeared in Kansas City, New York City, Washington, Chicago, Detroit, and Cleveland. Where next?"[124] Many black southerners embraced this New Negro mentality, and their demands for full inclusion into American society, politics, and economy frightened many white southerners.

White fears over the New Negro combined with legal breaches in the Jim Crow racial hierarchy. African American organizations, especially the NAACP, challenged segregation statutes in the Supreme Court throughout the 1920s, 1930s, and 1940s, with increasing success.[125] In 1927, for example, the U.S. Supreme Court overturned New Orleans's race-based residential zoning law in *Harmon v. Tyler*.[126] In 1935, the Supreme Court further challenged the tenets of white supremacy when it declared all-white juries unconstitutional in two cases, *Patterson v. Alabama* and *Norris v. Alabama*.[127] The federal government also pressured city governments to expand New Deal relief efforts to include African Americans. Southern whites viewed these challenges to white supremacy as an attack on the very foundations of Jim Crow social structures. In 1935, New Orleans's District Attorney Eugene Stanley declared, "At no time in the history of our State has White Supremacy been in greater danger."[128] The collapse of some of the formal and legal mechanisms ensuring black subordination sparked fear in many white southerners, who worried that African Americans were gaining rights at the expense of the white community.[129]

Concerns over challenges to white supremacy heightened fears of black violence targeting whites during the 1930s. Although rates of black crimes against whites remained low and declined throughout the decade, when interracial crimes occurred they were often amplified by southern newspapers.[130] News stories of black criminals assaulting white residents proliferated, and articles about black murderers, robbers, and "prowlers" who stalked through the city were mainstays in the white press. During the first four months of 1938 alone, the *Birmingham News* reported at least thirty-three stories regarding black criminals in the city.[131] In a typical example, the *Birmingham News* reported on April 24, 1938, "Negro Stomps, Robs Woman." The story warned residents in Birmingham of the dangers African American criminals posed for whites. Mrs. Irene White simply stood waiting on a streetcar when, according to the news report, "the Negro came up behind her and ordered her to give him her purse. She resisted . . . and the Negro knocked her to the ground, kicked and stomped her and then took the purse, which contained a small amount of money."[132] Crime became associated with blackness partially because of the media focus on black criminality and the threat black criminals potentially posed for white residents.[133]

Southern city officials turned to the police to assert greater control over the black population in response to these challenges to segregation and white concerns regarding black criminality during the crime panic of the late 1920s and 1930s. During this era, men such as NOPD's superintendent, George Reyer (1931–42); Memphis's commissioner of public safety, Clifford Davis (1928–40); Birmingham's police chief, Fred McDuff (1921–33); and, most infamously, Birmingham's commissioner of public safety, Eugene "Bull" Connor (1936–54), oversaw the assumption of the responsibility to maintain Jim Crow race relations by these more modernized police forces using violence, harassment, and arrests of increasing numbers of African Americans.[134] Many of these leaders of southern law enforcement agencies not only utilized police forces to maintain racial subordination, but also personally viewed African Americans as inferior and often collaborated with, drew political support from, or were active members of the Ku Klux Klan in the 1920s and 1930s.[135] The attitude of individual officers on the force often mirrored that of their leaders.[136] Under Commissioner Davis's tenure in Memphis, for example, as many as 70 percent of MPD officers were avowed members of the Ku Klux Klan.[137]

With white supremacist leaders and officers, southern police forces embraced racially discriminatory practices to maintain Jim Crow. Vagrancy

arrests proved an effective and time-tested way for southern law enforcement to arrest large numbers of African Americans.[138] Yet, vagrancy arrests
increased nationwide during the 1930s as the Great Depression thrust
millions of Americans into poverty and unemployment.[139] This rise in
vagrancy arrests also reflected concerted efforts by police departments to
assuage concerns among white Americans about black criminality.[140] The
combination of white fears of African American criminals and the high rates
of poverty and unemployment among black southerners during the Great
Depression meant that African Americans were especially vulnerable to
vagrancy arrests. African Americans were well aware of this exploitation
by police and frequently complained about it. In 1934, Elizabeth Madison,
a black woman from New York City, wrote a letter to the president of the
New Orleans branch of the NAACP inquiring about the whereabouts of her
brother, Albert Madison. She claimed he lived in New Orleans and that she
had not heard from him in some time. She suggested that he might be housed
in a local or state jail because he "was frequently being arrested by the police
for no apparent reason."[141] Vagrancy arrests were indicative of the way southern officials manipulated the expanded legal system to turn black residents
into criminals, extract fines and labor from African Americans, and maintain control over the black population under the guise of crime control.[142]

While vagrancy arrests removed many black southerners from city
streets, the police also launched massive, publicized campaigns targeting
large segments of the black urban population to appease white fears of violent
black criminals.[143] Following a 1929 holdup in New Orleans, the chief of
police demanded "'all suspicious negroes' be apprehended and searched for
concealed weapons." Again in 1932, NOPD detained upward of nine hundred
African Americans in the wake of a robbery-homicide of a white grocer.[144]
Indiscriminate round-ups such as these demonstrated to African Americans just how vulnerable they could be when police felt the need to make
arrests. But from the police perspective, these actions also provided the white
community with a perceived sense of safety from black criminals.

Police sweeps of black neighborhoods also involved nonviolent offenses.
In Memphis, police began raiding black saloons along Beale Street with
increased vigor throughout the 1930s.[145] On December 2, 1932, the *Memphis
Commercial-Appeal* identified a change in police strategy and stated that
the "first intimation of a 'shake-up' was noted this week with an unusual
number of negro gambling house raids. The raids have netted more than 50
negro gamblers."[146] Just six days later, the *Commercial-Appeal* detailed the

arrests of an additional ninety-five African American gamblers as police remained "determined to curb operations of alleged negro gambling houses, policy dives and other resorts which have served as hideouts for criminals."[147] Raids of this sort placated public fears over crime and vice, but perhaps more importantly for white residents, they demonstrated the transference of enforcement of white supremacy from the public to the police by bringing more African Americans under the control of the criminal justice system.[148]

As police sought black criminals (real and imagined), they often employed violence as part of their crime control strategy.[149] Aggressive policing led to the death of large numbers of African Americans throughout the Jim Crow period.[150] Police officers viewed African Americans as dangerous, unpredictable, and violent.[151] Although the number of police officers killed by African Americans was low, these instances tended to resonate within police departments for many decades.[152] Across the South, countless instances of police shootings of African Americans for resisting arrest or behaving suspiciously can be found in newspapers and police records. According to police homicide reports maintained by the MPD, between 1917 and 1945 police killed ninety-nine African Americans (see fig. 1.1). Moreover, when officers shot and killed African Americans, in 90 percent of the cases police claimed the black victim resisted arrest or attempted to escape.[153] On February 25, 1933, for example, six police officers confronted, bound, beat, and arrested nineteen-year-old Lavon Carlock in a back alley for allegedly assaulting a local white prostitute named Ruby Morris. When Morris identified the bound black man as her assailant, police reported that Carlock "jerked loose and attempted to make his escape with the result that Patrolmen Sanders, and Freeman started shooting at the Negro." Although the two officers said they fired only one shot, officials later determined that Carlock was struck by five bullets.[154] According to historian Michael K. Honey, police "regularly beat, shot, and killed enough blacks in Memphis that everyone knew the penalty for not living within the etiquette of Jim Crow."[155]

This type of violence was not confined to Memphis. According to NOPD records, police shot and killed fifty-nine people between 1926 and 1945.[156] Of these fifty-nine police killings, African Americans made up 61 percent of the victims (see fig. 1.2), even though they represented just 29 percent of the city's population. The NOPD officers typically shot African Americans suspected of disorderly conduct or suspicious activity, allegedly while they were resisting arrest.[157] When, for instance, Patrolman William Mellor and two other officers saw twenty-year-old Hamilton Duplessis driving an auto-

Fig. 1.1. African Americans Killed by Police in Memphis, 1917–1945. Source: MPD Homicide Reports, 1917–1945.

mobile while wearing a bathing suit on August 7, 1932, the officers demanded Duplessis take his car to the Fifth Precinct. Duplessis, who, according to the *Louisiana Weekly*, "had never before been arrested," refused and fled the scene. According to Mellor, as he chased the black man on his motorcycle he fell, and his gun discharged accidentally, fatally striking Duplessis. While at the hospital, however, Duplessis claimed, "Officer Mellor deliberately fired at him five times."[158] Duplessis died in the hospital twenty-one days later on August 28, 1932.

While the records of the BPD are not available, qualitative evidence suggests that police in the city also shot African Americans at alarming rates. At approximately 10:30 p.m. on December 31, 1932, three BPD officers shot and killed Edna Davis while she was at her home. The local black press reported several versions of the killing. Some said officers entered Davis's home to make an arrest and ordered all of the black men and women in the home to lie on the floor. Davis, according to this report, refused and demanded to put on her coat. At this point, "two officers of the law fired two shots into her body" and killed her instantly. Other reports claimed Davis "scuffled with the officers, resisted arrest, made an effort to get a shot gun from under a bed,

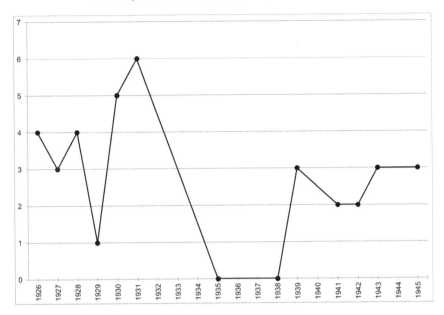

Fig. 1.2. African Americans Killed by Police in New Orleans, 1926–1945. Source: NOPD Homicide Reports, 1926–1945.

and in this attitude or disposition she was shot." According to yet another telling of the events, four officers all had guns and "not a Negro in the house was armed or in reach of any firearms." Regardless of how events actually played out, the local black newspaper declared, "The general sentiment leads to the point that the tragedy might have easily been avoided."[159] The *Birmingham Post*, a white newspaper, agreed. According to an editorial reprinted in the *Birmingham Reporter*, "Something is wrong when three able-bodied officers, with a clear chance to make a clean arrest cannot take a Negro woman into custody without adding another victim to the city's homicide rate."[160] Edna Davis was far from the only one. In 1932, sociologist Kenneth E. Barnhart studied homicide trends in Birmingham and paid particular attention to police killings of black suspects. He suggested that killings of African Americans by police for "resisting arrest" accounted for a large percentage of homicides involving blacks in Birmingham. "A careful check of police records for 1930," he noted, "shows that 18 negroes were shot in this manner. . . . No White males [or] White females . . . were shot by officers for 'resisting arrest.'"[161] In the context of white concerns over black criminality and an association of blackness with violent behavior, police violence against African American suspects proved commonplace as officers used lethal force as part of a broader crime-fighting strategy.

Even seemingly innocuous activities could turn violent for southern blacks. Around 8 p.m. on January 20, 1920, BPD officers H. H. Mooreland and W. M. Dews came across a black man riding a bicycle with two cartons of cigarettes on his handle bars. Something about this African American, whom officers later identified as Willie Lee Anderson, raised the suspicion of the officers. Officers Dews and Mooreland demanded Anderson halt, but he threw down his bike and ran. In a statement to the Jefferson County Grand Jury, Officer Mooreland stated, "I shot at him before he got to the corner." He missed. As the chase ensued, Mooreland yelled, "Wait a minute, boy. This is police, and I want to talk to you." Anderson, however, continued to run. Mooreland shot at him three more times and Officer Dew eventually caught up with Anderson, brought him to the ground, and arrested him for stealing cigarettes from the R. G. Patterson Cigar Company.[162]

A significant change in police violence against African Americans occurred during the 1930s. Police killings of suspects on the streets declined, while police abuse of African Americans during interrogations increased.[163] It is not that police violence against African Americans decreased: it simply changed locales. As historian Silvan Niedermeier argued, "as law enforcement officials gradually enforced the state's monopoly on the use of force in the South, they increasingly relied on methods of torture to obtain forced confessions and secure convictions of suspected offenders."[164] While use of the "third degree," or the use of physical or mental suffering to get information from suspects, was widespread, New Orleans gained a reputation as one of its most notorious adherents."[165] Out of 332 cities surveyed by the American Civil Liberties Union in 1939, New Orleans ranked as one of the worst three cities in the nation.[166] While black and white New Orleanians alike faced the threat of police abuse throughout the first three decades of the twentieth century, by the late 1920s and 1930s police violence became more racialized. Out of all suspects killed in police custody in the 1920s, black New Orleanians accounted for 50 percent of the total. During the 1930s, however, that total reached upward of 75 percent.[167] When NOPD arrested Loyd D. T. Washington, a forty-one-year-old black cook, on May 11, 1938, officers confined him to a cell, accused him of murdering a white man from Yazoo City, Mississippi, in 1918, and held him for thirty-three days without a warrant and never charged him with a crime. While he was in custody, officers interrogated him for several days and brought him into the "show-up room." As Washington remembered, police "tried to make me sign papers stating that I had killed a white man." Police kicked, punched, and severely beat Washington, knocked out five of his teeth, and broke one of his ribs. On June 13, 1938, the NOPD released Washington, finally admitting they had arrested the wrong man. Washington's experience was not atypical. The NOPD routinely utilized brutal tactics to thwart criminal activity and to extract confessions from African Americans.[168]

While New Orleans's police may have been the most notorious, police departments across the country employed the "third degree" as a tool in the police arsenal to gain confessions.[169] When the MPD arrested Willie Jones and accused him of stealing a purse from a white woman named Granville Garner, the officers dealt with him "extremely harshly," according to the leading black newspaper in the city. Once in custody, Jones denied his involvement, but police hit him in the mouth with their fists, beat him over the head with a board, hit him with a blackjack, and threatened him with a rubber hose. According to one witness, "I saw some white men striking him and he was crying for mercy."[170] The beatings were so severe that Jones eventually confessed to the crime. The BPD behaved similarly and, according to Charlie Jackson, BPD officers subjected him to the third degree, which caused him to confess to the murder of a white filling station operator named W. T. Smith on May 24, 1930. Jackson declared "they whipped me and threatened me there at the city hall.... There were about 15 of them had me in the room in the city hall. They dropped me down across the chair down there."[171] Law enforcement officials across the South used this method of forced confessions, in which interrogators typically made the defendant strip, laid them across a chair, bound them, anwhipped them across the back until they confessed to the crime for which they had been apprehended.[172] Subjecting African American suspects to these tactics reinforced notions of white supremacy by harkening back to the antebellum period when black slaves were often subjected to whipping punishments by white masters and overseers, and late nineteenth and early twentieth centuries when white mobs lynched, whipped, and physically assaulted thousands of black southerners.[173]

Maintaining control over swelling black populations involved more than a focus on perceived or invented criminal behavior in black communities. Southern city officials also viewed African American challenges to white supremacy as further attacks on law and order. Throughout the early twentieth century, African Americans formed a number of civic groups, fraternal orders, and civil rights and political organizations. White city officials tolerated some of these groups, except when organized blacks pushed the boundaries of Jim Crow and sought full inclusion into American political, social, and economic institutions. The National Association for the Advancement of Colored People (NAACP) drew particular ire from city officials and the police. Founded in 1909, the NAACP attempted to penetrate the South in the late 1910s. Although it enjoyed initial success, throughout the 1920s and 1930s law makers and law enforcement worked to limit its effectiveness. Across the South, states and cities passed ordinances that made the work of the NAACP and other civil rights organizations nearly impossible. In Birmingham, city officials passed a law under Section 5474 of the city code that prohibited posting of advertising matter on fences, buildings, and telephone poles. When local NAACP branch president E. W. Taggart distributed a poster denouncing lynching and promoting the NAACP in 1933, police quickly arrested him. According to NAACP officials, "Dr. Taggart was arrested because the Birmingham branch issued a poster and distributed it about the city protesting against lynching and appealing for members to join the branch."[174] City officials across the region passed a number of statutes to thwart black political organizing and used the police to enforce those laws and maintain white supremacy.[175]

Police also monitored African American political activities. Although disenfranchisement laws in Alabama and Louisiana did not completely eliminate black political activities in Birmingham and New Orleans throughout the Jim Crow era, those laws certainly curtailed formal activism. However, in Memphis, a significant number of African Americans retained the right to vote. The local police force often played a role in limiting the political power of African Americans if they challenged Edward Crump, boss of the Shelby County political machine.[176] Police repression of black political activists in Shelby County increased during the Great Depression as African Americans became more critical of Crump's political domination.[177] When local black businessman Dr. J. B. Martin, a well-known Republican, organized a series of campaign rallies in support of Republican presidential candidate Wendell Willkie and other Republican office seekers, Crump, a Democrat, demanded Martin call off the rallies or he would be "policed."[178] Martin refused, and the MPD stationed officers outside of his drugstore for nearly a month. Using a trumped-up drug distribution charge, officers harassed Martin and anyone who entered his store, including black children.[179] In a letter to President Franklin Roosevelt in 1940, Edward E. Strong described the harsh tactics of MPD toward black Memphians and claimed that "there is a concerted drive . . . to force Negro leaders out of business and out of town and to intimidate the entire Negro population by wholesale arrests every day and by placing heavy police guards in peaceful Negro neighborhoods."[180] Despite the ability of black Memphians to have some influence on local and state elections, if they openly challenged powerful white politicians they faced the threat of police harassment and abuse.

Labor activism among African Americans also threatened the Jim Crow racial hierarchy, and the police often played a role in undermining any attempt by black workers to unionize. As the Great Depression plunged Americans into poverty and economic hardships, the labor movement grew more radical and vocal. In the South, this radicalization challenged not only traditional political power but also the Jim Crow system of racial oppression. As historian Michael K. Honey stated, "Struggles for civil rights, civil liberties, and labor rights became inextricably intertwined. Without the right to organize, neither African Americans nor workers as a group could change their conditions, and that right could not be gained without seriously undermining the segregation system."[181] Unions faced many challenges organizing workers in the South as state and local governments typically worked to limit organizing. Yet, as unionizing efforts increased during the Great Depression, the Congress of Industrial Organizations (CIO) and the Communist Party USA further challenged southern laws and customs and promoted biracial unions.[182] The police worked diligently to harass union organizers because organized labor represented a threat to the business interests of southern cities in general, as well as the fact that interracial unions challenged the basis of Jim Crow and white supremacy.

Whether in Birmingham, Memphis, or New Orleans, police harassed, arrested, beat, and killed union organizers.[183] On October 8, 1932, the *Birmingham World* reported that several members of the BPD had monitored a meeting of the International Labor Defense (ILD) when they held their southern conference at the Colored Masonic Temple in Birmingham. The ILD was a legal advocacy organization supported by the Communist Party in the United States, and it posed a number of threats to Jim Crow as it supported interracial labor and political organizing. The ILD proved particularly attractive to working-class blacks in and around Birmingham because of its advocacy for labor rights, its protests against police brutality, and its decision to provide a legal defense for the Scottsboro boys.[184] When the organization held an interracial meeting on October 2, 1932, the BPD showed up in full force. According to the *Birmingham World*'s report, "there were in the building and on the outside at vantage points about seventy-five of Birmingham's police force" that monitored an interracial meeting of about three hundred people.[185] Approximately 26 percent of the Birmingham police force, then, was stationed in and around this meeting.[186] The police apparently did not arrest any of the attendees. Yet by monitoring the activities of this interracial group, the BPD sought to instill fear into the attendees and also to reduce public concerns of potential challenges to the Jim Crow social and political system.[187] As one black editorialist in the *Birmingham Reporter* understood, "Judging by the number of officers detailed to preserve order, there was the known necessity for extreme caution to prevent the occurrence of anything that [might] not add to the city's good reputation."[188]

While police monitored and intimidated black political and labor organizations, individual African Americans who challenged white supremacy also faced police violence and abuse. The case of Tom Watkins was perhaps the most blatant example of police abuse of black union organizers. At 2:30 in the morning, on May 26, 1939, Watkins, an organizer of dock workers on the Memphis riverfront, awakened to someone pounding on his door. When he went to the door he discovered two police officers waiting outside. The men came inside Watkins's house and told him, "We have some people who want to look at you." The two officers placed him and his wife, Arlene in handcuffs, put them in an unmarked car, and drove off toward the riverfront. Union activists and organizers in Memphis had a history of disappearing in the middle of the night.[189] Prior to this night, police had beaten Watkins severely on President's Island just outside of the city and arrested him on a charge of "communism"; the police chief, William D. Lee, told Watkins, "I'll get you if it takes me twenty years, you son of a bitch." Needless to say, Watkins surely knew he was in serious trouble. MPD officers took Tom and Arlene to a warehouse, bound her on a pile of lumber, and proceeded to beat Tom with a thirty-pound piece of oak timber used to draw barges to the docks, known as a capstan bar. Watkins fell to the floor and heard one of his abusers say, "Drop him overboard quick." As one of the men attempted to strike Watkins again, he missed, and accidentally struck his fellow officer. At this point Watkins scrambled to his feet and made a mad dash toward the Mississippi River. Police fired several shots at him during the chase. Watkins somehow managed to make it to the river and leap in. Police continued shooting into the river as Watkins clandestinely floated along the shoreline until they left. Watkins barely survived; his account illustrated the role of police in thwarting unionization of black workers in southern cities across the region.[190]

Throughout the 1930s and 1940s, southern police targeted black criminality and thwarted black political and labor organizing as part of a broader effort to maintain black subordination. As the economic depression of the 1930s descended upon southern cities, fears of black criminality among southern whites coalesced with more concerted and successful efforts by African Americans to challenge their subordinated status to produce more aggressive policing to maintain white supremacy in the face of these challenges. Police raided black establishments, monitored African American organizational meetings, and arrested black southerners at high rates. In so doing, the police demonstrated their commitment to protecting white communities from the perceived threat of African American criminals and to defending the Jim Crow racial hierarchy that permeated the South.[191]

At the end of World War II police departments in cities across the South looked remarkably different than their nineteenth-century predecessors. An NOPD publication entitled "Fifty Years of Progress," published in 1950, summed up the advancements made by departments across the region, "Fifty years which have seen the development of the science of fingerprinting, the use of automobiles, motorcycles, and even airplanes for patrol work, and great strides in communication by radio, telephone and teletype."[192] Through professionalization efforts, the police attempted to change their image from corrupt and inefficient to a more competent crime-fighting force that upheld law and order in the urban South. Law and order, however, became defined in racialized terms as white southerners not only relied on police to protect white lives and livelihoods, but also depended on them to bolster the racist structures that undergirded southern society. In other words, despite the fact that police departments in many southern cities continued to be mired in politics, inefficiency, and corruption, white southerners understood police officers and detectives as protectors of the Jim Crow racial hierarchy. In 1940, for instance, Memphis's police and fire commissioner, Joe Boyle, charged the MPD with keeping Memphis "a white man's country." He continued, "Any negro who doesn't agree to this better move on."[193] For black southerners, then, the transformation of southern police departments coincided with more coercive and efficient policing of the black community. Police placed more African Americans under the management of the formal criminal justice system, abused and killed black suspects at high rates, targeted black political and labor organizations, and maintained segregation statutes throughout the region. By the end of World War II, then, for white and black southerners the police represented the force that maintained white supremacy.

Despite their concerns over the role of the police in maintaining and enforcing Jim Crow, black residents also understood that the police had a key role to play in urban spaces. In their effort to reduce crime in their own communities, many African Americans believed that better policing offered a potential solution. While offering stinging criticisms of police abuse of black suspects, unnecessary arrests of black residents, and seeming disdain for black rights, calls for more police and better policing practices in black neighborhoods routinely appeared in the pages of the black press. These appeals to law enforcement to help combat crime in black communities reveal a legacy of criticism of and support for the police within the black community dating back to the early twentieth century.

CHAPTER 2

African American Responses to Crime in the Urban South

In an editorial published in the *Birmingham Reporter,* the major black newspaper of the city, on May 26, 1928, the author bemoaned a nearly decade-long crime wave that wreaked havoc in the city. While social scientists, city officials, and writers pointed to several potential causes of the nationwide crime wave, the editorialist declared, "However obscure [the causes of crime waves] are, there are definite results that leave no guessing about what is considered the most effective means of immediate relief from their effects. The centers from which they radiate are so elusive that it is idle to strike at the deep-seated causes for ultimate relief when the actual situation requires instant attention to insure public safety." The solution in the short term, according to this writer, rested not with public expenditures on parks, educational facilities, or access to better jobs. Instead, the editorialist declared, "the only immediate relief is police protection." In the author's view, the lack of adequate police forces in Birmingham, particularly in black communities, allowed criminal organizations to proliferate, expand their influence, and commit crimes with seeming impunity. He concluded, "Not tomorrow does Birmingham need better police protection, but today; in fact, it needed it yesterday and the day before."[1]

The concerns expressed in this editorial reflected the sentiments of many middle-class African Americans in the urban South in the first half of the twentieth century. As southern police forces evolved in response to white southerners' concerns over crime, violence, and black migration to southern cities, middle-class black residents articulated similar concerns over seemingly high rates of crime and violence that occurred in their own communities. In many ways, this was not surprising. Rates of violence in the black community, particularly homicide, far outpaced rates in white communities. White perpetrators of violence against African Americans rarely faced punishment, while punishment for black intraracial crimes also seemed lacking in the Jim Crow criminal justice system. Middle-class African Americans at the time understood the root causes of these disparities, including limited opportunities for economic advancement for African Americans, lack of adequate housing, and poor educational facilities. In response, middle-class black residents of the urban South routinely called for improvements in these facets of their communities in the pages of the black press. However, most understood that extracting the necessary funding from white city officials and government agencies would be difficult, if not impossible. Those demands represented an ideal, long-term solution.

For many middle-class African Americans, the best short-term solution involved equitable treatment by the criminal justice system for crimes committed against African Americans. The demand for equitable treatment became part of a movement focusing on the fair administration of laws in black neighborhoods that dated back to the late nineteenth century. Fair-administration advocates called for several structural changes within the local criminal justice apparatus that all centered on providing black communities with more protection from crime and violence. Part of that effort centered on better policing in black communities. Better policing involved more officers on the ground in black neighborhoods, equitable treatment of black residents, and consistent enforcement of the laws. This movement for better policing focused on two main tenets: an end to police brutality and the hiring of black police officers. In the eyes of black fair-administration advocates, these two goals would improve police departments' responsiveness to crimes committed against African Americans, promote positive interactions between officers and black residents, and decrease crime in black neighborhoods. As white southerners turned to the police to monitor and control swelling black populations in the urban South, middle-class black residents also implored the police to protect them from the threats to black lives and property in the Jim Crow South.

Crime and Violence in Black Communities

Discussions of crime in black communities proliferated in the United States throughout the late nineteenth and early twentieth centuries. By the twentieth century, white southerners viewed African Americans as dangerous, prone to criminal behavior, and inherently inferior.[2] Black scholars, such as W. E. B. Du Bois and Monroe Work, attempted to combat these negative characterizations by pointing out discriminatory practices within the criminal justice system and lack of services provided to black Americans as possible reasons for the racial disparities in incarceration.[3] However, their arguments fell largely on deaf white ears. Local and state legislatures across the South relied on the characterization, and white fear, of African Americans as violent and dangerous to justify racial segregation and disenfranchisement that became known as Jim Crow. By the dawn of the twentieth century, concepts of race and crime became central to defending and defining the Jim Crow racial hierarchy.[4]

Although African Americans argued against the notion of black criminality as indicative of black inferiority, concerns over crime in black communities reached a climax during the 1920s and early 1930s in response to a nationwide panic over criminal activity.[5] Much of this conversation focused on the high rates of black intraracial violence that racked southern cities in the early twentieth century. These writers challenged the arguments put forth by their white counterparts that African Americans were more prone than white Americans to criminal behavior. Nonetheless, instances of violence against African Americans routinely appeared on the front pages of black newspapers, black writers expressed their concerns over crime and potential causes of it in black communities, and black civic organizations expressed their dismay with crime in black communities as well.

On any given day, stories related to various crimes in black neighborhoods confronted readers of black newspapers in southern cities. On April 23, 1932, the front page of the *Louisiana Weekly* featured several crime-related stories with headlines that proved typical of any given issue. Articles such as, "Killer Evades Posse," "Killed as He Seeks Refuge from Gunman," "Hayes Gets Long Term for Murder," "Ito Jacques Sentenced to Hang in June," "Woman Held for Killing of Husband," "Called from Home, Shot," and "Wants Bath Tub Clean, Gets Shot," appeared on the front page.[6] Much of this coverage undoubtedly related to the fact that stories about criminal acts are attention-grabbing and help sell newspapers.[7] But the coverage of crimes committed in black communities and against African Americans also spoke to a real problem faced by black residents across the urban South.

Violence perpetrated by whites against blacks was a mainstay of the Jim Crow South. Lynchings epitomized the most horrific forms of white violence that black communities faced. Such sensationalized acts of violence remained a constant threat to black lives during the Jim Crow era. Yet, instances of mob violence dropped significantly throughout the first three decades of the twentieth century. But, although lynchings declined, less dramatic acts of homicide occurred with terrifying frequency.[8] According to available police reports, white residents in Memphis and New Orleans killed 271 African American residents between 1917 to 1945.[9] On July 4, 1924, for example, a forty-six-year-old black man named Will Moore sat down at the front end of a streetcar in Memphis and, more assertively, refused to move back when the operator M. F. Green demanded it. Green then took a switch bar and hit Moore on the wrist and forced Moore to the back of the car. Once at the back of the car, Moore allegedly opened his knife and stated, "I am going to get you now" and lunged at R. D. Ford, the other operator on the car. Claiming self-defense, Ford stabbed Moore three times. An emergency car took Moore to the General Hospital where he died at 3:40 a.m. on July 6, 1924.[10] Much like lynchings, these acts of violence concerned black urban dwellers in the South because of the frequency and lack of punishment for white perpetrators.[11]

The murder of Hattie McCray by Charles Guerand was perhaps the most infamous interracial murder case to arise in New Orleans in the first half of the twentieth century. On February 10, 1930, Guerand, an off-duty NOPD officer, killed Hattie McCray, a fourteen-year-old black girl. On the day of the killing, Guerand came into a local restaurant named Matt's Place where McCray worked as a dishwasher. Guerand, who spent the day drinking, went into the kitchen and "started fooling around" with McCray twice throughout the day. Both times she "repulsed" his attempts. At 3:30 p.m., Guerand returned for a third time to "have SEXUAL INTERCOURSE" with the young girl, and yet again she "repelled" him. At which point Guerand announced to the restaurant that he would "kill that God Damned Nigger wench" and went back into the kitchen, argued about having sexual intercourse with her. At some point during the exchange, Guerand shot McCray. Hattie McCray died later at the hospital.[12]

White residents' criminal and violent actions against African Americans remained an ever-present threat to black urban dwellers, yet throughout the 1920s, 1930s, and 1940s, black intraracial violence also proved to be a major problem in the black community. Between 1917 and 1945, black residents in Memphis and New Orleans killed 1,302 and 674 African Americans, respectively.[13] On the evening of May 12, 1927, for example, Eddie Hill killed twenty-one-year-old Clarance Williams. On the night of the incident, Williams came home from work and found his girlfriend, Beatrice

Frederick, hosting a party in their room with several other men and women. Williams asked Hill what he was doing in his room, at which point Hill "pointed to one of the other negro men in the room and said that he had came [sic] there to see him." Williams demanded Hill leave the room. Hill told Williams "to move from the path of the door-way and he would leave." Williams grabbed his girlfriend and moved out of the doorway. As Hill left, Williams followed him out into the hallway. According to the police report, at this point Hill "pulled a revolver from his person and fired two shots at Clarance Williams, one of the bullets striking Clarance Williams in the breast who fell back into the room." Hill fled immediately. Williams died at the scene.[14] Black intraracial homicides such as the Williams case represented an additional threat to black lives in the Jim Crow South.[15] The racist political, economic, and social restrictions placed on African American southerners in the early twentieth-century urban South largely underlaid the high rates of black intraracial violence.[16] The continued dispossession of black residents only exacerbated the problems to the point that rates of homicide among urban black communities reached levels seen in some of the most violent countries today.[17] If not troubling enough, higher rates of violence in black communities also provided fodder for white supremacists, who supported notions of inherent black criminality and the necessity for segregation as a safeguard for white communities.

High rates of intraracial homicides in black neighborhoods were not lost on black residents. Readers of local black newspapers routinely saw articles and editorials discussing the high rates of violence. Black writers expressed concern over the pervasiveness of this trend. In nearly all southern states and cities, African Americans killed each other at rates that far surpassed that of their white counterparts.[18] Across the pages of the black press, editorialists expressed their dismay with crimes committed in black communities. In an editorial published in the *Louisiana Weekly* on May 19, 1928, the writer commented, "Unless something is done to curb the lust for blood between members of the race and to protect the race from the affronts of organized bands of hoodlums, decent law-abiding colored persons will be afraid to be about on the streets after dark." The editorialists concluded, "Crime is just as bad when committed by one member of a race against another member of the same race as it is when a member of one race commits a crime involving a member of the opposite groups."[19] An editorialist in the *Birmingham Reporter* expressed similar concerns about violence in the black community. He stated, "Human life is cheap today. . . . The principal news displayed in

glaring headlines upon the front pages of our daily papers is that of murder."
He demanded a "halt to this wholesale slaughter of human beings of which
the associated press advises us daily."[20] These editorials indicated the frustration and concern that black residents across the urban South felt as they
attempted to navigate life in Jim Crow cities. Crime and violence against
black bodies affected not only the victims but all residents. Instead of serving
as a bulwark against white oppression, many black urban dwellers grew
concerned that their lives were not safe in their own communities.[21]

To understand the urban experience of African Americans in the early
twentieth-century South, an understanding of black residents' concern over
crime and violence in their communities is necessary. Interracial violence
proved an ominous threat to the security of black lives, livelihood, and property in the Jim Crow South, but so too did black intraracial crimes.[22] The
frequency with which black writers and black newspapers covered black
intraracial crimes indicated as much. This is not to suggest that African
Americans were inherently more criminally inclined than whites, as structural inequality, racism, and institutional barriers to black achievement,
among other things, contributed to the racial disparities in criminal statistics. However, to ignore criminal acts committed against black Americans
by black Americans is to overlook an important aspect of understanding the
relationship between African Americans and the police in the Jim Crow
South. The frequency with which black southerners committed criminal
actions against other African Americans was of major concern in black
communities and sparked debate among black residents over the best way
to combat the problem.

African American Responses to Crime in Black Communities

Much of the recorded reactions to crime in black communities reflected the
concerns of the black middle class in each city. Broadly speaking, the black
middle class was comprised black business owners, teachers, doctors, church
leaders, and other economically successful African Americans. Members
of the black middle class viewed themselves as distinct from the mass of
black workers not only in terms of economic status, but also in behavior,
education, and lineage.[23] As increasing numbers of African Americans
migrated to southern cities in the first decades of the twentieth century, a
growing demand for black businesses and enterprises that catered to African
Americans spurred the creation of a black middle class. In Birmingham and

Memphis, men like Reverend W. R. Pettiford, Andrew J. Beard, C. M. Harris, Robert Church, Jr., and J. E. Walker comprised part of the black middle class that established successful businesses largely catering to an African American clientele. These businesses included banks, funeral houses, insurance agencies, and rental properties.

New Orleans's black elite shared similar characteristics with their counterparts in Birmingham and Memphis, but differed in important ways. The most marked distinction of the black elite in New Orleans was the presence of large numbers of Afro-Creoles who descended from a long lineage of free people of color that dated back to the original French establishment of the city. The Afro-Creoles were often well educated and formed an identity that was fundamentally different from that of a "negro," or slave. Throughout the antebellum era, Afro-Creoles owned businesses, sought education, and participated in public life. Following emancipation and during the Jim Crow era, the community of Afro-Creoles remained better educated and more economically successful, and they defined themselves as a community distinct from African Americans. Yet, as Jim Crow laws sought to remove those distinctions, Afro-Creoles took up the mantle of resistance in an effort to safeguard their status.[24] Such differences notwithstanding, the black elite in southern cities typically saw themselves as a separate group and maintained exclusive social clubs, formed religious and literary societies, rarely interacted with working-class African Americans, and typically established important alliances with the white civic and business leaders to limit the negative effects of Jim Crow.[25] Their views of crime in black communities largely reflected their class status and backgrounds.

Reflecting the growing concern about crime sweeping the country in the late 1920s and 1930s, middle-class African Americans expressed their dismay with criminal activity in the pages of the black press. However, as opposed to white southerners such as Bull Connor and Clifford Davis, who emphasized stricter law enforcement and harsher treatment of black suspects, middle-class African Americans embraced a broad strategy to combat crime in black communities. Black social scientists and commentators had long pointed to many issues faced by African Americans as the root causes of black criminal behavior: lack of economic opportunities, poor housing, inadequate public education, alcohol consumption, the decline in religious morality, lack of strict parenting, and inequitable treatment of crimes committed against African Americans by southern courts.[26] An editorial published in the *Louisiana Weekly* on November 7, 1931, indicated the solutions African Americans had come up with in response to the wide-spread causes. "With our hands on the pulse of 120,000 Negroes in this city," the editorial proclaimed, "we would advocate sound parental teaching; more and better schools; a wholesome surrounding influenced by Christianity; Boy Scout organizations and Y.M.C.A.'s; playgrounds, community centers, a police protection that will destroy lurking evils, instead of encouraging them, and justice in the courts of law. Herein lies the making of good citizenship."[27] In other words, African American commentators believed that the best way to combat crime in black communities centered on a broad approach that eliminated discrimination in its various forms in the urban South, promoted morality within black communities, and increased protection of black lives and property by the expanded criminal justice system of the early twentieth-century South.

Middle-class African Americans frequently commented on the connections between structural inequalities that resulted from Jim Crow laws and customs and the prevalence of crime in black neighborhoods. Black critics argued the city needed to provide African Americans with better job opportunities and affordable housing to help combat the crime problem. These writers believed there was an inherent connection between poverty and crime. Racial restrictions on the types of jobs African Americans qualified for, according to these writers, contributed to high rates of unemployment and poverty in black communities. The lack of affordable housing in black communities compounded the economic problem because high rents syphoned off a majority of what little money black workers made.[28] Black residents in southern cities believed that alleviating some of the economic pressures on African Americans would decrease criminal activity. To combat the "numerous . . . shootings, cuttings and killings" in New Orleans, a writer for the *Louisiana Weekly* argued on July 26, 1941, city officials should get at the "source of the evil" and "attack the conditions under which the majority of the unfortunate victims live." To do so adequately, the writer stated, the city should embrace a multipronged approach and "build more government low-rent housing projects. Launch a widespread health and sanitation program. Sponsor recreational centers and parks for the use of adults and children. And most important, lift the taboos on economic opportunity, which is the real cause for low living standards." The writer concluded that if the city did not address these issues in the black community, "we will continue to get the criminals we make."[29] Proponents of better jobs and living conditions as a tool to combat criminal activity in black communities believed that providing black residents with ways to reduce poverty in their own communities would indelibly reduce the crime rate.[30]

While structural issues undergirded much of the crime problem, several black commentators also pointed to deep-rooted issues in black communities. These middle-class writers viewed crime as a class problem associated with a lack of morality and character within the working-class black community. This belief largely stemmed from the "politics of respectability" that shaped the black middle-class worldview in the early twentieth century. Adherents to the politics of respectability found fault with the black working class, often criticizing the leisure activities and, in their view, the moral depravity of many black residents. The politics of respectability was also a means of advancement for middle-class black citizens. Their disdain and criticism of the black working class reflected their concern that vice and crime in black communities damaged the credibility of the race as a whole and stifled black progress.[31] This movement was not confined to the South, as black reformers in the North also advocated for state and city governments to provide assistance to black families in order to inculcate middle-class standards of morality and respectability.[32] With this mindset, many black writers placed the blame for crime on the shoulders of the black poor, and largely the failures of child rearing.[33] On December 22, 1923, Carol W. Hayes, a black probation officer in Birmingham, explained that in order to fix the crime problem, African Americans needed to address "the weaknesses and lack of interest of many parents and children." He argued that the causes of "juvenile delinquency are attributed to parental ignorance or neglect, environment, and heredity. We find that the greatest of these three maladies is parental ignorance or neglect." According to Hayes, parents needed to devote more time to educating their children in proper morals, religion, and health.[34] The lack of education, which many black writers believed began at home, had real ramifications for crime. According to an editorial published in the *Birmingham Reporter* on August 9, 1924, "Negroes get into too many frivolous things that must be settled by court trial and they are in them largely because of ignorance and lack of contact with superior elements, or interested elements of both races." Reflecting the politics of respectability ideology, the writer concluded, "The advanced element of the Negro people must see the wisdom and convert themselves to social service work and become more missionary at home and reach the humbler member in the remotest section of the city and community life."[35] A class-based understanding of crime shaped these middle-class

African Americans' views on the issue. In their opinion, working-class blacks lacked the familial commitment to educate their children properly, and as a result, their children often got involved in criminal behaviors.

To make up for the lack of parental guidance among the working poor, several commentators pleaded for more after-school opportunities for black children. The issue could be solved, they argued, if the city provided more spaces for African American leisure. Some called for "places where [African American children] may blow off surplus energy," such as "playing space," or "recreational centers, a few more swimming pools, [and] one or two bathing beaches."[36] Others called for "corrective institutions," like the Young Men's Christian Association (Y.M.C.A.), that could "provide young manhood 'ways and means' to obtain clean recreation, education and the stimulation of good companionship."[37] For these writers, providing areas and institutions for black children would help reduce the likelihood of black youth becoming involved in illicit activities on the streets. An editorial in the *Birmingham Reporter* on March 5, 1932, stated, "A Negro Y.M.C.A. would afford a culture center through which much of the criminal tendency in the negro youth might be eliminated." In the author's view, "homicides are incidents in poorly regulated communit[ies]" where black children need more "opportunities to spend leisure in a healthy atmosphere and under supervision." By providing black youth with exactly these kinds of leisure opportunities, the Y.M.C.A. and other institutions could impart the kind of middle-class values and senti-ments that they felt were lacking in working-class black homes. This form of mentorship would, according to the writer, "contribute to the reduction of crime among Negroes, as well as operate in many ways otherwise beneficial to the community."[38]

In addition to ferreting out the root causes of criminal activity, African Americans also understood that the criminal justice system played a role in combatting crime. Dealing with the structural causes of crime in black communities was a long-term struggle. In the immediacy, African Americans turned to the criminal justice system to punish criminals and hopefully reduce criminal activities in black communities in ways that mirrored the demands of white southerners. In response to a series of ax murders that occurred over the course of several years in Birmingham, an editorialist commented on the role of the criminal justice system in cities. "Our laws," the writer stated, "are made as human restraints and not primarily to punish people, but as a warning against crime, and when the laws are broken by individuals or concerns punishment must follow as a remedy." Alluding to the fact that larger structural changes needed to accompany a criminal justice solution, the writer opined, "Our redemption in Alabama is coming through social service organizations, the Christian church, educational institutions, *and a fair administration of our laws* [emphasis added]."[39]

For African Americans, "fair administration of our laws" represented a clarion call for criminal justice institutions and law enforcement officials to treat crimes committed against African Americans the same way that these institutions and officials treated crimes against whites. For its advocates, fair administration meant more police in black neighborhoods, better police practices when investigating crimes committed against African Americans, better treatment of black residents suspected of criminal behavior, and harsher penalties for anyone convicted of committing a crime against an African American.

Support for fair administration in the black community emphasized due process, or a citizen's entitlement to fair treatment under the criminal justice system.[40] Demands for due process grew out of African Americans' long-standing concern over lynching. Although lynching did not begin in the 1890s, during that decade lynching became viewed as a racialized phenomenon and became a focus of black activism. White mobs lynched hundreds of African Americans, often with the assistance of local sheriffs or other law enforcement agents, and almost never faced any form of criminal punishment as a result. In response, black critics of lynch violence routinely called for criminal punishment of lynch mob participants, the removal of law enforcement officials who cooperated with or refused to punish lynch mobs, and demanded trials for all black victims of lynch mobs.[41] As early as 1895, Ida B. Wells articulated black support for due process in her famous pamphlet, *A Red Record*. She stated, "We demand a fair trial by law for those accused of crime, and punishment by law after honest conviction. No Maudlin sympathy for criminals is solicited, but we do ask that the law shall punish all alike."[42] Instead of relying on extralegal methods of punishment, critics such as Wells staked their opposition to lynching in terms that promoted the formal processes of the criminal justice system.

Writers in New Orleans echoed Wells's support for due process in response to lynchings. While no lynchings occurred in the city in the early twentieth century, black commentators often discussed lynchings that occurred throughout the rest of the South. In response to the decision of Bibb Graves, governor of Alabama, to call out the militia to prevent a lynching, writers for the *Louisiana Weekly* celebrated his effort to "preserve law and

order" and encouraged "more governors [to] take this attitude" to "eliminate this evil from the confines of the United States of America."[43] One year
later, editorialists blasted South Carolina senator Cole Blease's support for
lynchings by declaring their own support for due process. "Lynching is an
abomination within the sight of God," one writer declared. "Laws are made
to punish man for his misdeeds against society, but if persons are allowed
to take the law into their own hands, like it was suggested by the Honorable
Cole Blease in his latest tirade against the Negro, then may God help us."[44]
By offering both support for white officials who, in their view, upheld law and
order and criticism for those who opposed due process in favor of extralegal
practices, African Americans demonstrated their support for fair administration and an understanding of the dynamics they had to navigate to obtain
support from officials of the criminal justice system.

Fair-administration advocates' efforts to reduce criminal acts against
African Americans continued even as the number of lynchings declined
during the early twentieth century.[45] As extralegal violence against African
Americans became more clandestine and less frequent, and homicide and
crime rates increased, calls for fair administration of the law from leaders
of urban black communities shifted focus. While the threat of violence by
whites remained ever present, many leaders also recognized that crime
and violence from within the black community threatened the lives and
livelihood of many African Americans. To hopefully quell rising crime rates
in the 1920s, several African American leaders continued to champion the
cause of law and order. On March 20, 1927, Reverend G. H. Connor, the pastor
at Second Avenue Baptist Church in Birmingham, hosted a mass meeting
"for moulding [*sic*] sentiment in favor of law and order, better citizenship
and general community betterment." The pastor claimed, "Negro citizens of
North Birmingham can boast one of the most law-abiding communities in
Jefferson county" and were "the leading spirit in the movement" for "law and
order."[46] Three months later, Dr. P. W. Walls, the pastor of the Payne Chapel
African Methodist Epsicopal church in Birmingham, offered more support
for the law and order campaign in the city. He declared, "The tide of crime has
risen to phenomenal heights within the period since November 1918." His
solution focused on what he called "a genuine campaign for law and order."[47]
By the 1920s, then, black calls for law and order in their own communities
represented an extension of earlier due process demands made in response
to lynchings.

In demanding equitable enforcement of laws, black supporters of fair administration critiqued the dual system of justice that existed in the Jim Crow South. Across the region, local criminal justice institutions typically treated crimes committed against whites, particularly those allegedly perpetrated by blacks, rather seriously and crimes committed against African Americans with leniency. Moreover, African Americans faced the threat of criminal prosecution for many nonviolent offenses at rates that far surpassed those for whites. The Jim Crow criminal justice system treated blacks and whites accused of crimes in very different ways.[48] For fair-administration advocates, strict enforcement of the law and sure punishment for offenders, regardless of race, would do much to curb crime in black communities.[49] In New Orleans, black supporters of fair administration filled the pages of the *Louisiana Weekly* with demands for harsh punishments for criminals. "The man who commits a crime," wrote one editorialist on April 10, 1926, "whether he be 'Master Mind' or the man with a sub-normal mentality, should be dealt with to the fullest extent of the law and dealt with as quickly as possible." The writer argued against discriminatory customs, such as lighter sentences for crimes committed against African Americans and harsher sentences for crimes committed against whites, that often shaped the outcome of criminal trials. The author declared, "We simply believe that whatever the law says is right, should be observed and observed to the letter."[50] Echoing this sentiment, another black supporter of law and order wrote on June 2, 1928, "Crooks are crooks, no matter of what degree, and when they are caught they should be dealt with according to the law."[51] These two editorials reflected a law-and-order sentiment present in the black community that decried the dual system of justice that existed in the Jim Crow South: one for blacks and one for whites.[52]

Demands for equitable treatment under the law did not necessarily mean demands for more lenient treatment. Among many black fair-administration proponents, strict penalties for crimes would do much to combat criminal behavior in black communities. In response to a series of crimes committed in New Orleans, one editorialist declared on May 7, 1932, "Killings in New Orleans are far too numerous, and unless immediate steps are taken to severely punish those who hold human life so cheaply, this city at the end of the year, will find itself leading the list of cities in America for wanton murder." The solution, according to this writer, centered on the criminal justice system. He cheered the Orleans Parish's grand jury for the several indictments handed down the previous week, but knew that these indictments dealt with only the tip of the iceberg. If judges and juries refused to hold killers accountable, then indictments proved useless. For this writer, the solution to the increase in homicides rested in harsher and consistent sentences for killers. "There is only one way out of this," he said. "it is an easy way, it is the best way. Punish the killer, and make the future safe for citizens who are citizen minded."[53]

In order to promote the equitable enforcement of the law, black fair-administration advocates questioned the ability, or willingness, of an all-white criminal justice system to treat black victims and suspects fairly. An editorialist in the *Louisiana Weekly* expressed these concerns on July 30, 1932. The writer stated, "the unfortunate Negro has been getting so many rotten decisions at the hands of 'Louisiana Justice'" in the last several years that some remedy was required. He argued,

> We hate to think that we are living in a State [*sic*] where the courts of justice have been stripped of every vestige of plain and simple justice, a State [*sic*] where decisions are rendered according to a man's outward color and not according to the evidence of guilt or innocence; we would hate to think that we are living in such a State [*sic*] where the men who sit on its judicial benches have fallen so low that they would ignore every right of a helpless and defenseless people; we would hate to think that we are living in such a State [*sic*] where it is impossible to select a jury of twelve white men or women who have enough moral backbone to hang a white man for killing a Negro and who would not be willing to hang every Negro who accidentally steps on a white man's toes.

He concluded, "Recent court room decisions have been such as to almost force us to that conclusion."[54] According to these critics, as long as the criminal justice apparatus remained all white, African Americans would not receive fair treatment in the justice system.

By advocating for the inclusion of more African Americans on the enforcement side of the criminal justice system, black fair-administration proponents believed they had found a solution to the dual system of justice. African Americans were barred from jury service by law and custom across the Jim Crow South. For many black southerners, the lack of black representation on juries contributed to the discriminatory nature of the dual system of criminal justice because white juries were unconcerned with and unsympathetic to the plight of black residents.[55] An end to racial discrimination in jury selection and service offered a solution to legal discrimination for many fair-administration supporters. Following exoneration of Charles Hintz, a white welfare worker in Algiers, Louisiana, who shot and killed a sixteen-year-old black teenager named Ben Singleton on May 12, 1933, many black residents of New Orleans voiced their discontent. One editorialist commented on the killing the following day, "The brutal slaying of Ben Singleton . . . should move every 100 per cent loyal Negro to take immediate action to halt the promiscuous slaying of the members of their race in this city." The writer emphasized one thing that he felt black New Orleanians should understand about the case. "First, no Negroes will sit on the jury that will try Hintz, and most likely his pleas of self-defense will be accepted."[56] For black New Orleanians, this self-defense claim seemed dubious. Hintz shot Singleton in the back of the head. Despite this seemingly glaring contradiction to Hintz's self-defense justification for the killing, the grand jury, on which no African Americans served, returned no true bill against Hintz. In the eyes of black supporters of fair administration, this ruling, among many others, exemplified the problem of all-white juries. "The Orleans parish grand jury," argued one such supporter, "has justified this murder because there were no Negroes to sit among them."[57] Black editorialists for the *Memphis World* expressed similar support for black jurors. In an editorial on September 18, 1931, the writer declared, "If the certainty of punishment will lessen crime . . . let Negroes sit on juries unhampered and give the murderer and felon his just dues." He continued, "The inclusion of Negroes on juries to try Negroes would be a forward step."[58] While the demand for black residents to be included on juries spoke to larger civil rights issues related to proper roles accorded to American citizens and a fight against white violence committed against African Americans, it also spoke to the concern that black criminals were not being punished when they committed crimes against black victims. Thus, the call for African American representation on local juries became part of the larger fair-administration campaign of the 1920s, 1930s, and 1940s.[59]

In response to crime in black communities, African American commentators and residents in the South demanded a broad-based approach. As opposed to white city officials and commentators that used the issue of black crime to support segregation and disenfranchisement, black advocates largely blamed the Jim Crow hierarchy for the black crime problem. The limited access to jobs, poor housing, and dual system of justice resulting from the Jim Crow apparatus created by white officials promoted black poverty, affected parental relationships, and contributed to the seeming prevalence of crime in black neighborhoods. To combat this issue, black advocates demanded city officials alleviate these problems in several ways. Particularly important, however, was the emphasis on the criminal justice system. Black fair-administration advocates lamented the dual system of justice that was created and maintained by city officials and criminal justice representatives. While they offered critiques of the system, these critics also demanded the criminal justice system respond to the issue of black crime more effectively, reflecting a strain of thought that prevailed within the black communities in the Jim Crow South.

Black Perspectives on the Police and Crime

For black fair-administration advocates, the lack of police protection in black neighborhoods also contributed to crime in African American communities. Middle-class black residents demanded increased police presence in black neighborhoods throughout the interwar period. The struggle for better policing in African American communities did not indicate an uncritical support for Jim Crow law enforcement. Black residents' awareness of the unfair and often violent treatment they received at the hands of southern law enforcement officers meant that calls for better and more equitable policing of black neighborhoods occurred in conjunction with calls for a greater police presence. However, discussions about the necessity of improved policing in the black press only went so far. Disenfranchisement measures ensured that local city officials would not respond to African Americans' concerns as readily as they would cater to the concerns of the white community. Beginning in the 1930s, activist organizations, especially the NAACP, spearheaded campaigns against police brutality in several southern cities as part of a larger effort to secure better policing for black communities. Activists publicized cases of brutality, filed petitions with and lawsuits against police departments in response to abuse allegations, and, in some cases, proved somewhat successful in obtaining recompense for black victims of police violence. Campaigns against police violence developed into demands for black police officers. To these black activists, the presence of African Americans on southern police forces would reduce police violence, improve relations between black residents and law enforcement, and provide black neighborhoods with equitable and better policing. While fair-administration advocates and activists did not fundamentally alter the violent white supremacist culture prevalent in Jim Crow police departments, their efforts to reform legal institutions demonstrated their attempts to make Jim Crow police departments better serve the interests of black communities.

For decades, African Americans complained of being underpoliced in the sense that law enforcement officers typically showed little concern for crimes that involved black victims. Supporters of fair administration argued that would-be criminals knew law enforcement officers would not investigate crimes concerning black victims, which led to increased rates of violence committed against African Americans.[60] On April 14, 1928, the *Louisiana Weekly* published an editorial that expressed concern over the lack of police protection afforded black residents. "Negroes continue to kill one another and get away with it in this city while the police wink at the crime because only the colored man is involved, until all law breakers regardless of color or creed be brought before the courts and justice meted out to them crime will run rampant."[61] On April 15, 1939, in response to an "almost unprecedented wave of murders sweeping through the Negro population of New Orleans," one black resident argued that a "closer, more careful police patrol must be given those areas where the irresponsible element congregate, to the end that a fear of, and respect for, the law take deep root in their minds." The writer concluded, "This, and only this, will put an end to the murders which now terrorize the community and give to New Orleans a homicide rate almost second to no other urban center in the country."[62]

Black supporters of increased policing also demanded that law enforcement officers help crack down on some of the seeming causes of criminal behavior, particularly the consumption of alcohol. For example, following the killing of a black teenager named John Lowe, one black writer placed the blame squarely on the lack of police in black establishments. Local law enforcement did little to discourage underage African Americans from illegally consuming alcohol in taverns that catered to black patrons. He declared, "If local police were sufficiently vigilant as to patrol the various commercial establishments, they would see to it that girls and boys were not allowed to enter vice centers, not permitted to congregate on street corners in questionable areas." He concluded that the "all too few police assigned to neighborhoods thickly populated with Negroes" contributed significantly to Lowe's death.[63]

Aware of the threat of violence and discrimination that an increased police presence meant for black residents, African American demands for more policing coincided with a call for *better* policing in black communities. An editorial in the *Louisiana Weekly* entitled "A Need for Better Treatment," published on March 10, 1928, served as a case in point. The writer, concerned about several recent incidents of police mistreatment of African Americans and city officials' decision to eliminate upward of eighty officers from the force, hoped for "an order for better treatment of colored people" from the NOPD administration. "We cannot understand the point of view of policemen," he claimed, "who intimidate innocent, law-abiding Negroes, for certainly nothing but harm can come of it. We realize full well that there are suspicious characters who must be watched, but from what we can see, the activity seems to be directed solely to those of a darker hue." The editorialist demonstrated black residents' concern over crime in their communities and their desire to see more police officers in their neighborhoods. However, more precisely, the editorial articulated the concomitant demand for better treatment by the police of African Americans in general. Improved relations between the police and black community members, the writer believed, would lead to a decline in criminal actions. The writer concluded, "Better treatment of law-abiding Negroes will result in greater interest in the city in which we live, and develop a sentiment which will of itself eliminate the wrong doing far better than the law can ever hope to do."[64]

Black residents of southern cities articulated specific demands to make the police serve their communities better. Part of the fight for better policing focused on one of the main points of contention between black residents of the urban South and law enforcement: police brutality.[65] While critiques of police officers' treatment of black residents remained ever-present throughout the first several decades of the twentieth century, during the 1930s the fight against police brutality became a central component of black activism in many southern cities.[66] Throughout that decade, arrest, conviction, and imprisonment rates rose across the South as law enforcement officials used the criminal justice system to monitor and control the swelling black urban populations. As police targeted black communities, aggressive and violent tactics against African Americans became pillars of policing.[67] In Birmingham, Memphis, and New Orleans, black organizations such as the local branches of the NAACP and the black newspapers became vocal critics of and activists against police mistreatment of African Americans.

The issue of police brutality became part of a national conversation over the problems in the criminal justice system. The federal government commissioned a study on crime and the criminal justice system in 1929 (known as the Wickersham Commission) and reported its findings in fourteen different reports in 1931. One of the reports, the "Report on Lawlessness in Law Enforcement," was one of the first systematic investigations of police misconduct, and it criticized local police and exposed numerous ways that police across the country thwarted due process and abused people in their custody.[68] The Wickersham Commission also provided African Americans with a venue through which they could bring the issue of police brutality against African Americans to the attention of a broader audience of whites and blacks. Some southern African Americans contributed to the Wickersham Report to emphasize the widespread abuse of blacks at the hands of southern law enforcement. A. P. Tureaud, a black attorney and civil rights activist in New Orleans who had been concerned about the problem of abusive policing for many years, collected data on NOPD's abusive tactics as part of the report.[69] Tureaud requested that local black victims of police abuse contact him so he could compile a comprehensive list of incidents to submit to the Wickersham Commission. A front-page article in the *Louisiana Weekly* on August 2, 1930, stated that "it is understood that this data is being obtained for a subcommittee of President Hoover's Law Enforcement Commission. The data will not be used to punish offenders, but is to be made a part of the study by this subcommittee with a further view towards legislation by Congress."[70] Tureaud hoped that the information provided would help spur the federal government into action in ways that would ameliorate the problematic nature of local policing.

In addition to the efforts of African Americans like Tureaud to work through the federal government, at the local level the black press routinely offered criticism of southern police departments and individual officers for abusive treatment of black residents. These criticisms centered around the unnecessary violence used against African Americans that resulted from the unprofessional nature of policing in many southern cities. Following the killing of an African American man named George Simmons by NOPD officer Joseph Cronin in 1931, the *Louisiana Weekly* published an editorial offering a black perspective on the issue of police brutality in the city. Reflecting the larger concern over a lack of police protection in black communities, on May 30, 1931, the editorialist declared, "Time and again the cry has gone up that the city should pass laws to give the citizens more police protection. Indeed!" However, the writer also asked, "What about protecting citizens from cracked-brained, insane, and drunken policemen?" He continued, "The time has come when Negro citizens—and law-abiding citizens at that—have more to fear from some 'officers of the law' than from the most dreaded highwayman, bandits, cut-throats, and what-nots." The editorial also expressed the widely held view among African Americans that perpetrators of violence against African Americans rarely, if ever, faced punishment by the criminal justice system. The writer stated, "What is more to the point, the Negro victims of police brutality can expect little or no redress from our duly constituted courts of justice."[71] As this editorial demonstrated, African Americans recognized that instances of police brutality against African Americans were part of a larger, systemic problem with Jim Crow criminal justice.

Criticisms and demands in the black press coalesced with activism on the ground. The Wickersham Report highlighted the systematic use of violence in police interrogations, and growing reliance on violence by police against African Americans contributed to the development of the NAACP's anti-police brutality campaigns in the 1930s.[72] The NAACP traditionally reflected the views and approaches of the black middle class, especially that of working through official channels and relying on their relationship with powerful whites to promote change. These middle-class black activists typically favored formal protests of police brutality to city officials and public pressure campaigns designed to embarrass city officials into taking action. Yet, all of their protests and activism tended to work through official channels and fell short of large-scale challenges to white power structures in southern cities. Nonetheless, the NAACP's effort to combat police brutality demonstrated the larger concern of black communities about the lack of police protection in their cities.

Birmingham's NAACP branch took perhaps the most proactive steps in the fight against police brutality. NAACP organizers in Birmingham made the issue a springboard to attract new members in the 1930s.[73] The organization often used specific instances of police violence to proffer a larger critique of the BPD. The local branch's response to the killing of Edna Davis by BPD officers on December 31, 1932, represented the most aggressive response to date.[74] The organization delivered a petition to the commissioner of public safety demanding that the department do something to curtail the numerous police shootings of black suspects in the city. This petition addressed more than the single instance of Davis's murder. Instead, the NAACP demanded that the city commission reduce the number of violent officers within the department. The group's representatives claimed, "We have every confidence that this excellent Commission will close it's [sic] eyes and ears to that element that seeks to deny the Negro the right to live fully and safely, regardless to the POLITICAL outlook, and that it will pursue that course that will assure the negro Citizen the maximum security from violence of any nature." The petition demanded full investigations of homicides involving African Americans and asked for relief "from the atrocious legal murders, mistreatments of Negroes in various ways, miscarriages of justice, processes of intimidation and suppression of facts through threats of life by Officers of the law of this City."[75] Representatives of the NAACP presented the petition to the commissioner of public safety, John H. Taylor, in a private meeting. The commissioner, according to activists, "frankly admitted that what we were saying in the Petition was true." However, Taylor claimed he had no authority to bring charges against individual officers and that the decision rested with the Solicitor's office. He further obfuscated the issue and added that the other commissioners "were otherwise engaged" and would not be able to take up the matter. If city officials proved unwilling to act in this specific case, the NAACP representatives reminded Taylor, "The purpose of this Petition was not merely to seek an indictment so much as to prevent and put a stop to the very alarming homicide rate in our City," including those murders perpetrated by police. According to the NAACP records, little came from this meeting except a promise from the commissioner that he would call the police chief and "lecture to them and try [his] best to tone them down." Following the meeting, the local NAACP circulated the petition to the governor of Alabama, the attorney general, the Inter-Racial Commission, and several black and white newspapers to try and augment support for the group's efforts.[76] These tactics did not bring about any substantial departmental changes, yet they did work to highlight the problem and are indicative of the larger critique that black organizations offered of police tactics in the Jim Crow South.

In addition to protesting individual acts of police violence reactively, the local branch took a proactive approach to keep the issue of police brutality at the forefront of black activism and organizing in the city. This shift in approach mirrored changes in NAACP local branch leadership that occurred in cities across the South. A younger, more impatient generation of African Americans rose to leadership positions in these organizations. The broad change in leadership reflected the growth in labor militancy that occurred among African Americans in southern cities during the late 1930s and 1940s. As working-class blacks became more assertive in their demands, the new leadership within the NAACP branch used issues such as police brutality to help funnel that assertiveness into organizational growth.[77] In 1938, the president of the Birmingham branch, W. E. Shortridge, a former victim of police brutality, led the "Stop Police Brutality" campaign and made this the central slogan for the branch's membership drive.[78] The campaign proved particularly effective in the wake of the murder of John Lewis Smith, a twenty-year-old black man falsely accused of raping a white woman. Immediately following his trial, police were escorting Smith to jail when H. E. Colburn, the father of the woman Smith was accused of raping, fired four shots into Smith. During the killing, the county sheriff and two BPD detectives looked on and did nothing.[79] A committee organized by the NAACP raised money and retained a black attorney named Arthur Shores, a native of Alabama, one of the few practicing black attorneys in the state, and a strong advocate for black legal rights, to present the case.[80] Despite these efforts, the district attorney dismissed the charges against Colburn.[81] Despite this setback, the killing coupled with the branch's emphasis on police brutality as a campaign slogan proved very successful, and Shortridge noted that the "John Lewis Smith case was undoubtedly the greatest impetus in giving our membership campaign new birth just when it would appear to be a failure." The branch grew by 553 members.[82]

The branch followed up this successful campaign with a major legal victory against police brutality. On June 10, 1939, BPD officer George Williams drove up to Will Hall, a black man, as he sat on his front porch. Officer Williams shone a light on his face, and when Hall asked him to stop, Officer Williams got out of his car, and claimed, "Negroes are not permitted to talk to [me] in such a manner." Williams proceeded to beat Hall with his fists and a rubber hose, until a large group of bystanders crowded around the two men, and the officer then left the scene.[83] In response to the beating, the Birmingham NAACP filed a complaint with the Civil Service Board and, once again, hired attorney Arthur Shores. The hearing took place on July 26, 1939, in front of a large crowd of black observers. Under cross-examination by Shores, the officer admitted to the beating. The Jefferson Civil Service Board announced its judgment a month later and, to the surprise of the NAACP, decided that "Officer Williams was guilty of conduct unbecoming an officer." Although the board found that "there was provocation which mitigates the offense," they nonetheless placed Williams on probation for one year.[84] The NAACP announced the decision as "unprecedented" in the history of Birmingham.[85] As part of the organization's decade-long fight against police brutality, this victory demonstrated to black residents that the branch remained committed to the campaign against abusive policing and, more importantly, could get violent police officers temporarily removed from the police force.

The Birmingham branch continued its struggle against police brutality throughout the 1940s and cemented the organization's role as the most important civil rights institution in the city. The branch's "new approach to the problem of unfair police treatment" focused on filing complaints with the Civil Service Personnel Board.[86] In 1941, the branch also took up the case of John Jackson, a black man killed by police in Fairfield, a suburb of Birmingham. In the aftermath of the shooting, the NAACP "entered the case following investigation [sic] by two officials less than twelve hours following the slaying." The branch secured an attorney to try and "bring the guilty parties to justice." The NAACP held a membership drive and rally the following night, where a thousand new members signed up, and the branch passed a series of resolutions calling for officers involved to be discharged from the force and prosecuted for murder.[87] Although criminal charges never materialized, the Fairfield city officials dismissed the two officers from the force.[88] The Birmingham branch proved so successful that in 1941 the national office awarded it the Thalheimer Prize in recognition of its work. The announcement declared the branch "the most militant and outstanding" of all the branches. The group's "organized action in reducing police brutality" received special recognition.[89] In addition to the award, the branch membership expanded and reached unprecedented heights. By continuing to tackle these types of cases, the Birmingham branch solidified its status as the main black political organization in the city and by 1946 had 8,500 dues-paying members.[90] Similar to the Birmingham branch, NAACP branches across the South embraced the fight against police brutality during the 1930s and 1940s.[91] However, although individual branches such as Birmingham experienced some success in challenge specific cases of brutality, overall the NAACP and other activist organizations failed to radically alter the approaches of southern police forces in their dealings with African Americans.

The fight against police brutality and black critiques of police violence against African Americans should be seen as part of the burgeoning Civil Rights Movement, but also as part of a broader effort to combat crime and violence in black communities. Police officers accounted for a large number of black deaths. Sociologist Kenneth E. Barnhart, for example, studied homicide trends in Birmingham and suggested police killings of black suspects contributed to the elevated rate of homicide in the black community. "A careful check of police records for 1930," he noted, "shows that 18 negroes were shot in this manner. . . . No White males [or] White females . . . were shot by officers for 'resisting arrest.'"[92] Thus, a reduction in police killings would ultimately lead to a reduction in violence in black communities.

Police violence contributed to crime in black communities in other ways as well. Frequent violent encounters bred distrust between law enforcement and the black community. This distrust often discouraged black residents from assisting the police in their investigation of crime committed in black communities. Due to the fact that all-white police forces lacked an intimate understanding of black communities, black writers believed the effectiveness of the police would largely be determined by black residents' willingness to assist officers. Following an assault of two black women by black men in Jefferson County, Alabama, in August of 1931, an editorialist in the *Birmingham Reporter* declared, "the efforts of the law to effect his [the assailant's] capture should be seconded by citizens everywhere." He implored black residents to make it "impossible for him to escape immediate capture and the severest punishment." The writer, however, was also well aware that black cooperation with the police was predicated upon respectful interactions between officers and residents. After explaining the necessity of black assistance in the apprehension of the suspect, he declared, "The method of terrorizing and mistreating law-abiding Negro citizens in the course of a man-hunt does not enlist their co-operation. If it could be impressed that innocent people would not be fired upon and maltreated in a revengeful way in these man-hunts, the aid of Negroes could be made far more effective."[93] For this editorialist, and for other fair-administration advocates, part of the solution to the crime problem in black communities required cooperation and mutual trust between officers and residents.

For black fair-administration advocates the hiring of black police officers offered a solution to police abuse, the lack of trust and cooperation, and crime in black communities. Demands for black officers in these cities dated back to the early twentieth century, but had met with little success and much resistance.[94] Reflecting the growing militancy of black organizations across the region, at the end of the 1930s African American activists' calls for better policing in black communities became intertwined with demands for African American police officers. Black activists, however, lacked the political leverage that African Americans in the North utilized to secure black police officers. Southern African Americans, then, framed their arguments for black police officers as part of a larger effort to curb crime in black neighborhoods.[95] Responding to white fears over armed black police, these calls typically included an explanation that black police would serve only black communities. In an effort to combat "juvenile vandalism" and "'gangs of delinquent boys … terrorizing the district, destroying property and endangering public safety" several black community activists met with the local Negro Housing Project managers in New Orleans in August 1941. "To curb this wave of petty lawlessness," these activists decided, "Negro officers [should] be appointed to police the area. These officers," they pointed out, "would become members of the police force, but their duties would be confined to Negro neighborhoods."[96]

Arguments in support of black police officers mirrored that of fair-administration advocates who demanded black inclusion on juries. According to these proponents, black police officers could more effectively combat crimes committed in black communities. On August 9, 1943, an editorialist for the *Louisiana Weekly* acknowledged the necessity of black police officers to reduce vandalism in black neighborhoods. To assuage white residents' fear of uniformed and armed black police officers, the writer offered a potential solution: black officers would be confined to black neighborhoods. African Americans policing black communities, according to the editorialist, would "be the most efficient method to deal with the problem."[97] Two weeks later, another editorial championed the cause of black police officers. The writer declared, "Becoming more and more evident throughout the South is a desire for Negro policemen, a sentiment prevailing among both Negro and white leaders. Needless to say, this sentiment is on the increase much because of the widespread crime committed in Negro communities throughout the Southland, ranging from petty family fights to violent murder after murder." The editorialist then elaborated on some of the successes black police officers had achieved in other southern cities. Black police officers had distinct advantages over white police officers: "chief among them," the writer argued, "is the fact that Negroes are more familiar with the conditions under which Negroes live. They are a part of the Negro population and, therefore, are in a better position to curb law-making. As policemen they would be more efficient in seeing that law was observed in Negro communities."[98]

Black activists in Birmingham made similar demands on city officials. On September 7, 1943, an editorialist for the *Birmingham World* declared his support for black police officers as a way to reduce crime and promote cooperation between the black community and law enforcement. He wrote, "It is not arguable that denial of an opportunity for Negroes to participate in their own protection as police will tend to make them doubt the sincerity of those asking their cooperation with the police. It is extremely doubtful whether any other than Negro police can do the job necessary to clean up bad situations in Birmingham with respect to Negroes."[99] Mirroring the strategy of African Americans in New Orleans, African American writers in Birmingham often emphasized the success of black police officers in cities that employed them, and by 1945 a writer demanded the city commission hire black officers to combat crime in black neighborhoods in an editorial entitled, "Negro Policemen Now."[100]

In Memphis, William W. Gray, head of a black private detective firm, also advocated for the inclusion of black police officers on the MPD. Echoing the claims made in the *Louisiana Weekly,* Gray deplored the criminal conditions that existed among Memphis's black community. He believed the only solution rested in the hiring of black officers. He wrote, "There are no palliating circumstances, no mitigating conditions on God's green earth that will even to the slightest degree excuse this worthless class, except Colored Policemen on Beale street and other sections of the city." He praised the efforts of the MPD to date, but suggested "Negro policemen would be a vital link in the policing of the Negro race here, he knows the people better and could make arrest without very much racial fillings [*sic*]." He pleaded, "May some day by the help we may have the chance to prove our worth and ability, as a policeman in our city of Memphis."[101]

By the end of World War II, urban black communities across the South demanded better policing for their communities as part of a larger emphasis on fair administration of laws to combat crime. For them, better policing included an end to abusive police treatment of black suspects and serious efforts by police to apprehend men and women accused of committing crimes against black residents. The fight against police brutality represented one facet of the larger effort to improve policing in black neighborhoods. Black writers and activists critiqued law enforcement's treatment of black residents and used the issue of police brutality to garner support for their causes. However, the fight against police brutality also included efforts to improve policing practices. In cities such as Birmingham, Memphis, and New Orleans, where police forces remained all white, black critics also believed the hiring of black officers would offer the best, most feasible solution to policing issues in the black community. While none of the police departments in these cities hired black police officers before the end of World War II, calls for black officers became central to the demands of black writers and activists in the 1930s and 1940s, which eventually led to the hiring of black police officers in each of these cities by the 1950s.[102] Both the fight against police brutality and calls for black officers not only represented part of the larger civil rights struggle of the pre-World War II era, but also articulated demands for better policing to combat crime in black communities.

Concerns over crime and violence in their communities was a central focus of middle-class black activists in the Jim Crow era. While many white southerners used the notion of black criminality to justify disenfranchisement, segregation, and harsh policing tactics, for many black residents the realities of crime in their neighborhoods was of great concern. Keenly aware of the problematic nature of black crime statistics and institutional and structural reasons undergirding issues in black communities, many African American residents demanded that southern city officials do something to combat crime in black neighborhoods. Black activists and writers called for an end to employment and housing discrimination, more programs for black youth, fair treatment by criminal courts, and better policing in black communities. During the 1930s and 1940s, the fight against police brutality and the effort to achieve the hiring of black police officers to patrol black communities came to the forefront of black critics' campaign to fight crime in their communities.

These types of responses to crime in black communities largely reflected the black middle class's approach to activism in the Jim Crow era. However, utilizing the police to combat crime in black neighborhoods encompassed more than middle-class rhetoric and organizational actions. Much of the fair-administration effort occurred at the street level, led by working-class African Americans. Black victims and witnesses to criminal actions determined to utilize law enforcement to help make their communities safer, assisted the police in investigations of crimes in black neighborhoods, and, through their actions, demonstrated a commitment to fair administration as a solution to the problem of crime in black communities. Yet, as the next chapters illustrate, black crime victims and witnesses often had to rely on several strategies to cajole an otherwise reluctant police force into serving the interests of the black community.

CHAPTER 3

Police Investigations of African American Homicides

Around 1:15 a.m. on January 21, 1930, Benesta Burns, a black man in New Orleans, walked into the home of his common-law wife, Alma Cain. Burns lay down for a few minutes, got up, paced around their room several times, and, without a word, walked out the front door. Moments later, Cain heard "something like a shot being fired." When she looked outside to see what had happened, she saw Burns's car driving away. Thirty minutes later, Bose Clark, a friend of Burns, came to the door and told Cain that Burns had killed Fred Bernard. Cain ran out of her home, found her brother-in-law, Ned Thompson, at the Chauffeurs Club, and told him what happened. He suggested that Cain "better notify the police."[1] The owner of the club, Isaac Morris, echoed Thompson's suggestion and told Cain "that the best she could do was to report it to the police, and [Morris] walked to the Twelfth Precinct Police Station with her" and reported the homicide.[2]

The fair-administration rhetoric of the black middle class coincided with efforts by African American crime witnesses like Alma Cain to use the police to combat crime in black neighborhoods. While black writers and activists embraced fair administration and implored law enforcement to improve policing and reduce crime in black communities, these witnesses worked to make that abstract idea a reality.[3] As opposed to middle-class African Americans, these witnesses, who were largely from the working class, engaged with law enforcement for slightly different reasons. Although traditions of self-help or self-policing in black communities continued to influence African American witnesses' decisions to avoid law enforcement in the wake of a crime, many black witnesses chose to engage law enforcement in a seeming rebuke to those self-policing customs.[4] During the late 1920s and 1930s, as law enforcement attempted to place more African Americans under the control of formal institutions of criminal justice—police, courts, prisons—African Americans capitalized on the police departments' encroachment into black neighborhoods.[5] Proactive efforts to reduce killings proved difficult as gun laws were lax and rarely enforced in southern cities, and as there was a widespread availability of other weapons, such as knifes, bats, and bricks, that assailants used when they took a life.[6] Thus, reacting to killings after the fact was often the only recourse for African Americans. In the wake of a homicide, black witnesses exercised whatever leverage they could in their interactions with police officers in an attempt to improve the likelihood that the police would secure an arrest. By reporting potential homicides, acting as witnesses, and assisting police during investigations black southerners illustrated their dismay with widespread violence within their communities and their willingness to try and use the police to stop the problem. For these witnesses, self-policing strategies seemed to be ineffective, potentially contributing to increased violence in the community. Taking this into consideration, they engaged law enforcement in a larger effort to increase the likelihood of an arrest. Not only did black southerners use the police to try and make their communities safer, but because of their centrality to police investigations of black homicides, African Americans possessed influence over when the police came into black communities and how police proceeded with investigations. In the face of the overwhelming power imbalance that existed between white police officers and African Americans during interactions, black homicide witnesses proved to be quite capable of manipulating law enforcement into serving the interests of black communities.

Black murder suspects also managed their encounters with police in interesting ways. At times suspects dictated the nature of their arrest by choosing when and how to surrender themselves to police.[7] The harsh realities of life on the run, especially potential violence during the process of arrest or as retaliation from members of the black community seeking to avenge the killing, pushed some black murder suspects to turn themselves in, in order to try and mitigate these dangers. Black residents accused of homicide faced two unattractive options: life on the run or time in police custody. When surrendering, African Americans decreased the likelihood of violence faced at the hands of police or other African Americans while on the run, and they could chose the time, place, and circumstances of their arrest.

In the wake of a black homicide, African Americans demonstrated great acumen in managing their encounters with the police and shaping the outcome of homicide investigations. In addition, these efforts are representative of another form of activism among black southerners. By manipulating law enforcement officers to serve black interests, black homicide witnesses extracted civic services from a civic institution typically unwilling to serve black communities and, through their actions, articulated larger critiques of the state of criminal justice in the Jim Crow South.[8]

Police Investigations of Black Intraracial Homicides

Throughout the first half of the twentieth century, the police and city officials in Memphis, New Orleans, and Birmingham worked to reduce the incredibly high homicide rates that plagued their cities.[9] As city officials and law enforcement agencies targeted black communities and as the demands for greater police presence by middle-class African Americans increased, the interests of police and African Americans momentarily aligned. By arresting African Americans accused of killing other African Americans, the police addressed some of the demands for increased policing within the black community, worked to curb violence that plagued the city (and frequently made national headlines), and also brought more African Americans under the control of the criminal justice system.[10] The MPD homicide reports indicate that the police cleared, or arrested a suspect in, 76 percent of black intraracial homicide cases between 1920 and 1945.[11] As Figure 3.1 illustrates, the worst year for the MPD in terms of clearing black intraracial homicides was 1920, when the police arrested eighteen suspects out of forty total black intraracial homicides. Just four years later, the MPD cleared 86 percent of these cases. Over the next fifteen years, from 1925 to 1939, the clearance rate consistently ranged between 65 and 77 percent, and from 1940 to 1945, MPD cleared more than 90 percent of these homicide cases. The NOPD experienced similar success. From 1926 to 1945, officers and detectives arrested suspects in 498 cases out of 674 total black intraracial homicides, a clearance rate of 73.88 percent.[12] As Figure 3.2 indicates, from 1926 to 1931, NOPD clearance rates ranged between 52 and 79 percent. From 1935 to 1945, however, the rate never fell below 76.92 percent and reached as high as 90.91 percent. While the arrest statistics for Birmingham are lacking, from 1920 to 1932, a total of 572 homicide cases involving African Americans came before a grand jury in Jefferson County.[13] Taken together, the data suggest that police consistently arrested suspects in black intraracial homicides. In other words,

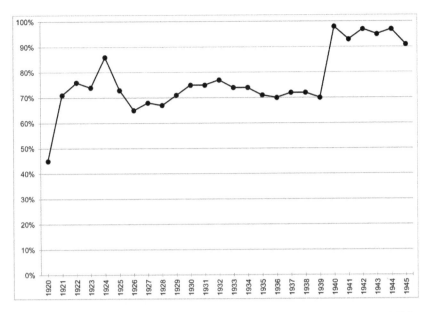

Fig. 3.1. Black Intraracial Homicide Arrests in Memphis, 1920–1945. Source: MPD Homicide Reports, 1920–1945.

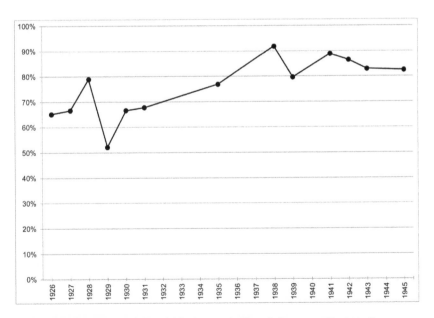

Fig. 3.2. Black Intraracial Homicide Arrests in New Orleans, 1926–1945. Source: NOPD Homicide Reports, 1926–1945.

as police forces across the country, embracing technological advances and improved training techniques, attempted to control and monitor African American communities, officers and detectives became more effective in arresting black homicide suspects.[14]

In addition to improved clearance rates, police officers and detectives proved fairly efficient when arresting suspects in black intraracial homicides.[15] In Memphis, police recorded the date an arrest was made, which makes it possible to determine the typical amount of time that transpired between the reporting of the homicide to the arrest. From 1925 to 1945, in 75 percent of cleared cases, MPD arrested a suspect in less than a week.[16] On February 19, 1937, for example, Lorenza Nelson, a forty-one-year-old black man, walked to his neighbor's apartment and called Willie Ray Haynes, a thirty-three-year-old black man, to the door. When Haynes opened the door, Nelson opened fire and shot Haynes four times in the abdomen. Nelson quickly fled, went to a nearby undertaker's office, and told them to send an ambulance to the scene. He then ran to another residence, hid the murder weapon under the house, and walked down Main and Auction Streets, where officers spotted him and placed him under arrest.[17] While it is unclear from the records how much time transpired between the shooting and Nelson's arrest, it happened on the same day as the crime. Instances such as this occurred throughout the 1920s, 1930s, and 1940s, as the number of arrests made in one week or less never dropped below 50 percent.

While most arrests occurred in a matter of days or weeks, in several instances a significant amount of time elapsed between the murder and the arrest of the main suspect. Following the murder of Leroy Robinson, a black male, on July 18, 1920, the suspect, Harvey Lobbins, made his escape. Three years later, on February 8, 1923, MPD received word from the St. Louis Police Department that their officers had Lobbins in custody. Authorities transported him back to Memphis, his case went to trial, and a jury found him guilty and sentenced him to serve between one to five years for the murder.[18]

As this example demonstrates, police departments in cities across the country also grew more interconnected throughout the early twentieth century with the introduction of improved communication technologies such as telephones and criminal databases.[19] These improvements extended the abilities of local police forces to track down suspects across the country.[20] The MPD tracked suspects in cities as far away as Oakland, Detroit, New York City, and especially in Chicago and St. Louis.[21] But communication between law enforcement officials also occurred between the MPD and smaller cities. Local authorities arrested suspects accused of murder in places like Ruleville, Mississippi; Hollywood, Tennessee; and Clarendon, Arkansas. The NOPD was similarly connected and made arrests in cities like Baton Rouge, Milneburg, Franklin, and Lockport, Louisiana; Biloxi and Picayune, Mississippi; and Chicago, Illinois. The BPD captured suspects in cities like Andalusia, Alabama; Pittsburgh, Pennsylvania; and Cleveland and Youngstown, Ohio. In other words, throughout the early twentieth century, law enforcement officials across the country became linked in ways that made the tracking of suspects possible in both small and large cities. This proved especially important in places such as Memphis and New Orleans where easy access to water and rail transportation made escaping the city fairly easy.

African Americans during Police Investigations of Homicides

While technological improvements made police work more efficient, the ability of law enforcement to arrest suspects in black intraracial homicide cases relied largely on the cooperation of African American witnesses. During black homicide investigations police officers and detectives became increasingly reliant on African Americans, who played crucial roles in the entire process of investigations of homicides in the black community. African Americans capitalized on city officials' and police departments' interest in arresting black residents, and by reporting potential homicides, acting as witnesses, and assisting police during investigations demonstrated their willingness to use the police to reduce violence in their neighborhoods.[22] Interestingly, at the same time that law enforcement officials like "Bull" Connor embraced racially discriminatory and violent policing practices, African Americans were largely responsible for the high rate of arrests made in intraracial cases by police because of their centrality to police investigations of black homicides. This is not to suggest that African Americans were responsible for those racially discriminatory police practices that targeted black residents, but instead that black southerners capitalized on the police presence in their communities in an attempt to assuage concerns over homicides in their neighborhoods.

By reporting potential homicides to law enforcement, African Americans demonstrated their willingness to utilize the police to remove violent offenders from their neighborhoods. On several occasions, police records indicated who contacted police headquarters to report a potential homicide; unfortunately, the records are far from comprehensive or complete. From 1920 to 1945, MPD homicide records identified in fifty-four cases when African Americans initially reported a murder.[23] In New Orleans, NOPD proved more systematic in their reporting. From 1926 to 1945, NOPD homicide reports contained a "By Whom Reported" section; however it was often left blank or filled in with phrases like "switchboard operator" or "charity hospital." Nonetheless, the homicide records listed 227 cases in which African Americans first reported a potential homicide to police.[24]

The surviving evidence demonstrates that African Americans routinely called the police to report potential homicides. In so doing, black southerners essentially 'invited' the police into their communities and urged them to investigate the deaths of their friends, neighbors, and relatives.[25] The circumstances surrounding how and why each of these African Americans decided to notify police are not completely clear in the extant records. There was a noticeable shift away from self-help strategies, or "informal, aggressive mechanisms of dispute resolution," among the black community in the late nineteenth and early twentieth centuries to an increased willingness to report incidents to the police in the 1920s, 1930s, and 1940s.[26] While middle-class black southerners often championed the increased involvement of police in black communities to reduce the black homicide rate, working-class blacks, the group most likely to be involved in or witness to a homicide, also believed police involvement could be useful in reducing violence in their community, or at the very least in removing violent individuals from their homes and neighborhoods. In January 1924, George Thomas, who did not see the murder but heard the shots, remembered the murder of Frank Sherrod and Jack Meadows by Perry Henry in Jefferson County, Alabama. Once he heard the shots and saw the bodies, he called the police and reported the incident. Thomas stated, "We didn't go out to where these two [dead] men were until the officers came. When the officers came we went."[27] Thomas did not feel it was safe to leave his home until the police arrived. The combination of gunshots and dead bodies frightened him, and, in this instance, the police represented safety from potential danger. When African Americans like George Thomas reported potential homicides to police, they took advantage of law enforcement's growing effort to bring more African Americans under the control of the formal criminal justice system and used police to try and combat the high rates of lethal violence in black neighborhoods.

It is impossible to say with any statistical certainty how many times and in what ways African Americans reported homicides due to the lack of consistency in police reporting; nonetheless, it is possible to make some generalized conclusions about the ways African Americans notified police of a potential homicide. When black residents witnessed homicides or found bodies, they often reported them to police headquarters. Such was the case in Memphis, on April 25, 1923, when Genie May Whitfield walked up the steps to her residence and heard a gunshot. Seconds later, her husband, John Whitfield, ran past her on the stairway and out the door without saying a word. Genie then continued up the stairs and looked into the room where she saw the body of John Henry Wooten, a twenty-five-year-old black male, lying on the floor dying from a gunshot wound to the head. Moments later, "she then went to [the] phone and called police headquarters" and reported the incident. Charles LeBlanc, a twenty-seven-year-old black New Orleanian acted similarly on July 13, 1942, when he called the NOPD and reported that Ella Davis had been fatally cut. LeBlanc, the superintendent of the Lafitte Housing Project, informed officers that Raymond Bailey, a sixteen-year-old resident of the housing project, called him and informed him of "some trouble" in the house. When LeBlanc arrived at the house, "he could only open the door about six inches, as something was against the door on the inside and upon looking in saw a woman lying on the floor in a pool of blood and he then notified at [sic] police."[28] On February 14, 1921, four black witnesses recounted the murder of Henrietta Walker by Pearl Harris. Emma Bryant, Walker's sister, remembered the evening. Bryant escorted Walker out of her home on the night of the murder. After she closed the door she heard several gunshots. Bryant immediately opened the door and witnessed Harris shooting her sister. Bryant claimed, "Henrietta turned around and started to me, and I went and called the officers."[29] In some cases, African Americans could be surprisingly persistent in their efforts to call police. In the early morning hours of April 14, 1929, Pauline Wade, a twenty-six-year-old black woman, stabbed Early Alexander, a twenty-two-year-old black woman, while she walked down Ayers Street in Memphis. Following the stabbing, Alexander's friend, Lena May Strickland, "attempted to call the police but no one in the neighborhood would admit her in the house." According to police, she then "remained [on the scene] until daylight and then got a phone and called in."[30]

In many instances there was no telephone near the scene, so African Americans asked other people to contact the police for them. In Memphis, on March 5, 1942, for example, "a negro man" witnessed Buster Jones stab Quintell Smith on the corner of Pioneer and West Trigg Streets. Shortly after the stabbing, the "negro man came back in [to a café near the scene] and told

[Mr. Lashee, the white proprietor of the café] that Jones had cut Quintell Smith and he called the officers."[31] Similarly, in New Orleans on the night of October 15, 1941, Josephine Reed, a forty-year-old black woman, sat on her porch and witnessed Dan Brown, who boarded at Reed's home, strike fellow boarder Charles Brooks in the head with an ax. According to the NOPD, immediately following the blow "Josephine Reed jumped up off of the steps and ran to the grocery store at the corner of S. Liberty and Clio streets and asked Mrs. Joseph Accardo to call up the Police [sic]."[32]

African Americans also reported homicides to police in person. On November 5, 1926, for instance, Gracie Robinson, who had just stabbed her husband, "came to police headquarters and reported the matter." Although she believed he was not seriously wounded, MPD officers proceeded to the scene and found Jerry Robinson dead. Officers quickly arrested Gracie.[33] Other times, individuals not involved in the homicide notified officers at police headquarters. At 9:00 p.m. on December 29, 1934, Robert Duncan "came to police headquarters and reported that his brother George had been killed." He relayed to police that while walking along Commerce and Main Streets, a black man named Jimmie Love stabbed his brother in the throat.[34] In New Orleans, Nellie Carter fatally cut her common-law husband, Thodile Jacobs, on Thursday, April 27, 1939, at 11:00 p.m., in the kitchen of the home. Following the fight and cutting, Louise Joseph, a boarder at the same house as Jacobs and Carter, fled the scene and ran a quarter of a mile to her cousins Frank Marshall's home. Once there, Joseph notified Dorothy Marshall about the cutting. Dorothy Marshall then ran another quarter of a mile to the home of her friend Oscar Hazet and "notified him of what Louise Joseph had told her." Marshall and Hazet then "went to the home of Jacobs where Hazet shook Jacobs and he did not answer him, both then left and notified the police."[35]

By reporting these killings, African Americans initiated the investigative process and demonstrated a desire to use the police to investigate homicides, but by acting as witnesses black southerners shaped officers' understanding of the crimes and increased the chances that the police made an arrest. The bulk of an officer's or a detective's work involved interviewing witnesses, determining what happened, and identifying suspects. Considering most black intraracial homicides occurred in black neighborhoods, black homes, and establishments for blacks, it is not surprising that at this point in the investigative process, African American witnesses played their most import-ant role in police investigations of black homicides. While the numbers are far from complete, the police reports documented 4,871 black witnesses who made statements to MPD officers between 1920 and 1945. In New Orleans, NOPD records indicated that 1,649 black witnesses made statements to police from 1926 to 1945. In Jefferson County, where Birmingham is located, grand jury indictment records indicate 1,918 black witnesses in murder cases from 1920 to 1932. Moreover, police interviewed black witnesses in the vast majority of black intraracial homicide cases. Out of a total of 1,218 black homicides investigated by MPD, police identified at least one black witness on their report in 1,127 instances. The NOPD noted at least one black witness in 600 homicide cases out of a total of 674. Jefferson County Grand Jury Indictment Records (JCGJIR) documented 546 cases with at least one black witnesses out of a total of 572 black intraracial homicide cases. Taken together, police in these three cities identified at least one African American witness in 2,273 black intraracial homicides out of a total of 2,464 cases (92.25 percent).

Ironically, as the police embraced more violent techniques in their interactions with black communities throughout the 1920s, 1930s, and 1940s, more African Americans provided law enforcement with testimony regard-

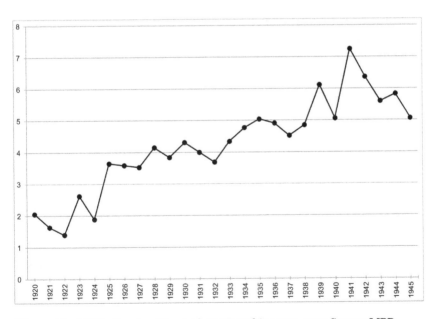

Fig. 3.3. Black Witnesses per Homicide in Memphis, 1920–1945. Source: MPD Homicide Reports, 1920–1945.

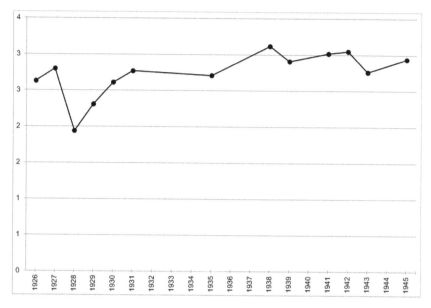

Fig. 3.4. Black Witnesses per Homicide in New Orleans, 1926–1945. Source: NOPD Homicide Reports, 1926–1945.

ing black homicides (see figs. 3.3 and 3.4). In Memphis, the most detailed recordings of black witnesses began in 1925, when police recorded an average of 3.5 black witnesses/homicide on their reports. Over the next twenty years that number steadily increased and peaked in 1941 at 7.25 black witnesses/homicide. In New Orleans, where reporting began in 1926, there was an average of 2.63 black witnesses/homicide. This average declined initially and in 1928 reached a low of 1.94 black witnesses/homicide. From 1929 to 1938, the number steadily rose and peaked at 3.12 black witnesses/homicide. Between 1939 and 1945, the average never fell below 2.75 or above 3.05. Although the change in New Orleans is much more nuanced and subtle, there was an increase in the overall average of black witnesses/homicide over the twenty-year period.

In Jefferson County, Alabama, the number of black witnesses/homicide listed slightly declined (see fig. 3.5). From 1920 to 1932, the rate dropped from 3.96 to 3.37. Outside of a major decline in 1929 and a subsequent jump in 1930, the number of black witnesses per homicide in Jefferson County, for the most part, consistently ranged between three and four per homicide case. The lack of increase in Jefferson County is perhaps related to the types of records utilized. In New Orleans and Memphis, police homicide reports detailed witnesses for nearly every homicide in the respective cities. However, the JCGJIR listed only those people called to testify before a grand jury. Perhaps the county prosecutors did not call all of the witnesses interviewed by police because they only needed to convince the jurors that there was enough evidence to prove the state's side of the case.[36] Or, as other scholars have noted, conviction rates for black intraracial homicides remained low throughout the 1920s, 1930s, and 1940s, so perhaps grand juries and prosecutors routinely dropped African American homicide cases because they assumed convictions would be hard to come by.[37] As a result, the number of black witnesses recorded on the grand jury records may have been incomplete as African Americans decided against making the trip to the city to testify in a case that would most likely be dropped. Despite the drop in Jefferson County, based on the data from New Orleans and Memphis, over time more black witnesses came forward and talked with police.

This general increase in black witnesses interviewed is indicative of several potential trends. As police investigated black homicides, it is probable that they simply recorded more witnesses in their reports. This could be the

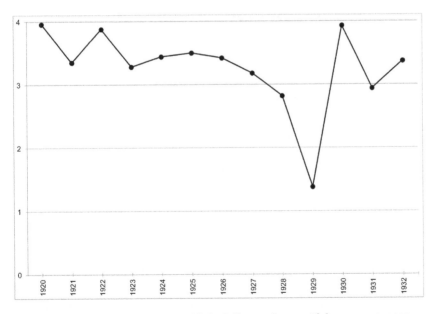

Fig. 3.5. Black Witnesses per Homicide in Jefferson County, Alabama, 1920–1932.
Source: Jefferson County Grand Jury Indictment Records, 1920–1932.

result of improved record keeping, professionalization efforts, and better training for officers and detectives. Or, perhaps officers and detectives actually interviewed more witnesses during their investigations. More witnesses meant more evidence supporting the case, which only increased the chances of an indictment and eventual conviction.[38] As police proved more willing to investigate cases, perhaps their record keeping and diligence resulted in more black witnesses being recorded in reports.

It is also likely that more African Americans actually witnessed murders and became more forthcoming with their statements over time. Two trends occurred that suggest this was partially the case. First, the urban black population across the South increased between 1920 and 1940.[39] While the population grew, black intraracial homicides comprised a larger proportion of the total homicides in the city. From a low of 47 percent in 1921, the percentage in Memphis steadily increased and reached a peak of 85 percent in 1939. Similarly, black intraracial homicides increased from 50 to 60 percent of all homicides in New Orleans in the mid-1920s to just over 70 percent of all homicides in the late 1930s and early 1940s. African American homicides in Birmingham jumped from just over 70 percent in the early 1920s to over 80 percent in the mid-1930s.[40] As the number of urban blacks increased across the South, racial segregation solidified, and homicides became more concentrated in the black community, the number of black intraracial homicides that occurred in public also increased.[41] As African American communities became more segregated and crowded, and violence more visible, black witnesses proved more forthcoming with their testimony.

In addition to the increasing number of black witnesses, the proportion of African American witnesses interviewed by officers relative to white witnesses also increased. In Jefferson County, the percentage of black witnesses in the early 1920s ranged from 72 to 79 percent; however, by the early 1930s that number reached between 88 and 98 percent (see fig. 3.6). In Memphis, African Americans typically comprised below 50 percent of the witnesses listed in the early 1920s, but by the 1940s that number rose to above 60 percent (see Figure 3.7). In New Orleans, the increase was not so drastic, as African Americans comprised 89 percent of witnesses listed in 1926 and reached a peak of 99 percent in 1941 (see fig. 3.8). Similar to Memphis, that number declined slightly by 1945 and totaled 96 percent. The percentage of black witnesses in New Orleans and Jefferson County is much higher than the percentage of black witnesses in Memphis. This is largely a result of recordkeeping, as MPD officers routinely listed white ambulance drivers

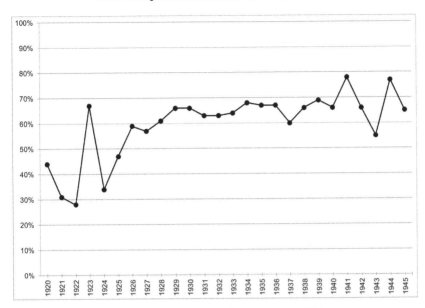

Fig. 3.6. Percentage of Black Witnesses in Jefferson County, Alabama, 1920–1932. Source: Jefferson County Grand Jury Indictment Records, 1920–1932. (The data for the year 1929 are excluded from this chart because the records indicated no races for witnesses.)

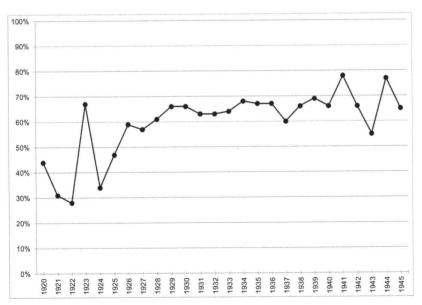

Fig. 3.7. Percentage of Black Witnesses in Memphis, 1920–1945. Source: MPD Homicide Reports, 1920–1945.

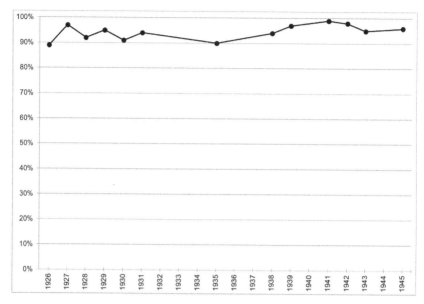

Fig. 3.8. Percentage of Black Witnesses in New Orleans, 1926–1945.
Source: NOPD Homicide Reports, 1926–1945.

and coroners on the homicide reports, while the NOPD did not. Despite that difference, the overall higher percentage of black witnesses over time in Birmingham, Memphis, and New Orleans is indicative of the growing segregation between blacks and whites throughout the early twentieth century. Throughout the 1920s, 1930s, and 1940s, the social lives of blacks and whites in southern cities diverged and instances of social interaction between the races became less common. As segregation solidified and black communities became more isolated from white communities, whites were less likely to witness a homicide involving African Americans.[42] Thus, black witnesses were the main source of information regarding black intraracial homicides in southern cities.[43]

Black witnesses ensured the police had the necessary information and evidence to make arrests of violent individuals in their neighborhood. By identifying the body, black witnesses helped begin the formal investigation process. When providing police with statements regarding events leading up to murders, they pointed police in the direction of the suspect and increased the likelihood of an arrest. African American witness testimony often countered the suspect's version of events, especially when a suspect claimed self-defense. In so doing, witnesses tried to make sure the killer would not be free to roam the streets. By providing the police with physical evidence, such as the murder weapon, black witnesses aided law enforcement officers in securing the arrest of a suspected killer, and in so doing benefited the black community. In other words, black witnesses shaped police interpretations of events surrounding homicides and oftentimes provided critical testimony and evidence that increased the likelihood that violent members of the black community would be captured.

African Americans routinely helped police identify bodies and begin formal homicide investigations by acting as corpus delicti witnesses. Out of the three cities under study, the MPD reports were the only ones to report who acted as corpus delicti witnesses. From 1925 to 1945, in 88 percent of cases MPD reports listed black corpus delicti witnesses.[44] These witnesses identified the victim's body and, in conjunction with doctors, embalmers, and ambulance drivers, established for the record that a particular person was the victim of a homicide. In homicide cases this usually meant summoning family members to identify the deceased, and coroners establishing the cause of death. Corpus delicti witnesses contributed to the initiation of formal homicide investigations, and in homicides involving black victims, black witnesses proved vital in this early stage of the process.

Perhaps most importantly, African Americans shaped the way police understood the homicides they investigated. They provided testimony to establish the cause of the murder, identified potential suspects, furnished descriptions of suspects who escaped, and informed police of family members and friends who might know the whereabouts of suspects. When, on August 22, 1926, for example, MPD officers arrived on the scene and found the body of Costie Louis Brown, they relied on the testimony of two black women, Dorothy Johnson and Mabel Simpson, to establish what had happened. Both women admitted they did not see the actual shooting but claimed that the victim, Costie Brown, and her husband had an argument the night before and that they overheard the latter, James Brown, yell that "[h]e was going to get his clothes and leave but that if he did the right thing he would kill her." A few minutes passed and the witnesses heard five shots fired. Based on this testimony, detectives listed James Brown as their main suspect, and using the description furnished by Johnson and Simpson, officers searched for and later arrested Brown near Horn Lake, Mississippi, on August 26, 1926. Two months later a jury sentenced Brown to life in the penitentiary for the murder.[45]

Similarly, when NOPD officer Dominick I. Curren investigated the murder of forty-four-year-old Oscar Hardin, on November 26, 1939, he relied on the testimony of Louise Thompson to identify the suspect. Thompson informed Sergeant Curren that on the night of the murder she and Hardin followed "a negro who was in the barroom" who told Thompson he would take her to a boarding house where she could rent a room. As Thompson and Hardin followed the unidentified black man down Clio Street, "the negro punched Oscar Hardin [on the] side of the face knocking Oscar Hardin to the pavement striking his head and Louise Thompson hollered and the negro struck her back of the head and knocked her over the stop and took her purse." The assailant then fled and made his escape. Thompson did not know the identity of the assailant, but "furnished the Officers with a description of the negro who assaulted Oscar Hardin and herself stating that he had a bandage on the side of his face." Soon afterward Curren saw a black man with a bandage on his face and proceeded with Thompson to the residence of Robert Moore. When Thompson saw Moore, she immediately identified him as her attacker and police placed him under arrest. Based solely on the testimony provided by Thompson, the NOPD charged Moore with Hardin's murder.[46]

At other times witnesses supplied police officers with testimony that conflicted with the accused's version of events. On July 2, 1927, Virginia Bullock and Thomas Lee Tapping brought Rayfield Bullock to the General Hospital in Memphis with a gunshot wound in his stomach. Hospital staff notified the MPD, and when officers arrived, Virginia Bullock, wife of Rayfield Bullock, claimed that she shot her husband by accident while trying to move their gun. She claimed "that she went to move [the] pistol from [the] mantel to [the] chifforobe drawer and it went off accidentally." However, Thomas Lee Tapping recounted a different story to police. When interviewed, he reported Virginia "tried to kill Rayfield that morning and that at [the] time of [the] shooting she unlocked [the] chifforobe drawer and secured [the] pistol and shot and seriously wounded her husband." Other black witnesses corroborated Tapping's version of events and when interviewed by police, they claimed that Virginia "made remarks recently that the law did not care anything about negro women killing men," suggesting that Virginia believed she could get away with killing her husband. Despite Virginia Bullock's initial self-defense claim, testimony from other African American witnesses brought her version of the murder into question. As a result, police arrested Virginia from the General Hospital, and she was tried for the murder of her husband.[47]

A similar incident occurred in New Orleans following the killing of Louis

Mitchell by Joseph Harris, on April 7, 1930. The NOPD quickly apprehended Harris, who claimed he had acted in self-defense. Harris reported to officers that he engaged in a fight with George Mitchell, the son of the deceased, and as he left the scene of the fight, Louis Mitchell "grabbed at me and I turned around and struck him with my fist."[48] Mitchell fell to the pavement and later died. Two black witnesses, Eddie Bell and Leona Charles, relayed a different version of events to the police. They described Harris as the aggressor and insisted that Harris came to Mitchell's residence and began arguing with several people. According to them, Louis Mitchell "tried to persuade Joseph Harris to leave." Harris "became more abusive, and then struck Louis Mitchell with his fist and knocked him down."[49] Based on the witness testimony, the police charged Harris with murder.[50]

Black witnesses also countered the claims of suspects who denied their involvement in a homicide. On a Friday evening in 1928 in Jefferson County, Alabama, Clayton Snow stabbed Fannie Simons twenty-seven times with a knife. The police arrested him on January 29, 1928. During his interrogation, Snow denied his involvement in the murder and instead stated "that he was at his brother's house at the time it was done." Despite his statement, Detective W. E. Garner claimed, "we have got witnesses to prove his whereabouts" and "one witness that saw him chasing [Simons]." Three black women, Jennie Mack, Clara Lewis, and Bertie Berry, all reported to authorities that they saw Snow in the vicinity of the murder on the Friday it occurred. Bertie Berry also recalled that Simons told her the day before her death that Snow was upset with her because she told him she was leaving him. When asked if Simons told her she thought Snow might kill her, Berry replied, "That is what [Simons] said. She said he was mad at her." Although Snow told police he was nowhere near the scene when the killing occurred, based on the witness testimony police arrested him and the grand jury returned a True Bill against him.[51]

Whether reconstructing events for the police, identifying potential suspects, or countering the claims of assailants, black witnesses shaped the way police understood the homicides, and by providing testimony, they pushed police to make arrests of violent individuals in their neighborhoods. Police needed the testimonies of black witnesses to reconstruct killings and determine their course of action. Black witnesses played a vital role in the way police interpreted events surrounding homicides, and affected how the investigations proceeded. Black witnesses often offered the only real evidence police could rely on to determine who their suspects were and what transpired prior to and after the killings. Their importance is encapsulated in BPD detective H. C. Jones's reply when asked about what he knew about the 1927 murder of Laura Hill by Dan Tweedy. In response to this question, he claimed in 1927, "[n]othing, only what the witnesses say." All five witnesses in this case were black women.[52]

In addition to interviewing witnesses, officers also needed to collect evidence. The murder weapon was one of the most important pieces of physical evidence, and black witnesses often turned weapons used in killings over to the police when they arrived.[53] After Walter Meek, a forty-year-old black male, killed Will Ross on April 23, 1932, in Memphis, he fled the scene by running through back alleys and at some point dropped the shotgun used to kill Ross. Susie Clark, a black woman with no apparent association with either the victim or the accused, found the weapon in the back alley and turned it over to the police.[54] During the January 1929 term of a Jefferson County grand jury, BPD detective J. T. Moser recalled his investigation of the murder of Arthur Albert by Jessie Albert. When the officers arrived on the scene, they arrested their suspect and interviewed several black witnesses. During the course of their investigation, the officers "recovered the pistol from a negro in the house at the time."[55] Black witnesses sometimes took the murder weapon from the killers in question. Following an argument over a crap game on October 9, 1933, Bill Looney shot and killed William Graham. Immediately after the shooting, "Walter Scott [a black man who witnessed the shooting] took the pistol away from Looney and kept it until [MPD] officers arrived and turned it over to them."[56] On July 23, 1939, Charles McCarthy fatally stabbed Elvira Peters in New Orleans. As McCarthy ran from the boarding house, three black men—John Frank, Thomas Snowden, and William Finch—chased after him. John Frank threw a brick at the fleeing suspect and hit him in the head, whereupon he fell unconscious on the ground. After McCarthy fell, Thomas Snowden picked up the knife used in the murder and "brought [the knife] into the station and turned it over to Desk Sergeant Albert Moustier."[57]

African Americans also helped police actually apprehend suspects. Some African Americans did so because it benefited them directly by minimizing their own role in a homicide and thus resulting in a reduced sentence. Other black witnesses seemed to have little to gain materially from assisting in the arrest of murder suspects. Instead, their concern with apprehending potential killers probably had to do with the welfare of their friends, family, and community.[58]

Information such as descriptions of suspects, their relatives, and their residences provided by black witnesses helped detectives track down the suspects. In Memphis, on September 17, 1922, John Coward and James Berry, two black men who witnessed the murder of Ike McKinney by Tommy Alston, chased the suspect for several blocks. Despite their effort, however, they failed to capture him. Nonetheless, when police arrived Coward and Berry informed officers that they knew Alston and where he lived. Police noted in their report that Coward and Berry "did good work in helping us locate Alston."[59] When Will Redford shot and killed Jim Hartley on November 17, 1929, in Birmingham, Redford fled the scene before police arrived. He evaded arrest for nearly a year. Throughout the year, however, Officer Jones of BPD stated, "[t]he negroes kept reporting to us they heard from him in Columbus, Ga." Based on this information, BPD officers notified authorities in Columbus, and they made the arrest on October 12, 1930.[60] Following the murder of Beverly Frank in New Orleans, on January 9, 1926, suspect Andrew Smith fled from the scene. Police arrived and interviewed three black witnesses, but never located Smith. Six years later, on March 23, 1932, Walter Martis called police and reported that he knew the whereabouts of Smith. Based on the information given to them, Corporal Edward Alberta proceeded to the location and "arrested the accused Andrew Smith, who admitted to his guilt."[61]

On a few occasions, black witnesses took a much more active role in apprehending suspects. Following the murder of Moses Hart by several black men during a botched robbery, Walker I. Koen, a twenty-seven-year-old black man, surrendered to police. Koen, who took part in the robbery, "informed [officers] that he knew who killed the man Hart." Koen then agreed "to put Wright, and Carter [two suspects] on the spot for us, saying he would get them on a street car, or rather a trolley, which he did." Once the two men were on the trolley, police rushed the car and arrested the two suspects. While Koen may have been coerced into helping police, the fact that he surrendered to them suggests he was willing to work with police in an effort to minimize his own role in the robbery. Nonetheless, the MPD charged Koen, and three other suspects, with murder, robbery, and carrying a pistol.[62]

African American witnesses also captured murder suspects and held them until police arrived on the scene. On the night of May 9, 1936, for instance, Cora Cole, Arcarrie Hudson, and Charlene Moss spent the night drinking at the Panama Café on Beale Avenue in Memphis. At some point during the night, Hudson gave Moss a nickel to put in the jukebox. Cole resented this and said, "Charlene was her old lady and [she] did not want anybody messing with her." An argument ensued and during the scuffle Cole stabbed Hudson in the heart, killing her immediately. According to MPD, Howard Evans, a black male, "grabbed Cora and held her until Patrolman J. D. Benson arrived on the scene and she was turned over to him."[63] Following the murder of Lucinda Thomas by Dorothy Askin in New Orleans, on February 3, 1931, Thomas Webbs, a thirty-six-year-old witness to the murder, chased Askin several blocks, eventually overran her, and held her until police arrived. According to Webbs's statement, "I took [Askin] in a grocery at Tulane Ave and S. Rocheblave St and held her there until the Police came." He continued, "Upon arrival of the Police I turned the woman that had killed the other woman over to the Police and went to where I had left my wagon ... and came to the First Precinct where I made this statement."[64]

Sometimes groups of African Americans held suspects for police. When Isaac Malone stabbed and killed Charlie Williams on March 10, 1934, in front of 379 North Dunlap Street in Memphis, a crowd of at least seven people witnessed the event. After the stabbing, "Malone was held by some of the crowd until the police arrived and took him into custody."[65] On June 8, 1941, New Orleans resident Ury Rousell and several other black men followed Leonard Matthews, a thirty-two-year-old black man who had just killed Solomon Sanders, several blocks. According to the NOPD report, when the men cornered Matthews, "Rousell having a pistol at the time, induced Leonard Matthews to return and wait for the arrival of the police." The group then escorted Matthews to the scene of the crime and had him placed under arrest by officers.[66] Although the police recorded these instances in only a few cases, it is important to highlight such moments because they are indicative of a larger trend in which African Americans risked their own safety to ensure police captured the suspect. In these few cases, black southerners did not resort to extralegal retribution against the suspect and instead relied on formal criminal justice institutions. African Americans who actively captured suspects and handed them to police must have believed on the whole that the police would not simply let the accused walk free.

From 1920 to 1945, the police made an arrest in the majority of black intraracial homicide cases. Improved technology and expanded police forces certainly contributed to these surprising statistics, but in reality, the high number of cleared cases mostly resulted from the actions of African Americans themselves. Despite the mistrust of law enforcement that permeated black communities, black witnesses initiated police investigations by reporting homicides and provided the police with most of the information necessary to apprehend suspects at increasing rates throughout the 1930s. In so doing, black homicide witnesses demonstrated their interest in using the police to reduce criminal activity in black neighborhoods. Equally important, the interactions between African Americans and the police in the wake of black homicides demonstrated how African Americans were capable of shaping the way individual officers understood the crimes and how they proceeded with their investigations.

Surrendering to Police

While most people fled following a murder, in a significant number of homicide cases black suspects surrendered themselves to police officers. In Memphis, this occurred in 23 percent of the reported cases. From 1920 to 1945, 272 African Americans who committed, or whom police suspected of committing a murder, surrendered themselves to MPD officers.[67] Over the twenty-five-year span, black suspects surrendering themselves to police became more common. As figure 3.9 indicates, in the early 1920s less than 10 percent of all black homicide suspects surrendered, whereas in 1935, 35 percent of homicide suspects did so. While the number of surrenders declined by the 1940s, it still remained above 20 percent. In New Orleans from 1926 to 1945, 145 African Americans surrendered themselves after a homicide. This represented 22 percent of the total homicide cases reported by the NOPD. Similar to Memphis, surrender rates never reached more than 50 percent of all cases, but the shifts in New Orleans were a bit more drastic, ranging from 11 to 42 percent throughout the period (see fig. 3.10). The lowest percentages for surrenders occurred between 1926 and 1930, when the rate hovered between 11 and 14 percent. The 1930s saw an upswing and ranged from 18 to 30 percent. By 1942, the surrender rates spiked to their highest point and totaled 42 percent of all homicides that year. By 1945 the rates fell back down to between 20 and 25 percent. In other words, between the early 1920s and the early 1940s, the number of black suspects who surrendered themselves increased. While it is impossible to know why each black murder suspect surrendered, as police clearance rates improved, and black murder suspects better understood the potential dangers faced while on the run, more of them decided surrendering proved the lesser of two evils. When police apprehended African Americans and brought them to precinct houses or police headquarters, they were often held incommunicado and faced the threat of violence, abuse, and lack of representation. By surrendering,

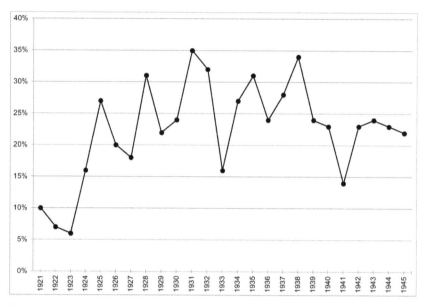

Fig. 3.9. Homicide Suspects Who Surrendered in Memphis, 1920–1945. Source: MPD Homicide Reports, 1920–1945.

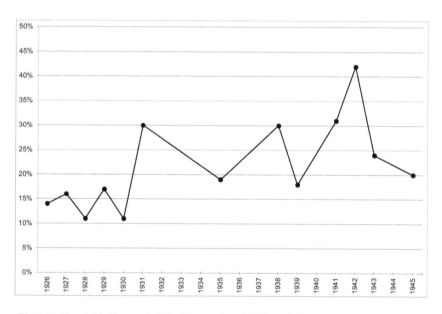

Fig. 3.10. Homicide Suspects Who Surrendered in New Orleans, 1926–1945. Source: NOPD Homicide Reports, 1926–1945.

African American homicide suspects tried to limit these possibilities and took control over when and how they were arrested.

Surrendering provided black suspects the most control over how, when, and where their arrest occurred. Over the span of two and a half decades, when black suspects turned themselves in, 63 percent of the time they did so at police headquarters. In Memphis, on June 29, 1937, for example, Henry Banks sneaked up on Charles Jackson as he walked to work and shot him once in the stomach. Banks, who according to police had a long criminal record, "came to police headquarters and surrendered [on the] same day as the shooting."[68] In just over 18 percent of cases of surrender, black suspects called police and awaited their arrival either at the scene, at home, or at another location. During a fight on the evening of May 26, 1934, forty-year-old Joe Ellis and forty-year-old Sylvester Harris got into a heated argument over Ellis's wife. As Harris attempted to walk away from the argument, Ellis followed him, when suddenly Harris turned and shot Ellis five times. After the shooting, "Harris awaited the arrival of officers and surrendered to them, turning the pistol, a .38 calibre Colt pistol over to them."[69] In 11 percent of the cases, black suspects surrendered to police officers on the streets of Memphis. On the night of May 29, 1928, a group of black teenagers played a baseball game in a vacant lot on Beale Avenue. During the game, a fight broke out between eighteen-year-olds Walter Brown and Walter Hoyle. During the fight, Brown ran at Hoyle with an icepick, but Hoyle struck Brown with his baseball bat and ran from the scene. Instead of fleeing the city or trying to hide from police, Hoyle hurried several blocks and "went to Beale and Orleans and surrendered to Patrolmen Luttrell and W. F. Turner."[70] As opposed to taking their chances on the run, African American suspects in homicide cases who surrendered determined the nature of their own surrender and exercised their own judgment in determining the best course of action.

Many suspects surrendered to support their claims of self-defense, accidental shootings, or defense of others. Mildred Lendsy, a sixteen-year-old black girl, killed seventeen-year-old Wills Lendsy on February 1, 1926. Immediately following the murder, Mildred "closed the door, went to Lawrence Jules room and informed him that she had just shot Wills and that she was going to surrender at the first precinct station." According to NOPD reports, Mildred surrendered the next day and also brought the murder weapon with her. Once in police custody, she claimed she had shot Wills in self-defense. She told the police that "Wills—who upon entering the room punched [her] in the left eye—and threw her across a Davenport in the bedroom and said 'I think I'll kill you—Mildred' then got up and back towards a safe drawer and reach[ed] for a revolver."[71] At that point, Mildred claimed she shot Wills three times in the back. NOPD officers seemed skeptical of Mildred's claim, noting that "at the time of her arrest [she] showed no blood stains or evidence of any black eye—or bruises," and she was charged with murder. When Gracie Robinson, a twenty-five-year-old black woman, came to police headquarters on October 31, 1926, after killing her husband in Memphis, her self-defense claim proved more convincing. During her interview, she told the police that "she and her husband had been having trouble for about four years and he often beat her and on the above date he came home and beat her up and then cut her on [the] leg with a knife and she got a knife and stabbed him several times." Robinson's claim of self-defense worked, and although police arrested her, a grand jury voted not to return the indictment, and Robinson was released.[72] Surrendering to the police provided black suspects with the ability to craft the narrative of events in a way that might ultimately benefit them and shape the way police, prosecutors, and grand juries understood the homicides.

Equally important, however, surrendering mitigated the potential for violence these suspects encountered while fugitives from justice. In cities across the South, rules and regulations provided officers much leeway in how they arrested fleeing suspects, especially in felony cases.[73] Southern law enforcement officers often relied on violence as part of a broader effort to control crime and preserve order.[74] Thus, when black suspects evaded arrest, the potential for violence remained ever-present. According to MPD records, from 1920 to 1945, officers shot and killed ninety-three African Americans, and eighty-four of these cases (90 percent) occurred while officers were attempting to make an arrest. African Americans were well aware of the potential for violence at the hands of police. While discussions of police brutality undoubtedly occurred between black families and friends, it also made the pages of the local black press. In an April 7, 1928, editorial published in the *Birmingham Reporter,* entitled "In What Will This Slaughtering End?" the editorialist stated, "Black people in the last few days have become greatly alarmed," and then continued, "Policemen in the past few days have been very free with their firearms and some five or six Negroes have fell [*sic*] dead from the results of their activities, and among this number some of the best characters of the state."[75] One black writer in New Orleans claimed in 1931 that "Negro citizens have more to fear from 'officers of the law' than from the most dreaded highwaymen, bandits, cut-throats and what-nots."[76] Police abuse and killings of African Americans continually circulated in the black press, and by 1942, Constant Charles Dejoie, editor of the *Louisiana Weekly*, dubbed the NOPD "the killer behind the badge."[77] These stories of brutality at the hands of the police were so well known that prominent black scholar Ralph Bunche proclaimed, "The only connection Negroes have had to the Memphis police force has been Negro heads colliding with nightsticks in the hands of white policemen."[78] Black southerners, then, were well acquainted with the potential for violence at the hands of police, and that possibility only increased if officers suspected them of a crime. By surrendering themselves to officers, black suspects avoided, or at least substantially reduced, the possibility of being abused during an arrest.[79]

Moreover, by surrendering themselves to police and then admitting to crimes, black suspects also potentially limited chances of police abuse during interrogations. As discussed in chapter 1, use of the third degree was widespread. The NOPD gained a reputation as one of the most notorious adherents to the practice of abusing suspects in custody. From the late 1920s to the mid-1940s, the NOPD's use of the third degree became more racialized.[80] In addition to the "third degree," the police employed a number of coercive techniques to try and extract confessions from suspects.[81] Many African Americans surrendered themselves to police with an attorney present, possibly to avoid any potential violence or other forms of coercion during the interrogation.[82] Moreover, by securing an attorney prior to surrendering, African Americans ensured that police could not deny them access to legal counsel.[83] Attorneys routinely advised their clients to avoid making statements and, in the case of abuse by officers, could act as witnesses on behalf of the African American suspects they represented. Melvin Williams, the African American suspected of killing Victoria Young, surrendered to NOPD headquarters four days after the killing with an attorney present and "refused to make a statement."[84] On the night of March 5, 1929, Annie B. Washington shot her husband, Mason Washington, during a fight. After the shooting, Annie immediately fled the scene before officers arrived. However, at 11:00 a.m. on the following morning, she appeared at MPD headquarters to surrender with her attorney, Ed Bell. Once she surrendered, "she was instructed by Bell not to make any statement whatever and she would not admit the shooting."[85] Although a jury eventually sentenced Annie Washington to five years in the penitentiary for the murder, by surrendering with her attorney, she, and other African Americans who did likewise, provided herself with both legal counsel and a bit of protection from the potential abuses and coercion that police in the 1920s and 1930s so infamously employed.[86]

While many African Americans surrendered because they feared potential violence during arrest, black suspects also surrendered to police because they feared extralegal retribution by other African Americans. While most instances of black intraracial lynching declined in the late nineteenth and early twentieth centuries, extralegal justice still permeated parts of the black community. On August 8, 1944, "a group of Negro citizens" of Memphis formed a posse and sought John Myers, a fifty-three-year-old black man who shot his estranged wife, Fredonia Myers. The day following the murder, the posse formed, found Myers, followed him several miles, and "just as he was about to enter some woods near where they found him, he told them again to stop following him and made a threatening move. It was then that Noel [a member of the posse] shot Myers in the leg."[87] Extralegal or informal justice did exist within the black community, and black homicide suspects sometimes surrendered themselves to police to avoid extralegal punishment from other African Americans.[88] Following the murder of James Kelly, a black man from Birmingham, suspect Clarence Reese found Officer L. B. Strong and surrendered. According to Strong, Reese claimed "the negroes were trying to kill him."[89] Although the Jefferson County grand jury returned an indictment against Reese, Officer Strong seemed to believe his self-defense claim and said as much to the jury. By surrendering, Reese crafted his self-defense narrative before police were aware of the crime, and he avoided potential violence at the hands of other African Americans. Considering the likelihood for violence existed from within the black community as family, friends, and neighbors sought out potential murder suspects, it is likely that several of them, like Clarence Reese, chose to take their chances with the criminal justice system and surrendered to police to avoid such violence.

Similar to black witnesses, black suspects faced a dilemma. They could choose a life on the run and face the threat of violence at the hands of police or other African Americans, or they could surrender to a criminal justice system that treated them unfairly.[90] Black suspects did not surrender themselves because they trusted the police, but rather because they did not. By turning themselves in, they limited the potential for violence during the process of arrest. By surrendering with an attorney present, black suspects decreased the chances of abuse or manipulation by police during interrogations. Finally, surrendering to police lessened the chances of any type of extralegal revenge at the hands of other African Americans. Considering all of the potential dangers faced by black fugitives, choosing the time, place, and way in which they were apprehended demonstrated their understanding of the complexities and dangers they faced both in the criminal justice system and in their own neighborhoods. While on the surface it might seem paradoxical to assume that black murder suspects would voluntarily turn themselves over to police, these surrenders actually revealed shrewdness and suggests how African Americans could, at times, use the police for their own benefit.

On the whole, African Americans played vital roles throughout the process of police investigations of black intraracial homicides. By reporting crimes, acting as witnesses during investigations, securing evidence, or capturing suspects, black southerners used police to remove dangerous African Americans from their community. The efforts of individual black southerners coincided with a larger push by law enforcement agencies to monitor and control swelling urban black populations through the criminal justice system during the late 1920s and 1930s. Within the larger context of a national "war on crime" that targeted African Americans to assuage white concerns over black criminality, black southerners took advantage of an increased police presence in their community to try and compel law enforcement officers to investigate homicides and arrest suspected killers. African Americans understood the potential for violence that permeated their interactions with police; however, by providing police officers with information regarding potential homicides, black witnesses attempted to ameliorate the chances of violence and instead to exercise some influence over the way police worked in black neighborhoods because of their centrality to the investigative process. Equally important, black murder suspects could, at times, shape the way they were arrested by turning themselves in to police. By surrendering, black suspects exercised the greatest control possible over their arrests by police, and by choosing the time and place of arrest, they could avoid particular detectives and precincts, whether or not they surrendered alone or with an attorney, and they could craft a self-defense narrative of the crime that improved their chances of release. Furthermore, black suspects who surrendered to police and admitted the crime, even if they claimed self-defense, reduced potentially violent encounters with police or other African Americans. In sum, whether aiding in police investigations or surrendering to police, African Americans found whatever leverage they could to use, shape, and manage the police. The relatively high clearance rate for black intraracial homicides during the early twentieth century largely resulted from these efforts.

While concerns over violent actions in black neighborhoods certainly motivated black homicide witnesses to engage with law enforcement, African American crime victims also sought out the police when victimized. An examination into the interactions between black theft victims and law enforcement demonstrates how widespread the concern over criminal activity in black communities was and further illustrates how African Americans influenced the actions of police officers throughout the course of an investigation. More importantly, a closer look at black theft victims' encounters with the police illustrates the circumstances surrounding thefts that largely determined whether an African American theft victim reached out to law enforcement.

CHAPTER 4

African Americans and the Police in Black Stolen-Property Cases

Around 7:30 a.m. on February 4, 1920, a black pressing-shop operator in New Orleans named Emerly West realized that someone had broken into his business during the previous night. When he arrived at work, "he discovered that some unknown party or parties had entered the place and stole one blue suit, a ladies [*sic*] overcoat, and one pair of black pants." All told, West estimated that the thieves had absconded with eighty dollars' worth of clothing. Quickly West called the third precinct station of the NOPD. Patrolmen William Bell and Joseph Leaber arrived on the scene and conducted their investigation, but there was little physical evidence, and West said he did not know who to suspect of the theft. Nonetheless, he informed the officers that he would "due [*sic*] his utmost to help the Police to locate the guilty parties."[1]

In his decision to notify the police of a theft and contribute to the investigation, West was not alone. African Americans often notified law enforcement of thefts and burglaries in the Jim Crow South.[2] As discovered in an analysis of over 1,325 black property-loss complaints filed with the NOPD, 604 documented black property-loss complaints found in the JCGJIR, and qualitative evidence culled from MPD homicide reports and black newspapers in Birmingham, Memphis, and New Orleans, black theft and burglary victims and witnesses engaged law enforcement in a variety of ways during the Jim Crow era.

Similar to African American reactions in homicide investigations, urban black residents throughout the 1920s, 1930s, and 1940s capitalized on law enforcement's presence in black neighborhoods and, despite the potential for violence or manipulation at the hands of law enforcement, used the police for their own ends.[3] In addition to urging the police to investgate homicides, black residents turned to the police with increasing frequency following thefts and burglaries. During the 1920s, the number of reported stolen-property complaints filed by black, and white, New Orleanians rose, but steadily receded during the Great Depression and World War II, reflecting a larger, national decline in crime rates during the 1930s and 1940s. At the same time, however, the percentage of black complaints increased relative to white complaints. Not only did African Americans report more stolen-property cases to the police between 1920 and 1945, but the police cleared black stolen-property cases at a higher rate than white cases. Yet, similar to the homicide arrest rates, this disparity was not the result of benevolent police action. Instead, African Americans were less likely than white southerners to report thefts and burglaries when they did not have any information relating to suspects. As a result, when black residents did file complaints, they supplied police officers with information regarding the suspect at higher rates than their white counterparts, which increased the likelihood of an apprehension. Officers' ability to secure an arrest in these cases also depended heavily on the efforts of African Americans who provided officers with information about the incidents and often tracked down, captured, and turned suspects over to the police.

In addition to black witnesses' behaviors in the wake of a homicide, these types of interactions support the notion that black residents increasingly embraced the rule of law as opposed to extralegal or self-help methods of dispute resolution.[4] The trends in black property-loss complaints suggested that just as white Americans became more reliant on formal criminal justice institutions to maintain social and racial order and promote economic growth, African Americans adopted similar strategies, albeit for more personal reasons. Black southerners harnessed the power of criminal justice institutions largely in an effort to safeguard their property or have it returned. While the protection of property seemed paramount, other victims and witnesses acted out of concern for their friends, relatives, and neighbors. As police forces expanded their presence in the black community in order to gain legitimacy in the eyes of white southerners beginning in the late 1920s, African Americans used those same police officers to mitigate the problems of theft and burglary in the black community. In so doing, black residents sought to make police more responsive to their concerns and make abstract notions of fair administration of the law a reality.

Stolen-Property Complaints

In an editorial published in the *Louisiana Weekly* on November 7, 1931, one black writer declared, "The rapid increase in crime is staggering.... What

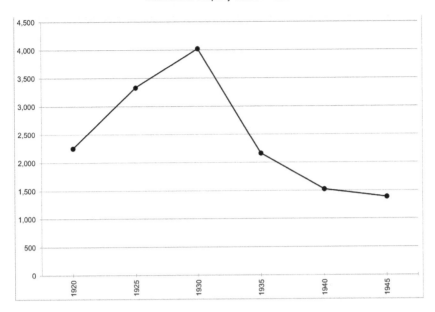

Fig. 4.1. Total Stolen-Property Complaints in New Orleans, 1920–1945. Source: NOPD Offense Reports, 1920–1945.

will society do to protect itself?"[5] Along with homicides, property crimes troubled white and black southerners in the early twentieth century.[6] Stolen-property complaints reported to the police illustrated southerners' concern over the problem. New Orleans residents, for example, reported 14,691 stolen-property complaints to the police between 1920 and 1945.[7] The number of complaints rose sharply between 1920 and 1930 and then declined more dramatically in the subsequent fifteen years (see fig. 4.1).[8] In 1920, New Orleanians reported 2,256 total thefts and burglaries, and by 1930, the total had reached 4,025. After reaching this peak in 1930, the number steadily declined until reaching a low of 1,388 complaints in 1945. Similarly, from 1920 to 1932 the total number of stolen-property complaints listed for Jefferson County totaled 4,291.[9] Stolen-property cases listed in the JCGJIR also rose fairly steadily from the early 1920s to 1926, and declined until 1932 (see fig. 4.2).[10] The decline in the 1930s follows the national trajectory as property crimes decreased for most of the 1930s.[11] Despite the drop in stolen-property complaints, concerns over crime and crime control continued to resonate in the black community throughout the era.[12]

The vast majority of these complaints came from white residents. Despite making up anywhere from 25 to 30 percent of the population of New Orleans

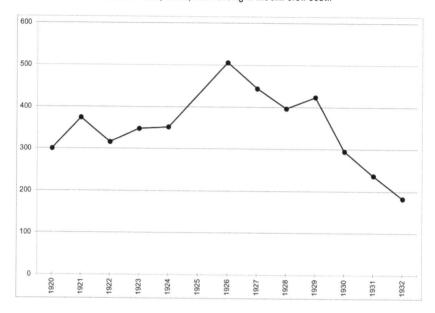

Fig. 4.2. Total Stolen-Property Complaints in Jefferson County, Alabama, 1920–1932. Source: Jefferson County Grand Jury Indictment Records, 1920–1932.

between 1920 and 1945, black residents filed just 9.0 percent of the total stolen-property cases. Jefferson County stolen property rates had similar racial disparities. The black population of Birmingham equaled nearly 40 percent of the city's total residents; however, black complaints equaled only 13.8 percent of all complaints listed in the JCGJIR from 1920 to 1932.

The racial differences in complaints suggested that most African Americans did not report property crimes to the police.[13] African Americans avoided reporting crimes to law enforcement agencies for a number of reasons. Many black residents feared the police and expected indifference from them.[14] The potential for violence and abuse pervaded encounters between African Americans and the police. One editorialist attested to this fear, describing the NOPD in the *Louisiana Weekly* in the following manner: "Negroes know here better than anyone else that the local police department has little or no regard for them. At least once a week some poor, unfortunate Negro is 'gone over' by our sadistically inclined police department."[15] African Americans had more to fear than just violence, however. Law enforcement agencies criminalized black behavior to such an extent that nearly all black men faced the threat of arrest for any number of reasons.[16] Even when black crime victims reached out to the police, they could find themselves in a precarious position. For example, when Benjimen Watson, a black resident of New Orleans, notified the NOPD that Laurence Lewis had stolen his watch, Patrolmen John C. Clark and Morris Milner placed Lewis and an accomplice under arrest. At the same time, however, the officers reported, "Benjimen Watson was also booked and charged with being drunk."[17] As law enforcement and city officials across the country criminalized various behaviors throughout the first half of the twentieth century, black residents, even victims of crimes, faced the threat of arrest for any number of trivial offenses, such as public intoxication or vagrancy.[18] As this example illustrated, calling the police invited a number of potential problems for the black resident making the complaint.

In crimes less serious than homicides, many African American urban dwellers relied on self-help strategies to resolve disputes and conflicts between one another.[19] When a young black man named James Morris Hardeman attempted to break into fifty-three-year-old Nettie Shorter's residence in Memphis, she did not inform the police. According to Shorter, "she had seen a burglar attempt to enter her home on Thursday night and that she had awakened and scared him away." She did not, however, make any attempt to involve the Memphis police. Instead, she "lay on her bed the rest of Thursday night with a shotgun beside her awaiting the return of the culprit." Although the burglar did not reappear Thursday night, early the next morning, on July 12, 1945, the intruder returned and "made an attempt to enter her home." Shorter "shot when she saw him start thru [sic], and he fell back into the yard mortally wounded." Despite the presence of law enforcement agencies across the urban South, African Americans did not always think it prudent to involve the police in order to protect their property. Instead, they relied on their own efforts.[20]

Not all African Americans, however, relied on self-help strategies. Unlike Nettie Shorter, an increasing proportion of black residents decided to report burglaries and thefts to law enforcement. In New Orleans, for example, African Americans notified the police in 1,325 cases between 1920 and 1945. In Jefferson County, 594 black stolen-property cases appeared in the grand jury indictment records between 1920 and 1932. Victims' motivations were multifaceted, but the protection or return of their property seemed paramount. In addition to concerns over their property, black victims and witnesses also notified and assisted the police to protect their friends, relatives, and neighbors from potential thieves and burglars. Similar to their counterparts in homicide investigations, these African Americans sought to use the legal system as a tool to safeguard themselves and their communities from suspected criminals.

African American victims often seemed more concerned with getting their property back than with ensuring the police arrested the suspect. During the January term of the 1924 Jefferson County grand jury, several African Americans recalled the events that led them to believe Ben Cleveland had stolen Peter Deed's pistol and jewelry. Virginia Carrington claimed that she saw Cleveland exiting Deed's house around the time of the alleged burglary. Martha Liggon and Andrew Carrington corroborated her statement, but none of the witnesses conclusively argued that they saw Cleveland steal Deed's property. Deed, however, remained convinced of Cleveland's guilt. In his testimony before the grand jury on March 25, 1924, Deed claimed that he saw the suspect wearing some of his stolen jewelry. He stated, "I caught the pin on Ben Cleveland." Apparently, this proved enough evidence to lead to the arrest of Cleveland. By the time the grand jury heard the case, Martha Liggon stated that Cleveland, "has not paid for any of this stuff yet and has not offered to pay for it." This was of paramount importance for Deed, who merely wanted his property back or to be reimbursed for the value of the stolen items. He informed the grand jury that "I don't want to send him to the penitentiary if I could get my stuff back."[21]

Arrests often proved to be an effective way to get stolen property returned. The JCGJIR documented several occasions when this occurred.[22] In his testimony before the Jefferson County grand jury on February 23, 1920, Hershel Brown recounted the day he realized someone stole his clothes. While Brown was away from his residence, Charlie Milton and Hope Bishop, two black men who boarded in the same building as Brown, informed their neighbor, Mary Adams, that they were returning back home. Adams recalled, "They carried the clothes off." According to BPD officer W. M. Burge, "We went over and arrested Milton." Once in custody, Milton "told us [the officers] where we could find the suit. We found it down at Clayton, Alabama." With the stolen property in hand and one suspect in custody, Burge then arrested Hope Bishop. In this instance, the police returned the stolen clothes to Brown. According to Brown's testimony, "I got [the clothes] back about 20 days afterwards. A detective got them for me."[23]

In other instances, a victim recovered their property much more quickly. When Robert Purdie, a black man who operated a shoe repair business in Birmingham, Alabama, realized someone had burglarized his shop one night in October, he quickly notified the police. According to the arresting officer, W. H. Fulghum, "We were on 14th Street and Woodland Avenue and there was a negro boy run up and hailed us and said there was a negro as 1415 Woodland Avenue and wanted him arrested for breaking in his store, and he told us it was a long slim man in a light suit, which we went up and found was John Williams." Purdie took police to the residence where the suspected burglars resided. Once there, police recovered several articles of clothing and eight pairs of shoes that had been stolen from Purdie's store. Purdie informed the grand jury that when the officers arrested John Williams, Will Davis, and Richard Myles from the residence, his property was returned. He said that he got them "out of [Williams's] house where he resides." Unlike Hershel Brown, who had to wait twenty days for the police to return his items, Purdie knew the location of the stolen shoes, took the police to the residence, and recovered his property the same day.[24]

While the return of or compensation for stolen property motivated many black victims, sometimes they used law enforcement to safeguard their neighborhoods. When two black men, Walter White and John Grayson, broke into Pearl Russell's home in Birmingham in 1927, she quickly summoned the police. According to Officer B. E. Riggins, "A negro woman called us in her house at 2612 2nd Alley, said she had been robbed."[25] According to Russell, the two men broke into her trunk, took fifty dollars, and taunted her by saying, "get it if you can." Shortly after Russell reported the crime, police arrested White and Grayson, and Russell positively identified them as the men who stole her money. Officer Riggins claimed, "We got $10 off of Walter White, and the Grayson negro gave the negro woman $2 of her money." But Russell was concerned with more than simply getting her money back; she wanted the two men removed from the community. When White and Grayson's lawyer offered to pay her the rest of her money back if she dropped the case, Russell refused. Her refusal suggested that she preferred that the legal system mete out punishment for the two men.[26]

Whether black residents notified the police for personal or for communal reasons, the number of African Americans who turned to formal legal institutions in stolen-property cases increased over time.[27] Between 1920 and 1945, black complaints comprised a larger percentage of total stolen-property complaints received by the NOPD. The number of black complaints rose and fell in ways that mirrored the trends in total complaints (see fig. 4.1). African Americans filed 181 complaints in 1920. That number grew to 310 and 309 in 1925 and 1930, respectively, then declined to 142 and 146 in 1940

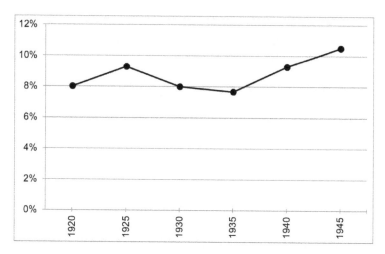

Fig. 4.3. Black Stolen-Property Complaints in New Orleans, 1920–1945.
Source: NOPD Offense Reports, 1920–1945.

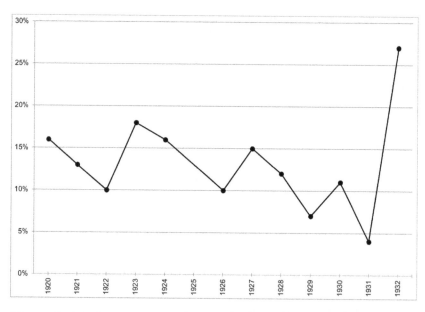

Fig. 4.4. Black Stolen-Property Complaints in Jefferson County, Alabama,
1920–1932. Source: Jefferson County Grand Jury Indictment Records, 1920–1932.

and 1945, respectively. This trajectory probably reflected the declining crime rates that occurred nationally during the Great Depression and World War II. However, as a percentage of the total number of complaints filed, black complaints increased during the twenty-five-year period. In 1920, black complaints totaled just 8.0 percent of all reported thefts and burglaries, but by 1945 that number had increased to 10.5 percent (see fig. 4.3). This represented a 31.3 percent increase. The rise in complaints far outpaced the growth of the percentage of African Americans in New Orleans during the same period, which grew by nearly 20 percent. This surge in stolen-property complaints coincided with similar increases in African Americans' involvement in homicide investigations and suggested that as police forces became more visible in black communities, African Americans proved more willing to report complaints to law enforcement officers.[28]

The trends of reported black thefts and burglaries in Jefferson County followed a similar trajectory. Recorded black complaint percentages remained low throughout the 1920s, but there was a noticeable increase in rates from 1931 to 1932. This upsurge coincided with the rise in reported black stolen-property cases in New Orleans that began in the mid-to-late 1930s. The black rate remained in the teens throughout most of the 1920s before dipping to 6.9 percent in 1929 and 11.0 percent in 1930, and 4.0 percent in 1931 (see fig. 4.4). However, the rate rose nearly six times by 1932 and totaled 27.0 percent of all reported cases in the JCGJIR.

The increase in black-reported crimes coincided with a growing police presence in black communities. As police departments expanded and embraced technology, city officials and white residents relied more heavily on formal law enforcement institutions to monitor the swelling black urban populations.[29] As the police presence in black communities increased, officers adopted aggressive techniques for handling black suspects as part of a larger "war on crime" that occurred in the late 1920s and 1930s.[30] Police officers brought more and more African Americans into contact with criminal justice institutions in an attempt to control these urban black populations. While city officials across the South embraced similar strategies of racial control, and police departments encroached on black neighborhoods, black victims of thefts and burglaries were more likely to report crimes to law enforcement.

The growing reliance on formal legal institutions crossed class lines in the black community. Unlike the case with homicides, which largely occurred in working-class communities, African Americans of working- and middle-class backgrounds reported stolen-property cases to the police.[31] Although African Americans occupied the lowest socioeconomic rungs in the urban South, throughout the course of their lives black urban dwellers acquired various types of possessions, such as clothes, jewelry, and money, and some African Americans owned so much property that they became part of a distinct middle class.[32] While it is difficult to discern the class background of victims, the NOPD offense reports provided a glimpse into the class background of complainants. One way to gauge the class background of victims is by examining the stolen items, and in New Orleans the types of stolen items reported to police varied tremendously. At 10:50 p.m. on December 2, 1934, for example, eighteen-year-old Alfred Pierce reported to police that Jee Jessie and Ferdinand Cavalier stole forty-three cents from him.[33] But almost seven months after Pierce reported the theft of forty-three cents, Louis Gelestin informed police on July 15, 1935, that someone stole his seven-hundred-dollar Chevrolet truck from outside his residence.[34] As these examples suggested, African Americans filed complaints for a broad range of items. Moreover, the average value of all stolen items reported by African Americans between 1920 and 1945 was just over $135. However, the

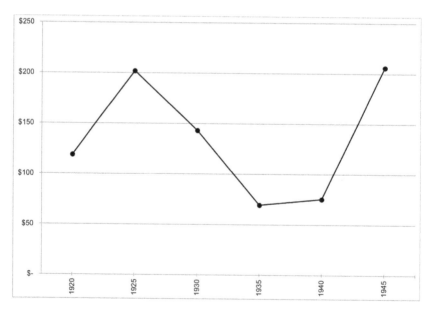

Fig. 4.5. Average Value of Items Stolen from African Americans in New Orleans, 1920–1945. Source: NOPD Offense Reports, 1920–1945.

value of items fluctuated over time (see fig. 4.5). The mean value of stolen items reported by African Americans rose from $118.97 to $202 from 1920 to 1925. Perhaps as a consequence of the economic hardships that resulted from the Great Depression, the average value declined sharply in the 1930s from $143.09 in 1930 to $75.42 in 1940.[35] As the U.S. economy expanded during World War II, the average value of items reached its highest level, at $206.15.[36] As a point of comparison, in 1940, out of 28,400 nonwhite families surveyed in New Orleans, 19,630 families earned between $200 and $999 per year.[37]

While class background did not necessarily dictate whether or not a black victim notified the police of stolen property, the gender of the victim did. Black men reported the majority of thefts and burglaries. The most complete information on the gender of black southerners who reported stolen property to the police is available in the NOPD Offense Reports. In New Orleans, black men reported 1,508 cases of stolen property to the NOPD between 1920 and 1945. Although men made up roughly 46 percent of the black population in New Orleans, black men filed complaints in 69.8 percent of all black theft and burglary cases brought to the attention of law enforcement.[38] This disparity resulted from the fact that thieves and burglars targeted black men more

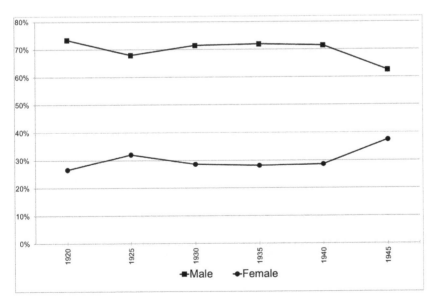

Fig. 4.6. Gender Breakdown for Reports of Stolen Property in New Orleans, 1920–1945. Source: NOPD Offense Reports, 1920–1945.

often than black women and that black men often represented their families in encounters with the police.[39] However, during World War II, as more men left to serve in the armed forces, the percentage of black women who reported stolen property increased. Black women made claims in an average of 28.8 percent of cases between 1920 and 1940. By 1945, black women reported 37.4 percent of all cases to the NOPD (see fig. 4.6).[40]

Regardless of class background or gender, African American victims, as opposed to witnesses, relatives, or employers, reported the vast majority of stolen-property cases to law enforcement. From 1920 to 1945, black theft victims reported the crime in 1,236 out of 1,325 offenses, which represented 93.2 percent of cases reported to the NOPD. Although JCGJIR were far less consistent in documenting who notified the police, the records indicate that black victims initiated contact with law enforcement in fifty-seven cases.[41] When victims reported cases, they did so in one of three ways. First, many black victims went to police headquarters or precinct stations to lodge a complaint. Although African Americans often faced police manipulation, abuse, and violence at precinct houses and headquarters, black theft and burglary victims often overcame those fears and entered these same spaces to try and use the legal system.[42] On the night of April 26, 1925, Cornelius B. Washington walked outside of his residence at 1323 South Rampart Street in New Orleans and noticed his Ford Touring automobile, which he valued at three hundred dollars, had been stolen. Immediately upon discovering the theft, he decided to notify law enforcement. According to NOPD clerk H. J. Mayeux, "at about 11:45 p.m. this Sunday April 26th, 1925, (One) Cornelious B. Washington . . . came to this station and complained that he had his Ford Touring Automobile parked in front of his residence . . . [and it] had been stolen." While at the station, Washington gave a full description of the automobile to the officers, and the clerk sent a message out to all NOPD stations detailing the theft.[43] James Burney, a black resident of North Birmingham, explained to a Jefferson County grand jury that on March 20, 1929, two black men, named Jerome Mack and Frank Patterson, stole one hundred dollars from him. Immediately following the theft, he "went right on to the police headquarters that evening."[44]

Other black victims notified the police using the telephone. On May 12, 1920, for example, John Simpson returned to his residence around 2:45 p.m. and discovered that someone had broken into his home at 2216 Cadiz Street. No windows or doors appeared to be broken, so Simpson believed an intruder had used a "duplicate key," entered his residence, went to his room, and stole a suit and three silk shirts. In his estimation, the loss of property totaled ninety-five dollars. Once he realized that a burglary occurred, he called the seventh precinct station. According to NOPD corporal Jarred C. Rankin, he "received a telephone message from John Simpson . . . that he was robbed and wants to see an officer."[45] Similarly, Samuel Garrett called the BPD to report the theft of his automobile on December 21, 1929. On the day of the theft, Garrett's Studebaker ran out of gas. He parked the automobile and went across the street to purchase some gasoline. According to Garrett, "I stayed a little while and come back and wasn't no car there." He searched the general area and found the automobile "jacked up and they had taken one tire off." Upon discovering the theft, Garrett "went to the restaurant and told a fellow, and I told them don't you all go no where [sic] and I called an officer."[46]

If black victims did not call or report offenses to the police station, they often found a police officer on the street and filed their complaints. On the morning of October 7, 1920, Georgia Douglas, a black woman from New Orleans, did just that. The reported incident occurred on the previous day, when Douglas realized that someone "effected an entrance of her residence" and stole $159 worth of clothing. The next morning, Douglas saw a police officer walking down Claiborne Street and "complained to Sergt Betbene while passing her residence."[47] Jesse Smith, a black man living in Birmingham, also found officers on their beat after Harrison Jackson "snatched" $22.50 from him in 1925. After stealing the money, the suspect quickly fled. Smith reported the crime to two BPD officers who were at a nearby post office. According to his testimony before the Jefferson County grand jury on October 6, 1925, he claimed, "I got two detectives over there in the post office building to arrest them."[48]

Although black victims were the most likely individuals to report thefts and burglaries to the police, they were not the only people to do so. In addition to the victims, other African Americans, typically either family members or witnesses, filed complaints in forty-two cases (3.2 percent) in New Orleans. Around 11:50 p.m. on November 14, 1945, twenty-seven-year-old Private First Class Rochel McLaurin "walked into the Struggle Inn slightly under the influence of liquor and ordered a drink." Stacy Bracken, a thirty-three-year-old black bartender, refused to serve him, after which McLaurin "sat on a stool and went to sleep." McLaurin slept for several hours, unmolested, until around 2:30 a.m., when a thirty-one-year-old black man, Arthur Ogden, who had spent the night drinking at the saloon, said to twenty-one-year-old Earl C. Palmer that "he was going to clip this negro soldier who was sitting at the bar asleep." Ogden walked up to the sleeping McLaurin and "took out of McLaurin's right hip pocket a brown leather wallet" which contained $325 and McLaurin's identification cards. With the wallet in hand, Ogden walked out of the Struggle Inn and continued down St. Ann Street for about ninety feet. Bracken, who witnessed the entire affair, called the NOPD and chased the suspect down the street. She "called [Ogden] back and brought him into the Struggle Inn and awakened the soldier and informed him that he had been robbed." When Sergeant John Cruso and Patrolmen Paul Gares and Earnest Rives arrived on the scene, Bracken told them what had happened and the officers arrested Ogden and took him to the fourth precinct station.[49]

When African Americans themselves did not report cases, white employers or witnesses occasionally did so on their behalf. Throughout the Jim Crow era, African Americans sometimes utilized whites as intermediaries when interacting with law enforcement institutions because they felt the latter would receive preferential treatment.[50] Nonetheless, in New Orleans, this occurred in only twenty instances (1.5 percent). On October 9, 1920, Lucien Pleasant, a black worker employed at Swift and Company, discovered the watch, chain, and diamond ring he placed in a drawer on the third floor of the Swift and Company offices were missing. Shortly thereafter, he alerted his boss, a white man named Charles Reichart. Seven days later, on October 16, 1920, Reichart notified the NOPD on behalf of Pleasant. Patrolman Thomas J. Kieran reported that he "received a complaint...from Mr. Charles Reichart, superintendent of the Swift and Co Plant." According to Kieran, Reichart informed him that "one of his employees, Lucien Pleasant...had been robbed."[51] While it is unclear why Reichart neglected to inform law enforcement of the theft for a week after the incident, it is probable that Reichart and Pleasant attempted to identify the person responsible for the theft prior to calling the police. Once the investigating officers arrived on the scene, Reichart informed them that he suspected another employee, a white eighteen-year-old man named Fred Casseriono, of the theft because "he was in possession of a key which opened the drawer from which the above described jewelry had been stolen."[52]

Police-officer-initiated arrests that occurred without a complaint being filed by black victims proved very uncommon.[53] Due to the fact that a large number of black thefts and burglaries went unreported to law enforcement, on occasion police officers arrested African Americans only to find out later that these same individuals had been involved in thefts or burglaries previously. At times, law enforcement officers noticed "suspicious activity" while walking their beats and discovered that a theft or burglary had occurred after questioning the suspect. Or, crowds of African Americans captured the attention of the police as an officer walked his beat. These types of cases, where white police officers initiated contact with black suspects without receiving a formal complaint occurred twenty-five times (1.9 percent) in New Orleans.[54] On September 20, 1930, for example, Sergeant Thomas Doody of the NOPD "noticed a crowd of Negroes chasing a negro man out Conti in the direction of the lake, and down North Robertson to St. Louis sts [sic], and [that man] was placed under arrest on St. Louis between North Robertson and N. Claiborne sts [sic]." Once Doody had the suspect in custody, several of the black men in the crowd informed the officer that the man had stolen $175 from a black contractor named Gilbert Guilyot. Guilyot explained how the suspect, Benjamin Kato, snatched an envelope containing the money off a counter in a crowded restaurant. Immediately after grabbing the money, Kato "ran out of the room running several squares to the place where he was arrested from." Doody searched Kato, found the envelope, and placed him under arrest.[55]

Thus, in the clear majority of black stolen-property cases investigated by law enforcement agencies, African Americans initiated contact with the police. Just as they did in homicide cases, black theft and burglary victims "invited" officers into their communities to investigate these stolen-property cases. By reporting these crimes to the police, African Americans attempted to capitalize on law enforcement institutions' assumption of the responsibility of monitoring and controlling the massive urban black populations in cities across the South in the 1930s and 1940s. Police departments encroached on black communities, arrested more African Americans, and placed them under control of the criminal justice system. Although police officers' interest in black crimes usually represented an effort to maintain black subordination, this provided black victims with an opportunity to try and use the police to help them regain their property and protect their community from suspected black thieves and burglars.

Arrest Rates for Stolen-Property Cases

While white and black southerners urged the police to investigate and solve thousands of stolen-property complaints in the early twentieth century, law enforcement seemed incapable of meeting the challenge. The ineffectiveness of law enforcement, however, was not confined to the South. According

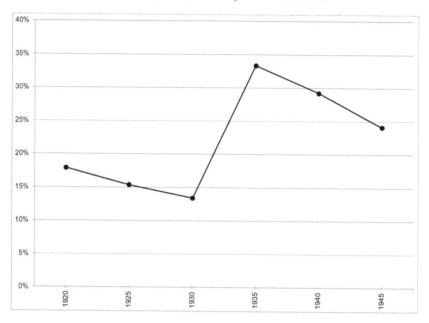

Fig. 4.7. Overall NOPD Clearance Rate for Thefts and Burglaries, 1920–1945.
Source: NOPD Offense Reports, 1920–1945.

to the FBI's Uniform Crime Reports for 1931, law enforcement agencies cleared just 29.1 percent of burglaries, 23.3 percent of larceny cases, and 10.6 percent of automobile thefts.[56] As crime rates dropped during the 1930s, clearance rates across the country improved slightly. By 1938, authorities cleared 35.6 percent of burglaries, 20.8 percent of larceny cases, and 20.0 percent of automobile thefts.[57] In southern cities such as New Orleans, the problem was greater. The NOPD cleared just 20.0 percent of reported thefts and burglaries from 1920 to 1945.[58]

While the overall clearance rate for the period remained low in New Orleans, the police became more effective over time (see fig. 4.7). From 1920 to 1930, the NOPD's clearance rate actually declined from 17.9 percent to 13.4 percent. This drop coincided with a rise in reported thefts and burglaries. As more New Orleanians reported more crimes, the clearance rates declined. However, the arrest rate surged to 33.3 percent in 1935. This increase was related to two trends. First, despite the economic downturn related to the Great Depression, the NOPD reorganized and expanded in the mid-1930s to include 817 police officers, the most officers employed by the department up to that point.[59] Second, the expansion of the police force coincided with a sharp decline in the number of reported stolen-property cases. As a result, police officers could allot more time to each case and the clearance rate improved. By 1945, however, the clearance rate declined to 24.1 percent, which probably was related to the war mobilization effort, the removal of officers to serve in the armed forces, and law enforcement agencies' increased devotion to maintaining black subordination in the face of increasing black militancy during the war.[60] As the clearance rate for stolen-property cases in New Orleans suggested, despite modest gains, law enforcement failed to make arrests in most theft and burglary cases.

Just as there was a gross imbalance in the rates of complaints between whites and African Americans (91.0 percent white and 9.0 percent black), there was also a gross imbalance in rates of arrest. Black complaints, surprisingly, ended in arrest at a much higher rate than their white counterparts. Out of a total of 13,366 white complaints, the NOPD cleared just 2,406 cases. This represented a clearance rate of 16.4 percent. The African American clearance rate, however, was more than double the white rate (39.8 percent). Between

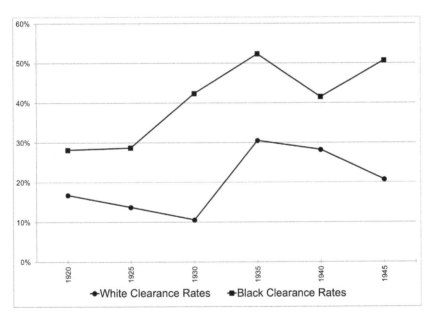

Fig. 4.8. NOPD Clearance Rate for Thefts and Burglaries by Race, 1920–1945.
Source: NOPD Offense Reports, 1920–1945.

1920 and 1945, the NOPD cleared 528 out of the 1,325 thefts and burglaries reported by black New Orleanians. In fact, in each year the clearance rate for black-reported stolen-property cases was higher than for white-reported cases (see fig. 4.8). The NOPD's clearance rate for white cases remained in the teens from 1920 to 1930, peaked in 1935 at a rate of 30.5 percent, and fell into the twenties in 1940 and 1945. The black clearance rate experienced a similar rise and fall. In 1920 and 1925, the rate remained in the high twenties, rose significantly in 1930, and peaked at 52.3 percent in 1935. The rate fell to 41.6 percent in 1940, and increased again to 50.7 in 1945. In other words, NOPD proved significantly more effective in making arrests in black cases than in white cases. While the white clearance rate never reached more than 31.0 percent, NOPD cleared black thefts in more than half of the reported cases twice, in 1935 and 1945.

This disparity suggested that police officers were more effective in handling black cases than they were in white cases. Yet African Americans were largely responsible for any success that the police department claimed in black cases. Black victims were less likely to report stolen-property cases when they did not have any information about the suspect than whites were. White theft and burglary victims reported cases to the police with no idea who was responsible for the offense in 72.0 percent of cases. When African Americans reported cases, they did so with no information regarding suspects only 58.0 percent of the time. The lower number of reported thefts and burglaries in the black community also suggests that African Americans did not report many stolen-property cases.[61] Since black southerners distrusted the police and initiating interactions with police officers could prove problematic for African Americans, it appears that black theft and burglary victims were less likely than whites to contact law enforcement when they did not have any information regarding suspects.[62]

While it is impossible to know how many African American victims did not report crimes to the police because they did not know who committed the offense, qualitative evidence suggested this occurred frequently. As Menola Stuart, a black woman from New Orleans, prepared herself for a church affair one evening in early February of 1945, she looked for a diamond ring to wear. After she searched her residence, she realized the ring was missing and concluded that someone had taken it. However, "she did not suspect anyone of the robbery and did not notify the police" in regard to the missing jewelry. Around 7:00 p.m. on April 23, 1945, Stuart received a telephone call from a young man from her neighborhood named Herman Johnson. Johnson informed her that Alvin Kendell, an eleven-year-old acquaintance of his, had stolen the ring. On the day the ring disappeared, Stuart sent Kendell to the grocery store to procure some food, and, according to Kendell, he stole "the ring while Menola Stuart was writing the note to the grocer." After receiving this information, Stuart notified the NOPD, informed them that Kendell had stolen her ring, and police officers arrested the suspect from his parents' residence on the same day. Importantly, Stuart did not involve law enforcement regarding the theft until she had an idea of who was responsible for taking her property.[63] Based on the racial discrepancies in reported cases, many African Americans acted similarly to Stuart and did not involve the police in cases where they did not believe police involvement would result in any action.

While black victims' decision whether to notify law enforcement of a theft affected clearance rates, so too did African American victims' and witnesses' efforts to assist the police. Most complaints that ended in arrest resulted largely from the efforts of African American victims and witnesses, not necessarily from the diligent investigating of police officers. Between 1920 and 1945, the NOPD made an arrest in 528 black theft and burglary cases, and in 80.5 percent of these cases African American residents provided law enforcement officers with specific information vital to the apprehension of the suspect.[64] The type of information provided by African Americans to the police ranged from names and addresses of suspects to identifying and even apprehending them. This type of assistance provided by black southerners also became more important to the ability of police officers to clear cases over time. For much of the period (1920 to 1935), African Americans supplied information necessary for the police to make an arrest between 76.0 percent and 83.1 percent of the time. This percentage declined to 70.9 percent in 1940, but rose to 88.0 percent in 1945 (see fig. 4.9). The high percentage of African American involvement in arrests was certainly related to the solidification of racially segregated residential areas in New Orleans. As African Americans became confined to specific sections of the city, the likelihood that victims and witnesses would see a theft or burglary occurring and know or be able to locate the suspect improved.[65] However, the sharp rise in 1945 suggested that something more than segregation affected these rates. Despite the hostility that existed between black residents, who challenged Jim Crow, and white police officers, who maintained the racial hierarchy, by supplying individual officers with information to ensure an arrest black southerners attempted to make the police work for them. This effort only increased during World

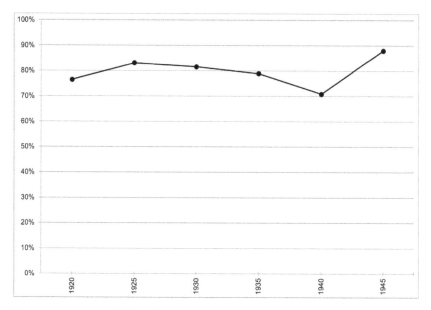

Fig. 4.9. Percentage of Cleared Cases with African Americans Providing Police Information in New Orleans, 1920–1945. Source: NOPD Offense Reports, 1920–1945.

War II, as African Americans across the country demanded government institutions be more responsive to their concerns.[66]

In cases brought before a Jefferson County grand jury, African American victims and witnesses also comprised the majority of individuals who provided testimony in cases with black victims. From 1920 to 1932, 1,014 African Americans provided testimony in black theft cases out of a total of 1,124 statements given. In other words, when the BPD conducted investigations into black stolen property claims, they relied on the testimony provided by black victims and witnesses much more than they did on that of white witnesses. Like New Orleans, as segregation intensified, black witnesses comprised a greater percentage of witnesses over time (see fig. 4.10).[67] The percentage of black witnesses was at its lowest point in 1920, when blacks comprised 73.1 percent of all witnesses who provided testimony before a Jefferson County grand jury. That percentage rose steadily throughout the 1920s and peaked in 1931 at 100.0 percent. Thus, black victims and witnesses became more important to police investigations of black stolen-property cases over time.

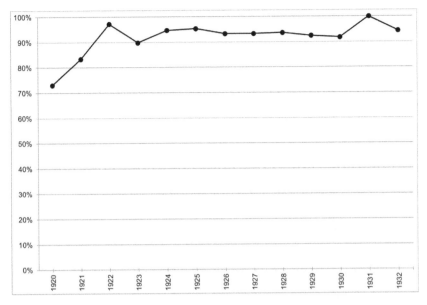

Fig. 4.10. Percentage of African Americans Providing Testimony in Jefferson County, Alabama, 1920–1932. Source: Jefferson County Grand Jury Indictment Records, 1920–1932.

Black southerners routinely provided law enforcement with the information necessary to secure arrests. The type of information supplied by victims and witnesses varied from general descriptions and names to the addresses or expected locations of suspects.[68] Around 1:30 p.m. on November 18, 1925, two black men approached Clara Syous, a black woman living in New Orleans, near Lafayette Square. The men engaged Syous in conversation and, according to Syous, eventually swindled her out of $105. Once she realized the men had taken her money, she notified the NOPD. Although she did not know much about the suspects, when the officers arrived on the scene she provided them with a description of the men. Nearly a week later, on November 23, 1925, Patrolmen Ed Rooney and Richard Durnin reported seeing two men on the corner of Poydras and Dryades Street who "answered a description of those [men] furnished by the Syous woman," and the officers confronted them. They questioned the two suspects on the street and eventually arrested them for "being well known Confidence Men." Then, back at the station, the NOPD reached out to Syous, and she "positively identified both Negroes as the ones that had taken her money." Although the arrest took several days, Syous's description of the thieves allowed the police officers to identify the suspects and make their arrest.[69]

When BPD officers arrested Willie Allen in Birmingham in 1927, it was the result of information provided by a black woman named Leola Wright. The theft occurred as Wright approached a Western Union office on First Avenue. Before she could enter the building, an unknown black man approached her and struck up a conversation. The black man asked her if she had any change. As soon as she pulled out her pocketbook, he "grabbed it and ran right on up the stairway." He escaped, following a short pursuit, and according to Wright, several witnesses "told me to go to police headquarters and report it." After making a statement, she provided BPD officers with a description of her assailant. Based on the information provided by Wright, Detective Paul Cole homed in on a man he knew named Willie Allen. According to Cole, "she gave a good description of him. She described his overcoat and his hat perfectly, and I arrested him on it."[70]

In cases where the victim did not come face-to-face with the suspect, African Americans often conducted their own investigations before notifying the police. When Joseph Toulme, a black man from New Orleans, arrived at his residence around 7:30 p.m. on December 26, 1935, he "discovered that the rear door which was secured with a thumb latch and a home-made wood latch, had been forced open." Toulme searched his home and noticed that his Ingersoll alarm clock, which he valued at five dollars, was missing. Upon realizing that a burglary had occurred, he asked neighbors if they noticed anyone coming in or out of his room. Carrie Mitchell, a black woman who lived above him, stated that she saw Cleve Thomas and Cleophes Thomas "leaving Toulme's room at about 7:15 this p.m." Toulme notified the NOPD and, together with Patrolmen Henry Luthjens and Henry Kirchmen, proceeded to 709 North Roman Street, where the suspects resided, questioned the two men, placed them under arrest, and charged them with larceny.[71]

Black victims also supplied the police with descriptions of the stolen items that led to arrests of suspects. At 2:30 p.m. on June 5, 1925, F. S. Lambert, a black mechanic, called the police and reported a theft. Several days earlier, on May 28, 1925, he remembered leaving a car tire in his garage. When he returned to work the next day, the tire was missing. In the days between the theft and when he notified the police, Lambert obtained "information that the tire was on a Page make automobile bearing the license 37680–1925," which he told the police was parked in front of 331 North Basin Street. NOPD officers proceeded to the address supplied by Lambert, towed the car, and learned that a black man named Henry Bailey owned the auto-mobile. When interviewed by police officers, Bailey informed them that he bought the car from an eighteen-year-old black man named Edward Boyer and provided officers with Boyer's address. NOPD officers Herman F. Stupey, Ishmeal Barrios, and Louis Verges went to Boyer's residence and placed him under arrest. Boyer's arrest, then, resulted from the initial investigation conducted by the victim, Lambert, himself. Without his crucial information regarding the whereabouts of the stolen tire and automobile, NOPD officers would not have cleared the case.[72]

While descriptions of suspects and evidence proved useful, when it was possible black victims provided law enforcement with the names and loca-tions of assailants. Armed with information this specific, police officers typically searched for the suspect at the address supplied by African Ameri-cans. On February 14, 1920, Ida Jones, a black woman living in New Orleans, notified the NOPD of a burglary at her residence. When officers arrived on the scene, Jones explained that at some time during the previous afternoon, someone had stolen several articles of clothing from her room. She informed the police that she suspected her neighbor's brother, Aaron Curtice, of the theft. According to Jones, Curtice had "just returned from the penitentiary, where he served a sentence from breaking and entering in the day time, and that she suspicioned Aaron Curtice of stealing [her clothes]." Based on her suspicion, the officers searched Jones's neighbor's residence and arrested Aaron Curtice.[73]

When African Americans assisted the police, they mostly provided general information, such as descriptions and names, but in some cases, they also took a much more proactive role. In 36.8 percent of cases in which Afri-can Americans assisted law enforcement in New Orleans between 1920 and 1945, they did so by identifying or capturing suspects.[74] In the same period, in 19.0 percent of all cases in which black victims and witnesses assisted the police, African American victims captured their suspects and turned them directly over to law enforcement.[75] In 17.8 percent of cleared cases, they explicitly pointed suspects out to law enforcement.[76] In these cases, they relied on the police only to remove the offender from their neighborhoods. While black residents may have been wary of police concern for black crime victims, by identifying and handing over suspects directly to officers they limited the likelihood that their cases would go uninvestigated or unsolved. Black victims and witnesses did not completely trust the police to investigate and solve cases on their own, and by limiting the amount of work individual officers had to conduct, they increased the chances that an arrest would occur.[77]

When African American victims apprehended suspects on their own and handed them over the police, they essentially did all of the work necessary to ensure that law enforcement arrested the suspect. This was exactly what happened when the NOPD arrested eighteen-year-old Claiborne Young for stealing a one-dollar bill from Richard Brown on May 14, 1920. The incident began when Brown attended a "prayer meeting" and took "some money from his pocket to give a dime to the negro preacher." As he pulled out his money, several coins fell on the ground. Brown bent over to pick up the change, and as he did he felt "Claiborne Young place his hand in his [Brown's] pocket" and remove a dollar bill. Young fled, and Brown pursued him. The two men ran down Saratoga Street and caught the attention of Patrolmen John Schiro and William Bailey. When Brown eventually captured Young, the two police officers appeared and "placed [Young] under arrest and charged [him] with larceny from person."[78]

Not all victim apprehensions occurred immediately following the incident. On December 20, 1920, Cornelius Mosely, a black man waiting for a train at Union Station in New Orleans, realized someone had stolen a suitcase containing clothes worth $111.75. The alleged suspect fled quickly after the theft, and Mosely had no idea who committed the crime. However, on December 27, 1920, as he walked down South Rampart Street, he noticed a black man in Cohen's Pawn Shop "trying to pawn the gray suit of clothes which was ... stolen from the Union Station." Mosely quickly confronted the man and "held on to the negro until the arrival of Patm. Jos. Fitzpatrick," who placed the suspect under arrest.[79]

While overwhelmingly done by men, black women also captured suspects.[80] When Mary Lewis, a black woman, suspected seventeen-year-old Seminole Jones of stealing four dollars, she apprehended her and brought her to NOPD. The incident began when Lewis asked Jones to go to her residence and "get four dollars in U. S. currency and her insurance book on the Home Life Ins. Co. and to pay her dues which amounted to the four dollars." Lewis later found out that, while Jones had taken the four dollars, she never paid the money to the insurance company. Lewis made "inquiries" in the neighborhood attempting to locate Jones and learned that she had kept the money and traveled to Gretna, Louisiana, which is across the Mississippi River from New Orleans. Lewis went to Gretna, located Seminole Jones, and "brought her to this precinct where on being questioned ... [she] admitted having taken the money and further admitted having spent the same." The NOPD charged Jones with petty larceny.[81]

Black witnesses also participated in the apprehension of black suspects.[82] While this was a relatively rare occurrence, witnesses proved more likely to get involved in a pursuit when a black woman was victimized. Black woman filed just 31.2 percent of stolen-property complaints with the NOPD; however, when black witnesses captured suspects, 45.5 percent of the time it occurred in cases with female victims.[83] When Henry Foster broke into Sadie Johnston's residence and stole several articles of clothing, an umbrella, and money totaling thirty-three dollars, several black witnesses captured the suspect. The incident occurred on April 8, 1920, when Ferron Clementine and several other black men noticed two black men had broken into Johnston's home and stole her belongings. The group of men immediately pursued the suspects for several blocks. Finally, "one of the negroes was captured [on the] corner of Gravier and White St by Ferron Clementine and several other men." Once Clementine and the other men in the group had the suspects in custody, Johnston notified the ninth precinct station, and mounted patrolmen George P. Weidert and Corporal Joseph Porett proceeded to the scene. When they arrived, Clementine "turned [Foster] over to Corporal Joseph Porett." The officers transported Foster to the Ninth Precinct station and charged him with petty larceny. In cases such as this, black men, whose self-perception of masculinity was often bound up in the responsibility to protect black women, interceded to capture the man suspected of stealing Johnston's belongings.[84]

Not all African Americans who located theft or burglary suspects apprehended them. Instead, they pointed out suspects to the police and allowed the officers to make the arrest. When the NOPD arrested Irene Duplessen, a nineteen-year-old black woman living in New Orleans, on January 23, 1935, Duplessen's black victim identified her for law enforcers. Duplessen's arrest grew out of an incident that occurred several days earlier. According to Laverich Smith, a black resident of New Orleans, around 8:30 p.m. on January 17, 1935, an unknown black woman approached him as he walked up South Rampart Street. The woman asked Smith if he "wanted to have a good time," and after negotiating a price, he followed the woman to 1403 South Rampart Street. Once inside, Duplessen led Smith to a room, and "after having a sexual intercourse with her he paid her 50 cents." Smith then left Duplessen in the room and went down the hall to use the restroom. When he returned, he noticed Duplessen had departed, along with his watch, which he had left on a nightstand. Smith then looked around the neighborhood for the unknown black woman and eventually found her. He "asked her about his watch." Duplessen equivocated for a few minutes, abruptly ended the conversation, and "jumped over [a] fence making her escape." On January 19, 1935, Smith finally reported the theft to the NOPD's second precinct. According to the officer in charge of the case, "Smith could only give a meger [*sic*] description of this girl and said that he only knew her by the name of Irene." With this information in hand, the police searched the area, but could not find anyone matching Smith's description. The officers "instructed [Smith] that in the event he sees the girl to notify the police." On January 23, 1935, Smith met Patrolman John McDermott during his regular patrol. Smith informed McDermott that the girl who he believed stole his watch the previous week was standing on Rampart & Erato Street. According to the NOPD, "the officer accompanied Smith to the above location where the woman was pointed out to him. She was taken to this station where she was charged with Petty Larceny of a watch valued at $35.00."[85]

As the Smith case illustrated, the police did very little to secure an arrest before Smith brought them to confront his assailant. Although Smith provided the NOPD with a description of the woman and the location of the theft, the NOPD proved ineffectual. Four days after he initially reported the incident, the case finally came to an end when Smith pointed out Irene Duplessen to a patrolman. While the reports indicated that the NOPD cleared the case, Smith's effort to solve his own case, and not the effort of NOPD detectives, proved to be the precipitating factor to the arrest.

In other cases, black victims rode around with the police to identify suspects. Despite all of the distrust that existed between the police and black residents, in instances such as these their interests converged. Early twentieth-century ethnographers routinely commented on the animosity that existed between black residents and white law enforcement agents, largely due to the violent treatment African Americans faced at the hands of the police.[86] Some black residents overcame whatever fear and distrust they may have felt when interacting with police officers in other circumstances and accompanied them on a search for suspects. When Percy Bickham, a black resident of New Orleans, learned that someone had stolen his automobile, he notified law enforcement on March 10, 1940. Patrolmen Robert Volten and Albert Roux proceeded to the scene, where they met Bickham. He informed them that "he had parked his Automobile on First St. at S. Claiborne Ave. and that he had gone into the Restaurant at the corner for several minutes and when he left the Restaurant discovered that the Automobile was not where he had parked [it]." Although he did not suspect any particular person of the theft, Bickham accompanied the officers as they conducted "a search of the immediate neighborhood ... in an effort to locate the stolen Automobile and the thief or thieves." When the initial search proved unsuccessful, Bickham continued his own investigation. Several hours later he once again called the NOPD and informed them that he "had found his Automobile at Second and S. Galvez Sts. with two men in the Automobile." Patrolmen Volten and Roux proceeded to the location and discovered Bickham talking to the two men he suspected of stealing his automobile. When the two suspects saw the police officers, one man fled. According to Bickham and the remaining suspect, Henry Watts, the fleeing man was responsible for the theft. Once again, Bickham rode around with the patrolmen to search for the guilty party, located him, and saw him placed under arrest.[87]

On occasion other African Americans also identified suspects for law enforcement.[88] In these instances, witnesses to an alleged theft or burglary typically informed the police of a potential suspect's location. This occurred on the night of November 13, 1945, when Isaac Weems stole $1,064 worth of jewelry from Cleo Smith, a twenty-four-year-old resident of New Orleans. Smith initially contacted the NOPD to report the theft at 7:45 p.m. Patrolmen William Conlin and Valentino Blaum arrived on the scene, and the victim recounted the events leading up to the theft. She explained that she had spent the evening at the Plum Room drinking, and at some point during this time she placed an envelope containing several pieces of jewelry on the counter so she could pay for some drinks. At that moment, another patron picked up the envelope and absconded from the saloon. The officers failed to locate the suspect in their initial search of the vicinity, took down a description, and left. Several hours later, however, the suspect returned to the Plum Room, whereupon one of the patrons, Joseph Ross, recognized him and notified the NOPD; the patrolmen returned and placed the suspect, Isaac Williams, under arrest.[89]

African American victims of thefts and burglaries did not passively wait for law enforcement agencies to apprehend potential suspects. Black victims were less likely than white victims to report thefts and burglaries to the authorities if they did not have any information regarding potential suspects. While this accounted for the great disparity in white and black complaints, it also contributed to the higher clearance rate in black cases. For the same reasons that many black crime victims did not report incidents to the police, it appears that black theft victims who notified law enforcement still did not fully trust the police to pursue their cases with the enthusiasm that they would in cases involving white victims.[90] To counteract their inequitable treatment, many black theft victims provided the police with as much information as they could to ensure the officers arrested a suspect, even going so far as to point out and capture suspects for the police. Thus, African American victims deserved much of the credit for the higher clearance rate for black stolen-property cases relative to white stolen-property cases.

Throughout the interwar period, black southerners' concern over stolen property offenses in their neighborhoods pushed an increasing number of victims to use law enforcement to have stolen property returned, receive financial remuneration, or punish criminals. Similar to black homicide witnesses, black theft and burglary victims became more likely to use legal institutions to protect themselves and their communities. In stolen-property cases, African Americans notified the police at higher rates between 1920 and 1945. This suggests that potential for violent interactions or apathetic responses to their concerns notwithstanding, black victims believed that contacting the police provided them with a viable option for getting their possessions returned or securing some type of punishment for the suspect. However, the likelihood of an apprehension largely rested on the amount of information or assistance that African Americans provided officers when making a complaint. From supplying information about the suspect or stolen property to identifying or capturing suspects, black residents demonstrated their willingness to assist the police when it served their interests. Due to these efforts, arrest rates in black stolen-property cases improved throughout the 1920s, 1930s, and 1940s. Black victims wanted their stolen property returned. If an apprehension precipitated the return of their property, or the threat of arrest meant a suspect would return their property, either way, their main objective was satisfied. Some African Americans, however, utilized law enforcement in a broader attempt to remove suspected thieves from their communities. Similar to African Americans who filed complaints in reported homicides, in theft and burglary cases black residents' self-interest in safeguarding their possessions and their neighborhoods sometimes outweighed their concerns with the potential negative consequences of inviting the police into their communities.

Concerns over crime and violence in their communities motivated African American victims and witnesses to reach out to and interact with law enforcement. In so doing, black residents displayed incredible acumen in finding ways to manipulate law enforcement into serving the interests of individual black residents and the community at large. Yet, black crime victims and witnesses did not always operate out of altruistic notions of improving the community or reducing criminal activity. In some instances, African Americans used the police for more personal reasons. An examination of interactions between law enforcement and black assault victims and witnesses illustrates the various ways that African Americans utilized law enforcement to mediate personal relationships with one another.

CHAPTER 5

African Americans and the Police in Assault Cases, 1920–1945

On September 23, 1928, Julian Jones, a black man living in Birmingham, Alabama, decided to leave Ada Deampers's rooming house and board with another black woman, Maggie Cox. This decision infuriated Deampers. What began as a "fuss" between the two women quickly escalated into threats of violence. Deampers went to Cox's residence and demanded she come outside. Cox exclaimed, "Come out the gate if you want to fight!" Deampers pulled out a gun and replied, "I am going to fix you." At this point in the argument, Cox replied, "I will have to get the laws for you." Deampers challenged her to "Get the damn laws, get the God damn laws." At some point Cox apparently did, because the police arrested Deampers the following day. The arrest, however, did not end the dispute. On September 29, the two women engaged in another fight, and according to Cox, "I turned around she was in my back and hit me and we got to fighting." During this second altercation, Deampers's brother called the police and had Cox arrested. The police released Cox that same day, and as she walked back to her residence, she once again crossed paths with Deampers. Deampers apparently sought to finish the argument, drew a weapon, and shot five or six times at Cox as she fled. While it remained unclear who reported this final altercation to the police, BPD officers arrested Deampers and the grand jury returned a true bill against her for "Assault with Intent to Murder" (AIM).[1]

Disagreements were frequent in the black community, at times leading to African Americans such as Cox and Deampers fighting, arguing, punching, stabbing, and shooting each other.[2] This is not to suggest that disagreements were more common than in the white community, but it emphasizes that despite their shared experiences of being on the bottom of the Jim Crow racial hierarchy, African Americans were not one unified mass. Undoubtedly, a large number of these confrontations went unreported to the police, as many African Americans lacked faith in the legal system or felt that these quarrels were best handled outside the purview of the criminal justice apparatus.[3] Those concerns notwithstanding, African Americans became increasingly interested in using the police to mediate disputes that turned violent during the 1920s, 1930s, and 1940s, as they embraced the rule of law as part of their larger effort to curb crime and violence in their own communities.[4] Yet, as with other aspects of black life in the Jim Crow South, criminal justice institutions did not always respond to black concerns with any sense of urgency. To increase the likelihood that law enforcement officers would respond to African Americans' concerns, black assault victims and witnesses relied on calculated strategies when engaging with the police.

Assault cases reveal more than black residents' ability to utilize law enforcement to serve black interests. These cases are most significant because the motivations of black victims and witnesses for using the police are more pronounced and complicated than in cases of homicide or theft. To explore these motivations, this chapter focuses on the two most common types of assaults in the black community: assaults growing out of minor disputes and intimate partner assaults. An examination of assaults stemming from minor disputes makes clear that African Americans often used the police to control community norms as these related to the acceptable use of violence.[5] Black residents did not notify the police of every dispute between African Americans.[6] Yet, in cases where assaults proved especially violent, black witnesses and victims were more likely to contact law enforcement. According to criminologist Henry P. Lundsgaarde, the decision to contact law enforcement following a violent attack reflected notions of "acceptable and unacceptable ways to employ violence in interpersonal relations."[7] In cases of intimate partner assaults, black women deployed law enforcement for myriad reasons related to altering the nature of their relationships with violent partners. Some used the police to help end a relationship, while others utilized law enforcement to renegotiate the nature of their relationships. When African Americans engaged with the Jim Crow criminal justice system, they faced a system that regularly denied them fair representation and failed to recognize their rights. Yet, as the assault cases revealed, despite the glaring inequities that they faced, black assault victims and witnesses did not always avoid interactions with the police and at times sought them out to try and make a corrupted institution work for black communities and individuals.

Disputes between African Americans

Throughout the Jim Crow era, black southerners bonded together to resist their subordinated status in several ways; however, significant differences and disagreements within the black community also occurred. Some of these disagreements focused on larger ideological issues, but others focused on the minutiae of everyday life. At times, these disputes turned violent. While the existing records do not indicate every assault that occurred in these cities, 302 cases of intraracial AIM cases were identified in the Jefferson County grand jury indictment records (JCGJIR), the *Louisiana Weekly* reported 223 cases, while the *Memphis World* covered thirty-one cases.[8] Editorials suggested the problem was much more widespread. An editorial published in the *Birmingham Reporter* on January 14, 1926, stated, "It is a common delusion among men that their differences maybe be settled by doing violence to each other."[9] An editorialist for the *Louisiana Weekly* wrote on January 18, 1941, "Cuttings and shootings set an astoundingly high record during last year." The writer continued, "Brawls . . . are all too common, so common, in fact, that they are hurting the whole race."[10] Understanding the nature of disputes between black southerners provides context to the larger issue of how African Americans such as Ada Deampers and Maggie Cox harnessed the power of the police to intercede in their arguments with one another.

Despite the differences between the black populations, economic foundations, and politics in each city, patterns of assault proved fairly consistent. Most of the assault cases in Birmingham, Memphis, and New Orleans stemmed from disagreements over minor issues.[11] This category of assaults encompassed altercations that grew out of "apparently insignificant concerns" like bumping into someone or disputes over small amounts of money.[12] Despite the relatively minor issue that sparked the initial confrontation, these altercations increased in the level of violence. Such quarrels comprised nearly half (49 percent) of the 302 black intraracial assault cases in the JCGJIR, 65 percent of assaults reported by the *Memphis World,* and 61 percent of all assaults identified in the *Louisiana Weekly.*[13] Men getting into violent altercations with other men comprised the overwhelming major-ity of such assaults.[14] Green Davis, for example, shot Jerry Lewis in one of Birmingham's black neighborhoods when Lewis asked Davis to stop cursing, drinking, and gambling on his front porch. According to Lewis's testimony given on October 6, 1924, "My wife was sick, and he was cursing, standing on my porch cursing, and I told him to get down off my porch, putting me in the dozen or playing the dozen, that my wife was sick and I didn't want that cursing." Davis then told Lewis that he "was not going anywhere" and challenged Lewis to make him move. During this heated exchange, Davis shot at Lewis one time, but narrowly missed him. This type of assault that began over a relatively minor issue, became more intense, and ended with a potentially deadly altercation is representative of the largest subset of assaults that appeared in court records and in the pages of the black press.[15]

Intimate disputes, or arguments between husbands and wives or boyfriends and girlfriends, were the second most common form of assault in the three cities. These altercations made up 23.2 percent of the total identified cases in Jefferson County, 25.8 percent in Memphis, and 25.1 percent in New Orleans. Intimate disputes where men assaulted women made up the clear majority of the cases: 74.3 percent in Jefferson County, 75.0 percent in Memphis, and 60.7 percent in New Orleans.[16] Contentious separations initiated by black women typically sparked these types of assaults.[17] The case against Manuel Gray, a black man living in Birmingham, provided a typical example. Gray stabbed his wife, Lucile Gray, several times. Lucile Gray claimed on May 24, 1922, that she had recently ended her relationship with Manuel and now lived with her aunt. On a Tuesday evening, Manuel Gray came to the door of her aunt's residence and demanded to speak with his estranged wife. Lucile recalled, "When I went out there to see what he wanted, he asked me wasn't I going home with him. I told him no, so he kept on talking; so I turned away from him ... and when I turned, he just cut me back here. He turned me loose, and I went to run, and he grabbed me by the hand, and cut me here." Because of her injuries, Lucile Gray spent two weeks in the hospital.[18]

The trends in types of assaults that occurred during the 1920s, 1930s, and 1940s underwent significant shifts. In Jefferson County, minor arguments remained the most common form of assault throughout the 1920s, but by 1930, minor arguments became less common while intimate disputes rose sharply (see fig. 5.1).[19] As the initial economic downturn sparked by the stock market crash of 1929 deepened, intimate disputes increased as a percentage of all recorded assaults. These trends suggested that as the Depression worsened, men engaged in less reckless behavior such as gambling, hard drinking, and public brawling, which typically encouraged minor disputes to erupt into physical altercations. At the same time, however, domestic disputes rose sharply as a percentage of all recorded assaults. Assaults in Jefferson County appeared to have moved indoors as black relationships faced great

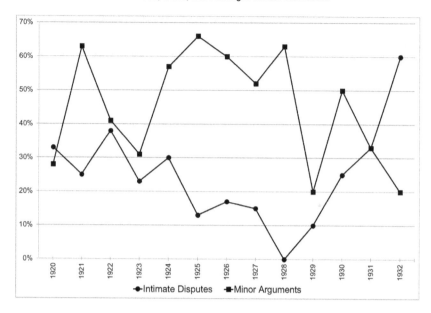

Fig. 5.1. Trends in Assaults in Jefferson County, Alabama, 1920–1932. Source: Jefferson County Grand Jury Indictment Records, 1920–1932.

strain because of the economic hardships they faced during the depths of the Great Depression.[20]

As these assault cases illustrated, significant disagreements occurred within the black community throughout the Jim Crow period, and at times these disagreements ended in violence. Highlighting these instances of violence between African Americans does not imply that African Americans were inherently more violent than any other racial community. But to understand why African Americans reported assaults to the police, it is important to recognize the divisions that existed *within* the black community.

African Americans Shaping Their Interactions with the Police

While the 556 reported black intraracial assaults identified in the JCGJIR reveal the broader nature of disputes between African Americans, these cases also expose the ways African Americans exercised influence over the police throughout their interactions with them. Jim Crow law enforcement officers and institutions, by rule and practice, were not created to improve the lives of African Americans. Black assault victims coaxed police officers into serving the interests of black residents in subtle ways throughout the entirety of their interactions. This process began with the reporting of the incident and continued throughout the investigative process as black witnesses shaped police officers' understanding of the assaults by providing most of the information and evidence used to make arrests. In the arena of assault investigations, African Americans, once again, illustrated that despite the power imbalance in their interactions with law enforcement, they exercised some influence over police officers' decisions and actions in their communities.

By notifying the police, African Americans initiated investigations and invited law enforcement officers into the community to investigate assaults and secure arrests of suspects. Although Jim Crow criminal justice institutions treated crimes committed against black residents less seriously than crimes committed against whites, black assault victims and witnesses reported these incidents in an attempt to make the law enforcement systems respond to their concerns.[21] Without these initial reports, police assaults in black communities would have gone largely unnoticed by law enforcement. Thus African Americans not only initiated the police investigation into the potential crime, but also began the process of extracting services from Jim Crow police forces. By contacting the police, black assault victims and witnesses signaled to the police a willingness to accept their authority or legitimacy. In so doing, victims and witnesses hoped that the police would believe their version of the events surrounding an altercation.

African Americans notified law enforcement of an assault in ways that mirrored their behavior in the wake of a homicide or theft (see fig. 5.2).[22] Considering most acts of violence occurred between members of the same race and in segregated spaces, African American victims and witnesses most likely alerted law enforcement to most of these assaults.[23] Just as black homicide witnesses and theft victims became more willing to utilize the power of the criminal justice system to alleviate some of the problems facing black neighborhoods, assault victims likely followed suit. Trends in black-reported assaults mirrored those of black homicides and thefts and became more common over time as part of a larger effort by black southerners to make the police better serve black interests.

As law enforcement homed in on black communities during the Great Depression, African American assault victims and witnesses continued notifying the police of altercations throughout the 1930s and 1940s. The *Louisiana Weekly* reported 200 black intraracial assaults between 1929

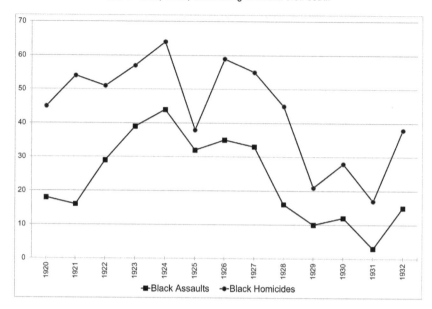

Fig. 5.2. Reported Black Assaults and Black Homicides in Jefferson County, Alabama, 1920–1932. Source: Jefferson County Grand Jury Indictment Records, 1920–1932.

and 1945. As was generally the case with national trends during the same period, assaults listed in the *Louisiana Weekly* declined (see fig. 5.3).[24] Nonetheless, the cases that made it into the pages of the black press illustrated that, much like black-reported homicides, which increased during this period, black victims and witnesses in assault cases, particularly those that involved deadly weapons, were willing to involve law enforcement following an assault. Although it is unclear from the data exactly what percentage of these assaults were reported by African Americans, it is likely that the trends in black-reported assaults followed the same trajectory as black-reported homicides.[25] The correlation between homicide and assault trends combined with the fact that law enforcement agencies across the country embarked on campaigns to arrest increasing numbers of African Americans during the 1920s, 1930s, and 1940s suggested that the police arrested more black assault suspects during the same period.[26] Thus, because most black assaults were intraracial, there is high probability that black victims and witnesses reported assaults at increasing rates throughout the 1930s and 1940s, reflecting African Americans' embrace of the rule of law.

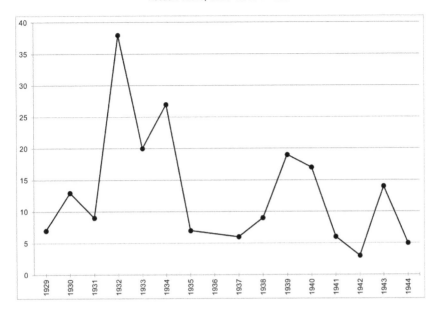

Fig. 5.3. Black Intraracial Assaults Reported in the *Louisiana Weekly,* 1929–1944.

African American assault victims often notified the police of attacks on them.[27] In so doing, they commenced the investigation and invited the police into their communities. Moreover, and more subtly, the initial report was the first step in the manipulative process designed to entice Jim Crow police forces into serving the interests of victims. When Cora Barnes shot at Annie Champion, the victim called the Birmingham Police Department. In a statement before the grand jury on May 20, 1926, Champion explained the events leading up to the shooting. On the night of the incident, Barnes found her ex-boyfriend, J. T. Mann, walking toward Champion's residence. Although Mann had severed romantic ties with Barnes, Barnes believed they maintained an intimate relationship. Mann walked up the steps toward Champion's front door, knocked, and when Champion opened the door she saw Barnes "come rolling out from under the porch." Barnes shouted, "You black bitch you, I am going to kill all of you black sons of bitches." Barnes quickly fired several shots in the direction of Mann and Champion but did not wound either one. As Champion ran inside, Mann turned toward Barnes and tackled her. When asked why she turned and ran inside, Champion replied, "I was scared she would kill me." As Mann restrained Barnes, Champion "called the officers." Together with Mann, she subdued the assailant and had the police arrest Barnes.[28] By contacting law enforcement and turning Barnes over to the police, Champion tried to frame the police officers' understanding of the assault. She provided the police with her version of the events that made her the victim, with a witness (Mann) to support her claim, as well as with the suspect.

In many cases, African American assault victims found police officers on the street or notified the police at the station or precinct house. The ability of African Americans to locate police officers near their residences or places of leisure suggested that the police departments in the Jim Crow South embraced the tactic of police visibility as a method of social control. This visibility increased during the 1930s as law enforcement focused even greater efforts on controlling black residents. Patrolling beats in uniforms or marked cars signaled white control in black neighborhoods.[29] At the same time, African Americans capitalized on this increased police presence to report crimes when victimized. On a Friday afternoon in April of 1930, Henry Holmes shot Robert Hayes at a barbershop on the corner of 26th Street and 3rd Avenue in Birmingham. The two men had had an argument the previous Sunday evening at church, when Holmes questioned why Hayes attended the service. Holmes allegedly stated, "You ain't got no business at the church." The two men cursed at each other, and Hayes later said that he told Holmes that "I had as much business as he did" being at the church. The men engaged in a series of heated exchanges throughout the week, exchanges which culminated in Holmes shooting Hayes at the barbershop. Shortly after the incident occurred, Hayes ran up to BPD officer R. G. Shirley, who "just happened to be passing there," and asked him to go take the pistol away from Holmes and arrest him. Shirley went to the scene, procured the weapon, and asked Holmes if he had shot Hayes. Holmes responded affirmatively, and the officer placed him under arrest.[30] John Walton, a black man from New Orleans, also notified the police that he was the victim of an assault. When Walton came home around 1:00 a.m. on June 18, 1933, he found Jesse McGee sitting on his doorstep. Walton "ordered McGee off his steps and an argument followed as to why McGee could not sit on the steps." At some point during the argument, McGee stabbed Walton and then fled the scene. Walton then "walked to the first precinct" and notified the police of the assault, whereupon the officers there rushed him to the Charity Hospital.[31] The police presence in black communities often signaled white control and authority over black communities. Yet, African Americans found ways to use this occupying force to their benefit by reporting assaults that otherwise would have most likely gone undetected by law enforcement.

While contacting the police initiated the investigative process, it was during the investigation that African Americans exercised the most influence over the course of police officers' investigations into assaults. By giving statements detailing the assaults, witnesses shaped the way police proceeded with their investigations. African American witness testimony often confirmed or refuted the victim's version of events, especially in cases where the assailant claimed self-defense. Black witnesses did more than confirm or counter narratives of assaults, however. By supplying or withholding evidence, African Americans largely determined what evidence police had at their disposal to proceed with an arrest. Finally, because police officers were from outside of the black community, they lacked a real understanding of the community, its residents, where people lived, and their relatives. When African Americans decided to reveal information regarding suspects and their whereabouts, at times capturing them for the police, black witnesses largely determined whether or not an arrest would occur. In the face of what must have seemed to be overwhelming power differentials between white police officers and black residents in the Jim Crow South, the ability of black witnesses to shape the actions and understanding of police officers in relation to assault cases demonstrated that African Americans could, at times, exercise influence over Jim Crow police officers.[32]

African American witnesses shaped the way police officers and detectives understood these assault cases. Due to de facto and de jure segregation across the South, it is not surprising that African Americans made up the vast majority of witnesses in assault cases involving African Americans. In Birmingham, between 1920 and 1932, African Americans made up 91.0 percent of people who testified before the Jefferson County grand jury in black intraracial assault cases.[33] As with black intraracial homicides and black theft and burglary cases, African Americans often supplied the police with information necessary to make arrests in assault cases as well. During the thirteen years for which the records remain for Jefferson County, the lowest percentage of African American witnesses occurred in 1929 when blacks made up 75 percent of all witnesses. More typically, the percentage remained above 90 percent and twice reached 100 percent, in 1926 and 1931 (see fig. 5.4).[34] It is also likely that witnesses' involvement in black assaults increased throughout the 1930s and 1940s in the same ways that occurred for black homicides. Much like the victims in assaults, then, black witnesses

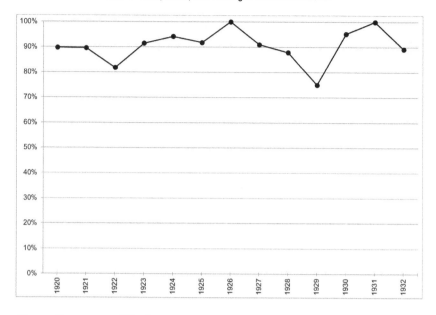

Fig. 5.4. Percentage of Black Witnesses per AIM Case in Jefferson County, Alabama, 1920–1932. Source: Jefferson County Grand Jury Indictment Records, 1920–1932.

embraced the idea of law and order at the expense of self-help at increasing rates.[35]

Law enforcement officers often spoke of the importance of black witnesses in their grand jury testimony. The BPD officer Lark Strong testified before a grand jury on February 11, 1924, and when asked what he knew about the assault case against Lucile Blount, he claimed, "I don't know anything about the case only I answered the call and just got a statement from the darkeys that was there at the house."[36] In his testimony regarding the stabbing of Pete Williams by Robert Griffin given before the Jefferson County grand jury on March 22, 1926, BPD detective J. T. Moser reiterated the significance of black witnesses to police officers' understanding of assault cases. He stated, "I don't know anything about the facts in the case other than what the other negroes told me."[37] Not only did African Americans comprise the clear majority of witnesses interviewed, but as these statements by law enforcement officers suggested, the only thing officers knew about the case often came from those black witnesses.

Witnesses provided much-needed context and confirmation to the version of events provided by those African Americans who were directly involved. When BPD detective J. T. Moser recalled his investigation of Jesse Hillman's assault on Willie Jay, he remembered that the suspect and the victim told him different versions of events. Hillman, according to Moser, "claimed that he cut [Jay] in self-defense." Jay countered, telling Moser "that Jesse Hillman cut him over a half dollar." With these conflicting accounts, Moser relied on the testimony of those who had witnessed the assault to determine the validity of both men's version of events. Moser claimed, "About twelve witnesses stated . . . that [Hillman] just jumped on this negro and deliberately cut him all to pieces." Although Moser did not say whether the witnesses knew the assault resulted from an argument over money, he affirmed that they disputed Hillman's claim that he acted in self-defense. In their minds, Hillman attacked Jay. When giving statements to the police, then, these witnesses painted Hillman as the aggressor and Jay as the victim. The police arrested Hillman for assault.[38]

Black witnesses played a similar role in the investigation of Sam Ardis's assault on his wife, Henrietta Ardis. In his testimony given on November 7, 1927, BPD detective W. L. Brannon recalled that Sam Ardis told him "that they were having an argument, and that she tried to cut him." Henrietta told a different story. She claimed Sam "shot me because I was quitting him," and she roundly denied having a knife. To reconcile these two competing claims, Brannon relied on the testimony of witnesses to clarify what happened. He mentioned that "no one saw the knife" that Sam Ardis alleged his wife tried to cut him with. Brannon's decision to arrest Sam Ardis for assault rested on the statements provided to him by the witnesses who challenged his claim of self-defense.[39]

The influence of black witnesses on police investigations of assaults involved more than shaping narratives for the police. Sometimes witnesses' testimony pushed black suspects to confess to assaults they had previously denied. In 1921, Noah Driscall accused John Culpepper of assault. Culpepper had fled immediately following the altercation. Driscall's family members put ice on his wounds to stop the bleeding and eventually took him to the hospital. It is unclear who called the police, but Officer W. T. Cochran reported that he "had a call down there," and "they gave us a description of him." Officers Cochran and O. D. Brown went to Culpepper's house, and his wife denied that he was there. Yet, when the police searched the house, they discovered Culpepper hiding inside. When the officers questioned Culpepper about the incident, he repeatedly denied his involvement. The investigating officers recalled that during their investigation, Culpepper "was identified by several negroes as being the one that hit this negro." When confronted with the witnesses' testimony regarding his involvement in the assault, Culpepper later "admitted that it was true." In cases such as this, black witnesses pointed the police to the home of the accused and provided police officers with enough evidence to elicit a confession out of a suspect who had initially proclaimed his innocence.[40]

While claims of self-defense were often refuted, in several cases African American witnesses corroborated the suspect's self-defense claims. When Carrie Roden shot her husband, Jim Holland, on February 23, 1924, she claimed self-defense. Holland explained to BPD detective C. E. McCombs that he and Roden had recently separated. He stated that he had decided to move his furniture out of their residence, and while he packed up his things, Roden came up to him and "just walked in the house and blasted down on him. She shot him twice." Holland further claimed that "he wasn't doing anything to her at the time she shot him." Roden, however, told a different story. She stated, "At the time I shot him he had a knife on me. He broke the door open, and he had the knife up right this way (indicating), and he come in there and I shot him." With two conflicting stories to reconcile, the police relied on black witnesses before coming to a conclusion in the case. Persuaded by witnesses' testimony, the police charged Holland with assault with intent to murder. Detective G. M. Bragan declared, "From the evidence of the witnesses there, mostly women, he was after her with a knife." As in the case of Roden, when the victim and assailant told different versions of the assault in question, black witnesses often influenced police officers' understanding of the assaults in ways that could significantly affect the outcome of the investigation.[41]

While refutation of or support for self-defense claims represented one of the important ways black witnesses affected police officers' understanding of assaults, they also sometimes provided testimony to the police that excused the violent behavior in question. On January 22, 1940, Peter Gaines, a thirty-one-year-old WPA worker from New Orleans, stabbed his wife, Viola Gaines, through the neck with a pair of scissors. On the night of the assault, Peter Gaines came home from work and found his food uncooked in the kitchen. Enraged, he threw it into the yard, woke up his wife, accused her of poisoning him, and attacked her with the scissors. Viola's mother rushed her to the hospital. The police later arrested Gaines, who "was full of blood, but no wounds were found on his body." During their investigation, police interviewed Peter Gaines's mother, who told officers that he was "a patient in the mental observation ward of the Charity Hospital." Witnesses informed the police that Peter Gaines "had been acting queerly since last Saturday" and that he had repeatedly accused his wife of poisoning him. The investigation never uncovered any evidence of poisoning. While the conclusion of the investigation was not elaborated on in the newspaper report, in providing testimony linking the commission of the assault to a history of mental illness, witnesses seemed to downplay the significance of the attack in an attempt to persuade the police not to arrest him.[42]

In addition to testimony, African Americans contributed directly to the arrest of black suspects. By holding suspects until the police arrived or pointing police in the direction of someone who fled the scene of an assault, black witnesses demonstrated that they were not content to let the police investigate on their own. Instead, they recognized that the likelihood of an arrest increased significantly if they limited the amount of time and effort that southern police officers had to exert in tracking down black suspects. The BPD officer W. L. Brannon testified before the grand jury on May 18, 1926, regarding the assault of James Clark by Luree Williams. He stated that after the shooting Williams "tried to escape, and [James Clark] caught her and took the gun away from her and held her until the officers came."[43] The BPD detective Woody Sandefer made a similar claim when he recalled John Fifer's assault of Arbell Lipscomb. According to Sandefer's statement given on August 25, 1924, Fifer fled the scene after the shooting. When Sandefer arrived on the scene, he and his fellow officer Mr. Watson "ran him all around back over there and some negroes helped us catch him at about 29th Street and 9th Avenue."[44] Juvenile Court officer C. H. Hamilton recalled an instance when black witnesses captured a suspect for police in his statement before the grand jury on June 10, 1930. After Paul DeJarnett cut Willie Mae Threadgill, several black men chased DeJarnett around the neighborhood. As these men pursued DeJarnett, they caught the attention of Officer Hamilton and his partner Officer Bell, who "got out and run down the alley and asked who did it." Black witnesses told the officers where they believed the suspect went, and according to Hamilton, "a negro with us said he saw him going up 12th Street and I jumped in the car and went around there and he said he went in the house." When Officer Hamilton approached the house, "a negro brought him out on the other side of the house and says 'Here he is Cap.'" Officer Hamilton quickly placed DeJarnett under arrest.[45] In five reported incidents, black witnesses in New Orleans held suspects until police arrived on the scene to make an arrest.[46] In the early morning hours of July 11, 1938, for example, several black witnesses surrounded Daniel Zander, who had just stabbed Nathaniel Carey in an argument over Zander's wife. According to the *Louisiana Weekly*, "Zander was held following the cutting until police arrived by several men who had formed a ring around him."[47] By holding suspects and turning them over directly to the police, African American witnesses did not engage in extralegal punishment for perceived offenses, but instead utilized formal institutions of criminal justice to mete out punishment. Moreover, by holding suspects until police arrived, they limited the likelihood that suspects would evade arrest.

Black witnesses proved adept at managing the way police engaged with their communities. During their investigations, police relied heavily on the testimony of black witnesses to understand the assaults, track down suspects, and gather evidence, all of which contributed to the officers' decision to make an arrest. By aiding the police in their investigations, black witnesses largely determined how the police interpreted the assaults and the likelihood that the police would apprehend an assailant.

From the point of contact between black victims or witnesses and the police, a process played out that in many cases ended in the arrest of a suspect. Once victims or witnesses reported a crime, police officers or sheriffs spoke with witnesses and individuals involved in the attack and, ideally, tried to make an arrest.[48] Although Jim Crow criminal justice institutions did not take criminal acts against African Americans as seriously as those committed against whites, in the case of black intraracial assaults arrests were not unheard of. In each of the 302 cases of intraracial AIM cases identified in the JCGJIR, law enforcement officers in Jefferson County arrested a black suspect.[49] Reports in the *Louisiana Weekly* stated that police arrested an assailant in ninety-four cases, while the *Memphis World* noted arrests in ten cases.[50] The police did not make an arrest in each reported assault case and typically did not treat black intraracial violence with the same attention as they did cases of violence against whites.[51] However, that did not necessarily discourage African Americans from trying to use the police in the wake of an assault. Although Jim Crow law enforcement agencies became more aggressive in their arrests of black residents in the 1920s, 1930s, and 1940s, African Americans attempted to manipulate the ways in which agents of criminal justice institutions engaged with and did their jobs in black communities. The efforts of black victims and witnesses to use and manipulate the police in the wake of an assault bore some fruit. In at least

406 cases the police arrested the assailant based on those black complaints.[52] Those arrests would not have occurred without black victims and witnesses reporting incidents, providing testimony, securing evidence, and giving information about suspects to law enforcement.

Using the Police during Disputes over Minor Issues

Understanding how black victims and witnesses manipulated the police during assault investigations reveals an important aspect of the relationship between police and African Americans in the Jim Crow South: namely, as indicated above, that black residents exerted some influence over police officers in their encounters with law enforcement. Yet, more so than in homicide and theft cases, the reasons black victims and witnesses chose to engage with law enforcement in the wake of an assault were complicated, nuanced, and indicative of the complex ways black residents living in the Jim Crow South negotiated their day-to-day lives under the confines of the racial caste system. Delving into the specifics of assaults stemming from minor arguments explains why African American victims and witnesses involved the police in violent confrontations with one another.[53] Witnesses and victims probably contacted the police for similar reasons.[54] Protection from violent individuals probably prompted much of their decisions to involve law enforcement.[55] What comes through in minor dispute assaults, though, is more than just concerns over one's safety. Instead, by contacting law enforcement regarding an assault, African Americans attempted to enforce communal views of acceptable and unacceptable forms of dispute resolution. Arguments between individuals did not typically prompt a victim or witnesses to contact law enforcement. Even aggressive confrontations often did not come to the attention of the police. However, when an argument or dispute turned potentially deadly, in the eyes of the victim or witnesses the altercation violated what they considered were acceptable forms of dispute resolution.[56] In these instances, African Americans utilized law enforcement to try and regulate behavior in the black community, especially as it related to the use of violence during disputes.[57] Attempts at regulating behavior through law enforcement in these instances seemingly outweighed the potential negative consequences of engaging with the police in the eyes of victims and witnesses.

Most minor disputes documented in the JCGJIR between 1920 and 1932 (73 percent) began as small arguments and rapidly escalated into violence.[58]

A typical example occurred in Birmingham in 1922, when Will Green shot Vennie Lee Bagby. As Bagby left a dance one evening in 1922, Green stepped on her, so she asked him to get off her foot. Green, who was drunk and upset that Bagby had refused to dance with him earlier in the evening, cursed her and said, "I'll blow your God damn brains out." After this outburst, Bagby claimed, "I didn't pay him any attention," and she and her husband walked out the door of the dance hall. As she exited, Green drew a gun out of his pants and fired several shots at Bagby, hitting her in the shoulder. It is unclear who called the police, but Officer W. K. McAdory noted, "We answered a call over there at a negro dance." It is probable that a witness reported the incident to the police, considering Bagby went to the hospital after the shooting.[59] The relationship between the witness and the victim was unclear. If the witness who reported the shooting did not know the victim, perhaps he or she called the police because the idea of someone discharging a weapon at a crowded community dance threatened his or her safety. Or, if the witness knew the victim, perhaps he or she reported the incident to the police to punish Green for nearly killing Bagby. In these instances, the altercations escalated quickly and often ended in serious, life-threatening injuries. For African Americans in the Jim Crow South, the use of potentially life-threatening violence often dictated whether to call the police.[60]

In the remainder (27 percent) of the minor AIM cases, a series of confrontations occurred prior to the incident that prompted the arrest. On July 6, 1920, for example, Vonnell Barron and Ed Mustin got into an argument that eventually turned into a fistfight. Mustin apparently bested Barron in the fight. The extent of injuries to Barron or Mustin could not be determined from their statements, but at no point after the altercation did anyone notify BPD. Nonetheless, Barron harbored bad feelings toward Mustin. One night in November, Barron saw Mustin standing in a restaurant. Without a word, Barron walked into the restaurant and opened fire on Mustin. He shot Mustin four times. Mustin spent four or five weeks in the hospital as a result of his injuries, and while he was there his wife "swore out the warrant for [Barron]."[61] As this example indicates, fistfights or arguments involving minor injuries may not have prompted black victims or third parties to notify the police. Altercations that resulted in major injuries and involved weapons, however, prompted African Americans to report incidents.[62]

The use of a weapon on an unarmed victim also appears to have violated acceptable forms of conflict resolution. On the night of January 21, 1925, Albert Gray yelled at his coworker Randall Baker, "Well, hurry, let's go." Baker replied, "You kiss my ass." At that point, Gray jumped off the truck and ran at Baker. Each man drew a knife, they scuffled a bit, and both combatants suffered minor injuries before several other coworkers "got them separated." However, every time the crowd separated Baker and Gray, they quickly reengaged each other. After the third altercation, the coworkers convinced Gray to leave, and he went into a room to change his clothes and told the group, "I am through. . . . I will put my knife in this locker." At no point during any of the altercations did any of the onlookers contact the police, which suggested that neither of the combatants violated the onlookers' sense of acceptable forms of confrontation. However, after Gray stashed his weapon in the locker and walked back out the door to continue working, Baker "[j]ump[ed] on him and cut him up with a knife." Gray suffered wounds in both shoulders. At this point, witnesses notified police and BPD officers arrested Baker.[63] As this case illustrated, in the initial altercations between the two men, although they involved weapons, neither man suffered serious injuries. Even as the men continuously engaged in fights throughout the evening, no one notified the police. It was not until the final altercation, in which Baker stabbed Gray, who was unarmed, several times with a knife, that witnesses contacted the police.

Whether the minor arguments escalated immediately or over a series of months, the decision to call the police rested largely on whether or not the altercation proved life-threatening. Minor quarrels without significant injury, such as the initial fights in the Barron and Baker cases, did not necessarily prompt witnesses or victims to notify law enforcement. Once those altercations crossed the threshold of acceptability and turned potentially deadly, however, victims, witnesses, and victims' relatives seemed more likely to notify the police.[64] While the police certainly represented white supremacy, enforced Jim Crow laws, and abused African Americans, in these cases black southerners capitalized on the increased interest by the police in black communities to their own benefit. Black victims of and witnesses to violent assaults used the pillars of the white racial system, the law and the police, to protect themselves and their community by punishing individuals whose violent altercations violated notions of acceptable dispute resolution.[65]

Using the Police in Intimate Disputes

Domestic quarrels afflicted white and black romantic relationships across the country during the 1920s, 1930s, and 1940s.[66] While not unique to the southern black, urban communities, these issues seemed particularly pronounced within black working-class families because of the cramped living quarters, poverty, racial discrimination, loss of political power, and daily humiliations of Jim Crow.[67] In New Orleans, for example, African Americans comprised 29 percent of the city's population but committed nearly three-fourths of spousal homicides.[68] The poverty and other pressures that resulted from Jim Crow created potentially volatile situations for black men and women in relationships with one another. Precluded from venting their frustrations against white southerners, at times black men lashed out at the people closest to them.[69] The most common form of intimate dispute involved African American men abusing African American women.[70] Black women, however, were not defenseless in these instances and employed a number of techniques to manage their intimate conflicts.[71] Many of these disputes were handled outside the formal criminal justice system, as black women often relied on their community relationships or self-help strategies to extricate themselves from volatile relationships.[72] Yet, as the police presence in black communities strengthened in the 1930s and 1940s, African American women incorporated law enforcement into their efforts to ameliorate domestic abuse.[73] In cases of intimate partner violence, African Americans often used the police to resolve these quarrels and establish or renegotiate social hierarchies within relationships.[74] The decision to notify police of an altercation rested on several factors.[75] Similar to disputes over minor issues, the threshold for reporting intimate violence to law enforcement was related to the use of a weapon or the severity of the injury. The desired resolution of these disputes, however, often varied. Victims of abuse turned to the police to sever ties with an abusive partner or to use an arrest, or the threat of an arrest, as a negotiating tool with their partners.

Contentious separations initiated by black women typically sparked these types of assaults. The case initiated by Beatrice Lee, a black woman living in Jefferson County in 1921, is a typical example. Lee and her husband, Nathaniel Carter, lived together for some time, but the relationship soured, and Lee moved out of their residence and in with her brother. Upset with Lee's decision, Carter told her, "You stay over there [with her brother] another night, you better stay every night." Carter then told her that she had better leave their residence, to which she responded, "Well, it's my house. Nathaniel, look like if [anyone] was going to leave it, looks like you were [the] one going to leave." Carter left for twenty minutes, but returned and continued the argument. He asked Lee if she really meant to end their relationship, to which she replied, "Me and you cannot get along together, and it is best for you to get you a room and go somewhere and stay. . . . I ain't going to stay in the house with you anymore. I'm scared of you." Once again, Carter left their house. Not ten minutes later, he returned and without a word, walked up to Lee, stabbed her in the chest, and shot her in the shoulder. Violent assaults of this kind appeared frequently before the Jefferson County grand jury. It is important to understand the causes of these violent encounters in order to better understand how and why these black women used the criminal justice system to respond.[76]

In the wake of violent assaults by their husbands, black women often turned to the police, and by extension the court system, to put their violent spouses in jail and out of their lives. In 15 percent of intimate dispute cases in the JCGJIR, black women stated that they wanted their partners prosecuted and incarcerated.[77] Despite the distrust black women must have felt toward the police and the larger Jim Crow criminal justice apparatus, in reporting assaults to the police, these victims believed that an arrest, conviction, and sentence were possibilities. The experience of Georgia Parker, a black woman from Birmingham, illustrates how black women utilized the police as part of a larger effort to end an abusive relationship and have their partner incarcerated. In early 1923, Georgia's abusive relationship became unbearable and she left her husband, Sylvester Parker. Sylvester became increasingly agitated following the separation, and on March 5, 1923, he came to Georgia's residence and stabbed her. Following the altercation, she ran to her neighbor's house and notified the police. According to witnesses, the Parkers had had a contentious relationship for some time. Georgia's mother, Mamie Owens, claimed that Sylvester Parker "beat my daughter up a time or two," indicating that the most recent stabbing was not an isolated incident but rather the culmination of a series of abusive encounters between the couple. Like minor disputes, when the abuse turned potentially life threatening, victims and witnesses seemed more likely to report the assaults to the police. In testimony given before the Jefferson County grand jury on March 21, 1923, Georgia Parker claimed, "My husband stabbed me because I quit him. I am not living with him now. I didn't say anything to him before he stabbed me. I didn't do anything but leave him." She concluded her statement by saying, "I am not going back to him. I don't love him. I want to send him to jail." These statements illustrated that Georgia Parker's decision to report the assault to police was part of her struggle to bring her abusive relationship to an end. After her initial decision to leave her husband, he had continued his harassment of her. His violent assault proved the tipping point for Georgia, who believed contacting law enforcement would land her estranged husband in jail.[78]

Hattie Hawkins had a similar experience in Birmingham. In a statement given on December 6, 1932, Hawkins recalled the series of disputes that ended with her estranged husband, Ernest Hawkins, shooting her. According to witnesses, the argument began when authorities arrested Ernest Hawkins on burglary and grand larceny charges and placed him in jail. When Hattie Hawkins met with her husband in jail, she refused to bail him out and encouraged him to "tell the truth about what he had done . . . to make it easy on [himself]." It is not clear whether he took her advice or not, yet three months later, authorities released him. Shortly after his release, troubles between Ernest and Hattie worsened. Hattie claimed that she "couldn't get along with him and he got mean and wanted to kill me." As tensions mounted between the couple and in fear for her life, Hattie Hawkins swore out a warrant for him and put her husband under a peace bond. After issuing the warrant, Ernest avoided Hattie for two months. Eventually, however, he ignored the warrant and resumed his harassment. Late one evening, he came to her residence and "started fussing." She demanded he leave, but he shot her instead. While she recovered from her wounds, Ernest's threats continued. On the night of his arrest, he came back to Hattie Hawkins's residence and begged her to "take up the warrant." Once again, she refused, but this time she also contacted the police. Officers arrived relatively quickly on the scene and arrested Ernest. When asked by the prosecutor during her grand jury testimony what she wanted to happen to her husband, she replied, "I want him put in; I don't want him to kill me."[79] Hattie Hawkins, much like Georgia Parker, informed the police of her assault in the belief that his arrest could lead to his eventual prosecution and incarceration. This decision did not come lightly to Hattie Hawkins. She tried to use the threat of arrest to manage her relationship with her estranged husband in the form of a warrant, and repeatedly refused Ernest's requests to rescind it. When it appeared that the risk of arrest would not work and after Ernest's violent assault, she delivered on the previous threat. By contacting the police and having Ernest arrested, she illustrated her commitment to using the police and courts to ensure her safety from her husband.

Black women who reported cases of abuse to the police did not always require a long sentence for their efforts to bear fruit. Oftentimes the initial arrest or short stints in the local jail or workhouse provided them with the necessary time to end abusive relationships without interventions by their intimate partners. Between the time of an arrest, prosecution, and sentence, African American women moved out of shared residences, filed for divorce, or separated informally from their partners. In Memphis, Minnie Gilliam employed the police to arrest her husband for abuse, and while he spent time in the workhouse, she filed for divorce. Minnie and Conright Gillman had been married for several years, and according to MPD records, she worked several jobs, and her husband "lived off her earning, he having never worked." By July of 1936, the relationship soured and turned violent. According to the police report, he "had been in the habit of abusing Minnie." She eventually had him arrested when the abuse became unbearable. Conright Gillman was convicted and spent twenty-five days in the workhouse. The MPD records indicate that "while he was confined [at the workhouse], she arranged with Attorney Holman to obtain a divorce."[80] While the arrest of an abusive spouse itself provided some respite from violence, black women also capitalized on the time their husbands spent confined by the criminal justice system to end their relationships.

Although the possibility of a conviction motivated some black abuse victims, incarceration was not always the intended outcome when contacting the police in abuse cases.[81] In some instances, black women testified that they did not, in fact, want their husbands prosecuted and put in jail.[82] These women's decision to have their attackers arrested, but not prosecuted, was complex and defied easy explanation. Nonetheless, some of their statements provided insight into why this might be the case. At some point in 1922, Jack and Millie Ward got into a heated confrontation. Jack "thought [Millie] was out with some man" and during the fight stabbed her twice. Millie fled to a nearby friend's residence and "begged" her friend not to let Jack kill her. Her friend, Bettie Beasley, pulled out a gun on Jack Ward when he entered the residence. He quickly fled the scene. While it is unclear whether Millie Ward or Bettie Beasley notified the police, the BPD eventually arrested Jack Ward for the assault. When Millie Ward testified before the grand jury on February 2, 1922, in the case against her husband, Jack Ward, she implored the prosecutor and the grand jury not to send him to jail. She stated, "I don't want nothing done to him." Despite the fact that witnesses claimed that Minne begged them not to let her husband kill her during the assault, she repeatedly downplayed the attack, claiming, "He didn't do nothing much. He didn't hurt me much." Although she never specifically stated why, she repeatedly told the prosecutor that they were married for thirteen years and she was "the mother of nine children for him." By reiterating this phrase, she indicated to the prosecutor and the grand jury that her concerns with how she would afford to raise nine children without her husband's financial support outweighed her desire to see her abusive husband sent to jail. Her plea that her husband not be prosecuted suggested that she perhaps had other motivations in using the police. During the initial attack, she feared for her life. Her initial decision to notify the police and have her husband arrested was probably related to the violent and potentially life-threatening nature of the assault. However, between the time of the incident and her appearance before the grand jury, it appears her concerns with her personal safety were somewhat alleviated and, as a result, she did not want Jack Ward prosecuted. Instead of viewing successful prosecution as the ultimate outcome or desire of these women, it is likely that African American women, like Millie Ward, often deployed the police to secure their safety in the moment of an assault.[83]

In other cases, black women used an arrest as a negotiation tactic.[84] When these women were attacked and had to spend time in the hospital, the expense incurred could be daunting. Thus, by having their partners arrested and threatening them with prosecution, black women could leverage that threat into making their abusive partners demonstrate contrition or ask for forgiveness. By paying medical expenses for injuries incurred during an assault, abusive partners attempted to demonstrate contrition. Black women frequently reported as much in the testimony before the grand jury. When Laura Patterson testified on January 28, 1920, for example, she declared, "I don't want him prosecuted." Although she did not explicitly state why she came to that decision, she testified, "He said he didn't aim to do it. He paid my doctor's bill. He is taking care of me while I was sick."[85] Lillie Starnes, whose husband stabbed her in the abdomen, made the connection much more explicit. According to the detective involved in the case, Starnes "said she didn't know whether she wanted to prosecute him or not." Her decision hinged on whether "he paid the doctor's bill." As these examples suggested, and as reported above, black women's decision to have their abusive partners arrested did not always stem from a desire to put them in jail for extended periods of time. Instead, some women chose to have their partners arrested as part of a larger negotiation. In these two cases, that negotiation hinged on whether or not the men paid the medical bills. While that decision may have been made out of economic necessity, it could also indicate that black women viewed their partners' agreement to pay medical expenses as an act of contrition.[86]

Having abusive partners arrested also placed considerable financial obligations on arrestees. Arrests could prove quite expensive even if the accused did not end up in jail. Regardless of whether an arrest led to an indictment and conviction, involving law enforcement placed these men under considerable financial burden: some paid fines, posted bond, hired attorneys, missed several days of work, or lost their jobs because of their arrest.[87] Take, for instance, Louis Jones, who shot and seriously wounded his wife, Ola Jones. According to the statements of several witnesses in the January 1926 term of the Jefferson County grand jury, at 8:15 p.m., Louis shot Ola five times on the porch of their house. The shooting was the culmination of an evening spent "fussing and quarreling," which both witnesses acknowledged. Louis fled the scene after shooting his wife, and their neighbor Pearl Jones, who was not related to either of them, ran over and found Ola groaning on the porch. It is not clear in the statements who called the police; however, Birmingham detective H. C. Jones noted that he "took that warrant" and arrested Louis Jones. Following the arrest, Detective Jones, in consultation with Louis Jones's attorney, allowed Jones to "make a three-hundred dollar bond."[88] The arrest forced Louis Jones to pay a three-hundred-dollar bond to get out of jail, a considerable amount considering the average annual wage in Alabama totaled $727.49 in 1931.[89] Moreover, by bonding himself out of jail, Louis Jones would forfeit the bond if he failed to appear for his hearing.[90] From the time of his arrest and trial, Louis Jones was placed under the surveillance of the local criminal justice system, limiting his freedom.[91] By calling the police during an intimate dispute, then, black women sometimes punished their lovers and spouses by inflicting significant hardships that fell short of jail time.

On other occasions, black women did not intend for the police to inflict any type of punishment on their abusive spouses. Instead, they used the *threat* of the police to deescalate tensions during potentially violent arguments. To force their partners to leave a residence or place of business, on several occasions black women threatened to or actually called the police. Concerned about the possibility of an arrest, male partners often fled the scene. On May 24, 1931, Julia Cook used the threat of the police to deescalate a confrontation with her husband, Roy Cook. On the night of the argument, Julia recalled that her husband came home and "was drunk and raising sand [making trouble or raising a fuss]." At some point during the argument, Julia Cook became worried about her safety and she "called the law." Realizing that Julia had just contacted law enforcement, Roy Cook fled the scene. While it is unclear when the police officers arrived at her residence, once they were there, Julia informed them that she did not want her husband arrested. The police left, and Roy Cook stayed away from the residence he shared with Julia for three days. Despite the fact that her husband threatened her repeatedly, it appeared that Julia Cook did not necessarily believe that he posed an imminent threat. Instead, it seemed that, in an effort to calm the situation, she contacted the police to deescalate the argument and get her husband to leave the residence and stay away for several days.[92]

Black women attempting to use the police to help mitigate potentially violent intimate disputes was not confined to Birmingham. Throughout the evening of May 5, 1929, Wesley Johnson, a thirty-eight-year-old black male, fought with his wife, Willie Johnson, at their residence in Memphis. During the series of fights, "the police were called two or three times." However, when Willie notified law enforcement, "Wesley would escape every time before they would get there."[93] While the police never arrested Wesley Johnson, the fact that Willie Johnson notified the MPD several times during the altercation and that her husband fled as a result, demonstrated that during domestic quarrels, contacting law enforcement could have an immediate impact. The threat of arrest encouraged an abusive partner to flee the scene prior to the arrival of the police, perhaps preventing an argument from escalating to violent levels. A similar incident occurred in late September of 1934. Lilly Gage and Jesse Travis lived together, but their relationship was fraught with problems. MPD officers reported that "Jesse had beat [Lilly Gage] up" and she had sworn out a warrant against him. In between the time that Gage swore out the warrant and the police arrived on the scene, Travis escaped. Although officers never arrested Travis, it seems that the possibility of the police coming to the residence to arrest him proved enough of a risk for him to flee. Gage did not see Travis for "several days" following the issuing of the warrant.[94] Whether it be an hour or a few days, the specter of an arrest often proved real enough for abusive partners that black women repeatedly notified law enforcement of assaults and black men left the scene to avoid apprehension. In these cases African American women appeared to use the threat of an arrest to reduce tensions during an altercation and force abusive partners to leave.

Despite the seeming willingness of black women to report instances of abuse to the police, that decision also came with potential risks, including retribution from an abusive partner.[95] Several instances of abuse occurred on the heels of black women attempting to have their partners arrested. On February 3, 1932, Roberta Wallace explained to the grand jury that her husband, Floyd Wallace, had stabbed her twice because she "had him arrested for non-support." According to Roberta, Floyd told her "[she] would be sorry" if she did not remove the warrant for his arrest. Sensing his anger, Roberta tried to avoid Floyd and spent a week boarding at another residence. Floyd eventually found out where she was staying, came to the residence, and demanded Roberta come talk to him. She refused several times and claimed, "I didn't want to speak to him." Her reluctance infuriated Floyd, who yelled, "You God damn son of a bitch, I will give you something to have me arrested for." He charged at her, yelling, "God damn you for having me arrested," and stabbed her two times.[96] Attempting to mitigate abusive relationships through the local criminal justice system was fraught with problems for black women. In addition to concerns over police brutality, wrongful arrest, or lack of enforcement of laws when black women were victims, black women who reported crimes against abusive partners also faced the potential of retribution from the person they needed protection from. While in some cases an arrest provided relief to black assault victims, in other cases the decision to report issues to the police escalated tensions and turned violent.

African American women used the police in a variety of ways to mitigate their intimate arguments with black men. Some women called the police to punish violent men, others used the police as part of a larger negotiation whereby they tried to extract something from their abusive partners, and others used the threat of the police to end abuse as it occurred. These cases signify some of the larger ways in which African Americans, particularly women, attempted to alter gender expectations within relationships by using the police. The traditional male-headed household of middle-class American life was challenged in many working-class black households.[97] Black women contributed financially to their family incomes and had a sense of economic independence unknown in most middle-class white households.[98] This gender dynamic within working-class black households, however, did not mean black men did not attempt to exercise control over their intimate partners.[99] At times, these issues boiled over into physical altercations.[100] As these intimate dispute cases illustrate, however, black women attempted to use law enforcement to resist black men's patriarchal demands and reject subordination in their relationships.

An examination of black intraracial assault cases between 1920 and 1945 sheds light on the ways in which African Americans deployed the police to mediate their social relations with one another. Disputes in the black community did not typically result in violent altercations, but when they

did, black victims and witnesses often turned to law enforcement to intercede. Black southerners' grievances with one another often outweighed the
combatants' negative or hostile view toward the police. In conjunction with
the behavior of black homicide witnesses, victims and witnesses to black
intraracial assaults involved law enforcement in disputes at increasing rates
throughout the period. By notifying the police of an assault and providing
investigating officers with information, African Americans demonstrated
their willingness to engage with law enforcement and their ability to shape
the way law enforcement agents worked in black communities. In black
intraracial assault cases, as in homicide and theft cases, African Americans deployed several strategies designed to influence the understanding
and behavior of police officers. Perhaps more importantly, the assault cases
demonstrated the multifaceted motivations that led African Americans to
involve the police in their affairs. In assaults stemming from minor issues,
black victims and witnesses routinely deployed the police as part of a larger
effort to regulate the use of violent behavior in these heated exchanges. Some
altercations, even violent altercations, seemed to fall below the threshold
of contacting law enforcement, while those that involved deadly violence
prompted many black victims and witnesses to turn to the police. Similarly, in cases of intimate partner violence, black victims and witnesses
also deployed law enforcement in a variety of ways to end or negotiate
relationships with abusive partners. In so doing, these African Americans
harnessed the power of law enforcement and attempted to bend it to their
own particular desires. As police departments across the country moved
into black communities to increase control over minority populations, black
assault victims and witnesses capitalized on the interest of the police and,
in turn, used the police to help mediate disputes within their communities.

Conclusion

In 1903, W. E. B. Du Bois famously, and presciently, proclaimed, "The problem of the twentieth century is the problem of the color line."[1] In the aftermath of emancipation and Reconstruction, white southerners reestablished the racial hierarchy, or the "color line," through elaborate customs that dictated blacks behave in subservient ways when interacting with whites, segregation laws physically separating the races, and black political disenfranchisement.[2] African Americans did not quietly accede to these efforts at subordination and resisted the implementation of the color line.[3] As a result, the veneer of white supremacy required constant surveillance and enforcement by whites. In many instances, efforts at "policing" the color line erupted into grotesque displays of communal violence in the form of spectacle lynchings, which occurred at alarming rates between the 1890s and 1920s.[4] Regardless of how effective extralegal violence may have been at fending off black challenges to white supremacy, by the twentieth century, these forms of violence threatened the economic viability of the South.[5] To combat these threats to economic growth, state and city officials worked to supplant extralegal methods of maintaining racial control by expanding the capabilities of criminal justice institutions.[6] By at least 1920, police officers, as opposed to ordinary white citizens, emerged as the foot soldiers in the battle to maintain black subordination in cities across the South.[7] Although consistently underfunded and undermanned, law enforcement agencies employed violence against black residents, arrested increasing numbers of African Americans, enforced segregation laws and customs, and consciously neglected some complaints by African Americans in a larger effort to ensure black southerners remained at the bottom rung of southern society. According to sociologist Gunnar Myrdal, "In the Southern cities where the two racial groups [were] more separated, the duty of policing the population [became] a continuous and specialized task. The police then also [became] more directly important for interracial relations."[8] Thus, understanding the ways in which African Americans responded to the growth of police departments and the encroachment of police officers into black communities to maintain white supremacy provides an important, and understudied, venue from which it is possible to understand aspects of race relations in the Jim Crow South.

The interactions between law enforcement and southern blacks in the first half of the twentieth century must be placed in the larger context of black reactions to the implementation of Jim Crow in general. Sociologist Charles S. Johnson's ethnography *Patterns of Negro Segregation* provides a useful framework. Johnson, who published his study in 1943, argued that blacks' responses to Jim Crow fell into one of three categories: avoidance, aggression and hostility, or acceptance.[9] According to Johnson, avoidance, or a "precautionary effort to avoid certain types of racial contact" in an attempt to "avoid conforming to the patterns of expected behavior," was the most common response.[10] Aggression and hostility, or the "active expression of an antagonistic attitude" toward whites and Jim Crow, was the least practiced response because of the violent consequences a black man or woman faced for this type of behavior.[11] Finally, African Americans widely practiced acceptance, or a willingness to conform "to the expected modes of behavior" dictated by Jim Crow. However, while outward conformity to expected behavior suggested black southerners accepted their subordinated status, "it [was], of course, possible to conform externally while rejecting the race system mentally and emotionally; and there are evidences in Negro behavior of widely varying degrees of acceptance."[12]

African Americans responded to the encroachment of law enforcement into black communities in the early twentieth century in similar ways. Most African Americans attempted to avoid interactions with law enforcement as much as possible. While it is difficult to know exactly how often this happened, the notion of self-help identified by a number of scholars suggested that black residents decided against involving law enforcement in intraracial issues.[13] Because many African Americans believed white-controlled criminal justice institutions would not treat black intraracial crime seriously and feared violence at the hands of police, they avoided contacting the police in the wake of a crime.[14] For example, the small number of thefts reported by African Americans in New Orleans indicated that most black theft victims did not lodge stolen-property complaints with law enforcement. The high number of black intraracial homicides was also a sign of self-help strategies as oftentimes the decision to employ violence resulted from disputes over property, debts, and perceived affronts. In many cases, homicides and assaults represented retribution on the part of an aggrieved party who operated outside of the formal criminal justice system.[15]

If avoidance represented the most common strategy employed by African Americans, violent resistance to the Jim Crow police was the most uncommon response,[16] Robert Charles's no-holds-barred resistance to police harassment being the most famous example (see chapter 1). Charles's resistance to law enforcement and white mobs made him a champion to many African Americans, who were frustrated with the state of race relations in the late nineteenth and early twentieth centuries.[17] Ida B. Wells-Barnett famously described Charles's defiance as heroic and declared him a martyr to the larger effort to fight back against segregation, disenfranchisement, and racial violence.[18] Wells-Barnett's support for violent resistance to racially discriminatory policing was echoed by other African Americans who, according to Johnson's observations and conversations with black southerners in the Jim Crow South, "secretly admired" men like Charles, who refused to submit to white supremacy.[19]

Despite the glorification surrounding resistance by men like Robert Charles, most African Americans did not express their frustrations with Jim Crow police forces violently. Instead, they expressed their aggression or hostility toward the police organizationally.[20] Across the South, a number of local black organizations materialized in the early twentieth century which developed strategies designed to lessen the worst abuses of the Jim Crow South. Organizations such as the NAACP developed campaigns against police brutality designed to punish violent police officers and change departmental policies, while they also worked to enhance the reputation of the civil rights groups. That black urban dwellers responded positively to these efforts is not all that surprising, considering they faced police manipulation, abuse, and violence. The resentment felt by black southerners built up over time. These types of organizations provided aggrieved blacks with a venue through which they could express their frustrations. Their protests and formalized efforts to combat white supremacy emerged as logical outgrowths of the oppressive nature of the Jim Crow legal system.

Black avoidance or aggression to the development of police departments as enforcers of Jim Crow seemed like obvious responses. However, the decisions of large numbers of African American residents to contact law enforcement, act as witnesses, turn over evidence, and capture suspects following the commission of a crime were more unexpected. Given that discriminatory treatment occurred at the hands of police, prosecutors, judges, and juries across the Jim Crow South, the notion that African Americans voluntarily invited the police into their neighborhoods and residences seemed counterintuitive. These decisions represented a third type of reaction by black residents. By contacting the police and assisting them throughout their investigations, black crime victims and witnesses signaled that they accepted the authority of law enforcement.[21]

In the South, police officers sought legitimacy and respect for their authority. According to Myrdal, the typical police officer in a southern city was "a low-paid and dependent man, with usually little general education or special police schooling. His social prestige is low." Despite this low standing in society in general, employment as a police officer offered poor white men one advantage: authority. Police officers represented the law, carried and could use a gun, and had the authority to arrest individuals. Myrdal concluded, "It is not difficult to understand that this economically and socially insecure man, given this tremendous and dangerous authority, continually feels himself on the defensive." Southern society emphasized status and hierarchies, both within racial communities and between them. While on the job, police officers "expect[ed] to be challenged when about routine duties.... This defensive attitude makes the policeman's job tedious and nerve-racking, and leaves the public with the feeling that policemen are crude and hard-boiled." In interactions with African Americans, Myrdal suggested, "There [are] practically no curbs on the policeman's aggressiveness when dealing with Negroes whom he conceives of as dangerous or as 'getting out of their place.'" Myrdal's description of southern police officers provided insight into what police officers sought when interacting with individuals: respect and recognition of their authority.[22]

African Americans often deployed a number of signals to illustrate to law enforcement their willingness to cooperate. In the eyes of the police, cooperation meant acceptance of their legitimacy. By using these signals, black crime victims and witnesses attempted to assuage police officers' fears of African Americans' resistance to white authority. Across the Jim Crow South, racial etiquette dictated how black and white residents should behave when interacting with one another so as to solidify the racial hierarchy.[23] White southerners, including police officers, routinely made a distinction between "good Negroes" and "bad niggers."[24] Law enforcement officers often described "bad niggers" as "those who 'give them trouble,' who are 'uppity' in manner, or who do not show proper respect for their authority."[25] "Good

Negroes," however, were often described in much different terms. In the presence of whites, these African Americans were appropriately deferential and "[knew] their place and stay[ed] in it."[26] In addition to the rules for interactions with whites in everyday settings, when engaging with a police officer African Americans offered other cues to demonstrate, at least on the surface, their support of the police. African Americans who lodged complaints with the police and assisted them throughout their investigations of crimes in the black community undoubtedly understood the history of abuse black suspects faced in the hands of southern criminal justice institutions. However, by employing law enforcement to respond to a criminal act these black victims and witnesses gave the impression that they accepted the legitimacy of the police.

While deferential attitudes toward police officers were certainly not confined to the South or to black interactions with the police, southern African Americans' reliance on deference when encountering law enforcement proved especially significant in the South. In northern cities, African Americans, especially by the 1930s, made up sizeable voting blocks and could attempt to assuage problems in black communities through the electoral process or by extracting services from politicians who relied on black votes. Moreover, in cities with black police officers, which almost all northern cities with sizeable black populations had by the 1930s, black crime victims and witnesses and community members concerned about crime and violence in black neighborhoods could interact with black police officers. Black southerners faced a different dilemma.[27] Electorally handicapped and lacking representation on police forces in cities like Birmingham, Memphis, and New Orleans, they deployed strategies designed to appeal to the white supremacist nature of southern police officers, while also extracting services from them.[28]

The signals offered by African Americans differed from the customary forms of deference that dictated other interactions with whites. When engaged in conversations with whites, racial etiquette typically demanded blacks remove their hats, avoid eye contact, walk slightly behind whites, and exhibit other subtle indications of white superiority.[29] While these forms of etiquette undoubtedly applied to encounters between African Americans and the police, black crime victims, witnesses, and suspects also used other signals designed to demonstrate their nominal acceptance of white police officers' authority.[30] First and foremost, black crime victims and witnesses contacted law enforcement.[31] By notifying the police of crimes, African

Americans sent a message to law enforcement agencies that, as opposed to self-help supporters, they accepted the police departments' sovereignty over criminal investigations, at least on the surface. In addition, by notifying law enforcement of crimes, black victims and witnesses invited the officers into their neighborhoods and homes, which also worked to disarm some of the fear that police officers held regarding African Americans in general.

All of the witnesses who provided information to police following a crime indicated to the police that they accepted police authority in much the same way that African Americans who notified law enforcement of a crime did.[32] White southerners relied on black informants dating back to the antebellum days, and when black residents provided white officers with information relating to black suspects it demonstrated a support of white authority in a way that also harkened back to the days of slavery.[33] But this was not the only way. Black men and women who supplied the police with information regarding crimes typically waited for the police to arrive on the scene. By voluntarily offering up information and not making police officers seek out black witnesses, African Americans tried to disarm any concern the officers may have brought with them regarding resistance from blacks.[34] Assistance conferred a sense of legitimacy in the eyes of the police.[35] In addition, black witnesses often offered to ride around with officers in search of a suspect. On March 29, 1931, for example, Granville Magnard, a thirty-one-year-old black longshoreman from New Orleans, saw Sanford Toliver shoot Henry Bailey. Toliver fled immediately following the shooting, but Magnard remained at the scene and waited for the police. When the officers arrived, Magnard "took Detectives Dillman and Russo to several places where [Toliver] hangs out at and located him . . . and pointed him out to the Officers who arrested him."[36] While this is not stated in the reports, African Americans most likely sat in the back of the police automobile, denoting their deference.[37] By riding around and identifying suspects, black witnesses allowed the police to assume a position of authority over black subordinates throughout the investigations.

By walking into police headquarters and precincts, African Americans also indicated to law enforcement their acceptance of police authority. Police precincts and headquarters were intimidating places, especially for African Americans.[38] Black suspects in jail routinely faced the threat of police abuse and manipulation, in addition to worry about the history of southern law enforcers handing black suspects in custody over to lynch mobs.[39] Black victims, witnesses, and suspects who came in to police headquarters understood this history, and by entering the police officers' space demonstrated a willingness to work with law enforcement, by filing a complaint, making a statement, or surrendering. Thus, the black southerner who walked into a police station sent a powerful signal to the police that they intended to voluntarily cooperate with the police and, by extension, they indicated a broader acceptance of police authority.

But the outward appearance of acceptance and subservience often masked African Americans' true intentions. As police officers across the country began arresting black residents with greater frequency, they provided African Americans with an opportunity to exploit the growing interest of criminal justice agencies in black criminality to remove violent and criminally inclined people from black neighborhoods.[40] Although black activists pushed local governments to address the underlying conditions in black communities that affected crime rates, often the only government agency they could access was the police.[41] Despite the obvious negative consequences of police encroachment into black neighborhoods, black crime victims and witnesses sought to use the police to mitigate problems facing their communities. The decision to call the police and assist them during investigations, while ultimately done to serve black residents' personal interests of protecting themselves and their possessions, was also related to what Du Bois called African Americans' "double-consciousness." Du Bois explained that African Americans in the Jim Crow era grappled with their "twoness,—an American, a Negro; two souls, two thoughts, two unreconciled strivings; two warring ideals in one dark body."[42] In black spaces, African Americans likely expressed their disillusionment with the police and supported the actions of black men like Robert Charles and organizations like the NAACP. The realities of Jim Crow made actions like Charles's suicidal and support for civil rights groups dangerous.[43] Moreover, a reliance on self-help strategies often increased violence within communities. In the wake of a theft, homicide, or assault, black victims and witnesses found another way to manage their interactions with the police: they gave the impression of subservience and acquiescence to the authority of white officers, while subtly and cleverly extracting from law enforcement services that benefited African Americans.

From the vantage point of law enforcement, the signals provided by African Americans established black acceptance of police authority; however, these interactions looked somewhat different from the perspective of black southerners. By giving the outward appearance of submission to white, and police, authority, black residents actually placed demands on the same institution designed to maintain African American subordination. In much the same way that a black carpenter seeking employment by a white homeowner might remove his cap and avoid direct eye contact in accordance with racial etiquette to make the homeowner feel more comfortable and hire the black worker, the variety of signals deployed by African Americans that demonstrated to police officers that they accepted police authority was also used to increase the likelihood that the police officers would serve the needs of African Americans.[44] The thousands of black victims, witnesses, and suspects discussed in the preceding chapters all used various rituals denoting racial submission to cast themselves as the "good Negro" in order to make demands of the Jim Crow police. By signaling their intention of cooperating with law enforcement, either by contacting police, pointing out suspects, or walking into police stations, these African Americans used the "mask of subservience" to invert the racial hierarchy by manipulating the police to serve their needs. In removing violent individuals from their neighborhoods, protecting their property, or altering the dynamics of gender roles in black relationships, under the guise of accommodation to police officers, black southerners deployed subtle strategies bound up in racial etiquette to make law enforcement work for them.

In sum, African Americans in the Jim Crow South engaged with the police in ways that mirrored their behavior in other interactions with whites. Some avoided interactions with law enforcement at all costs and relied on self-help strategies to resolve disputes and protect themselves and their property.[45] But while self-help remained a powerful force within the black community throughout the Jim Crow era, from 1920 to 1945 interactions between African Americans and the police became more common. Violent resistance to the encroachment of criminal justice institutions into black neighborhoods occurred infrequently; however, black organizations such as the NAACP engaged police departments and challenged law enforcement's discriminatory and violent treatment of black residents. This type of interaction represented a form of more aggressive resistance to Jim Crow.[46] While these forms of engagement have garnered the most attention from scholars, African Americans who gave the appearance of accommodating the police while actually using officers to their own advantage represented a third and increasingly important way that black residents managed their interactions with law enforcement. By acting in ways that made police officers believe that these African Americans accepted the superiority of individual officers and the police as an institution, black southerners attempted to manipulate the police into acting in ways that benefited the black community. While police forces in the Jim Crow South imposed white supremacy on black southerners and possessed almost unmitigated authority in their interactions with African Americans, that does not mean that black residents were powerless. Black organizations and individual African Americans developed and employed a variety of strategies to manage and influence Jim Crow police officers.

Unfortunately, the criminal justice system that developed in the early twentieth century was merely a precursor for a more robust, racially discriminatory, and damaging criminal justice apparatus in the twenty-first century. The growth of police forces, the reliance on improved technology, the militarization of law enforcement, and racial disparities in terms of enforcement, arrests, and incarceration continue at exacerbated rates. Despite the efforts of activists during the 1930s, and beyond, the inclusion of black police officers, and diversity and racial bias training for law enforcement officers, the main criticisms of policing still remain as pertinent today as they were in the Jim Crow era. Moreover, disparities between white and black communities are glaring in terms of investments in education and access to job opportunities, healthcare, social services, and even healthy food.[47] As a result, black communities today face similar issues that their predecessors did in the Jim Crow era: police violence, crime, and a lack of community investment from governmental agencies, among others. While significant gains were made in the post-Civil Rights era in terms of racial equality and gains for black communities, the growth of the criminal justice apparatus over the last fifty years has created a new system of racial oppression following the collapse of Jim Crow.[48]

As this book demonstrates, despite all of the problems related to African Americans and the police, for nearly a century African Americans have tried to reform, work through, and join law enforcement to help combat problems in black neighborhoods.[49] African Americans deployed several strategies for multiple decades to improve policing and public safety whether through the subtle strategies described here, larger protest movements, inclusion of black police officers, pushing for federal oversight, or increased training for law enforcement. However, the recent killings of Michael Brown, Eric Garner, Freddie Gray, Tamir Rice, Keith Lamont Scott, Terence Crutcher, Philando Castile, Breonna Taylor, George Floyd, and Rayshard Brooks have illustrated to the wider American public that there continue to be systemic, racial problems in policing and criminal justice in the United States. So much so that many black, indigenous, and people of color (BIPOC) communities and white Americans have abandoned efforts to reform police. Recent protest movements demanding defunding and even outright abolition of the police are indicative of the realization of these activists that efforts to work through or with law enforcement have not borne the type of change necessary to improve public safety in their communities. Recognizing the shortcomings of past efforts at reform, these groups are calling for new and innovative ways to improve public safety and introduce into their communities plans that curtail or eliminate police departments. As activist Mariame Kaba stated, "We don't want to just close police departments. We want to make them obsolete. We should redirect the billions that now go to police departments toward providing health care, housing, education and good jobs. If we did this, there would be less need for the police in the first place." She concluded, "The protests show that many people are ready to embrace a different vision of safety and justice."[50] These calls for abolition are a direct result of the failures of the police to address the issues faced by black communities who, for nearly a century, worked through and with law enforcement to try and remedy those problems. Despite the diligent efforts of African Americans, it has become glaringly obvious today that in myriad ways the police have failed black communities.

NOTES

Abbreviations Used in Notes

BPD Scrapbooks	Birmingham Police Department Scrapbooks, 1910–1969, Archives and Manuscripts, Birmingham Public Library, Birmingham, Alabama.
JCGJIR	Jefferson County Grand Jury Indictment Records, 1920–1932, Archives and Manuscripts Department, Birmingham Public Library, Birmingham, Alabama.
MPD Clippings File, 1800s–1930s	Memphis Police Department Clippings File, 1800s–1930s, Memphis and Shelby County Room, Memphis Public Library, Memphis, Tennessee
MPD Clippings File, 1938–1949	Memphis Police Department Clippings File, 1938–1949, Memphis and Shelby County Room, Memphis Public Library, Memphis, Tennessee
MPD Homicide Reports	Memphis Police Department Homicide Reports, 1917–1946, Shelby County Archives, Memphis, Tennessee.
NAACP Administrative File	Papers of the National Association for the Advancement of Colored People, Part 1: Administrative File, 1885–1949, Manuscript Division, Library of Congress, Washington, DC.
NAACP Branch Files	Papers of the National Association for the Advancement of Colored People, Part 12: Selected Branch Files, 1913–1939, Series A: The South, Manuscript Division, Library of Congress, Washington, DC.
NAACP Branch Files 1940–1955	Papers of the National Association for the Advancement of Colored People, Part 26: Selected Branch Files, 1940–1955, Series A: The South, Manuscript Division, Library of Congress, Washington, DC.

NOPD Homicide Reports	New Orleans Police Department Homicide Reports, 1925–1945, New Orleans Police Department, City of New Orleans, Louisiana Division/City Archives, New Orleans Public Library, New Orleans, Louisiana.
NOPD Offense Reports	City of New Orleans Police Department Offense Reports, 1920–1945, New Orleans Police Department, City of New Orleans, Louisiana Division/City Archives, New Orleans Public Library, New Orleans, Louisiana.
NOPD Witness Transcripts	Transcripts of Statements of Witnesses to Homicides, New Orleans Police Department, City of New Orleans, Louisiana Division/City Archives, New Orleans Public Library, New Orleans, Louisiana.

Introduction

1. William Glover on police brutality in Memphis, 1938, Folder 39, Carton 6, Series II, Robert R. Church Family Papers, University of Memphis Special Collections, Memphis, Tennessee.

2. Instances when African Americans were subjected to horrific police violence and brutality have commanded copious attention from historians. See esp. Gunnar Myrdal, *An American Dilemma: The Negro Problem and Modern Democracy* (New York: Harper & Brothers, 1944), 535; Marilynn S. Johnson, *Street Justice: A History of Police Violence in New York City* (Boston: Beacon Press, 2003), 12–180; Khalil Gibran Muhammad, *The Condemnation of Blackness: Race, Crime, and the Making of Modern Urban America* (Cambridge, MA: Harvard University Press, 2010), 226–68; Jeffrey S. Adler, "'The Killer behind the Badge': Race and Police Homicide in New Orleans, 1925–1945," *Law and History Review* 30 (May 2013): 495–531; Simon Balto, *Occupied Territory: Policing Black Chicago from Red Summer to Black Power* (Chapel Hill: University of North Carolina Press, 2019).

3. Myrdal, *American Dilemma*, 535.

4. Leon F. Litwack, *Trouble in Mind: Black Southerners in the Age of Jim Crow* (New York: Vintage Books: 1998), 263; Dwight D. Watson, *A Change Did Come: Race and the Houston Police Department, 1930–1990* (College Station: Texas A&M University Press, 2005), 4; Leonard N. Moore, *Black Rage in New Orleans: Police Brutality and African American Activism from World War II to Hurricane Katrina* (Baton Rouge: Louisiana State University Press, 2010), 1, 19; W. Marvin Dulaney, *Black Police in America* (Bloomington: Indiana University Press, 1996), xi, 39; Edward J. Escobar, *Race, Police, and the Making of a Political Identity: Mexican Americans and the Los Angeles Police Department, 1900–1945* (Los Angeles: University of California Press, 1999), 12.

5. Moore, *Black Rage in New Orleans*, 37.

6. Much of the scholarship on the development of police departments focuses on the urban North in the late nineteenth century. For some of the more important examples, see Roger

Lane, *Policing the City: Boston, 1822–1885* (Cambridge, MA: Harvard University Press, 1967); James F. Richardson, *New York Police: Colonial Times to 1901* (New York: Oxford University Press, 1970); Robert M. Fogelson, *Big-City Police* (Cambridge, MA: Harvard University Press, 1977); Sidney L. Harring, *Policing a Class Society: The Experience of American Cities, 1865–1915* (New Brunswick, NJ: Rutgers University Press, 1983); Wilbur R. Miller, *Cops and Bobbies: Police Authority in New York and London, 1830–1870*, 2nd ed. (Columbus: Ohio State University Press, 1997). Studies of the development of southern police departments also focus on the nineteenth century. The best example is Dennis C. Roussey, *Policing the Southern City: New Orleans, 1805–1899* (Baton Rouge: Louisiana State University Press, 1996). One of the only examinations of the institutional changes in a southern police department in the Jim Crow South is Watson, *A Change Did Come*. However, Watson's narrative begins in 1929 and devotes little time to a discussion of the changes that occurred in policing in the early twentieth century. Jeffrey S. Adler also explores the changing in policing patterns in Jim Crow New Orleans and focuses specifically on the Jim Crow period. His arguments emphasize the relationship between violence and perceptions of violence to the development of the police and criminal justice systems in Jim Crow New Orleans. See Jeffrey S. Adler, *Murder in New Orleans: The Creation of Jim Crow Policing* (Chicago: University of Chicago Press, 2019).

7. C. Vann Woodward, *Origins of the New South, 1877–1913* (Baton Rouge: Louisiana State University Press, 1951); Edward L. Ayers, *Vengeance and Justice: Crime and Punishment in the Nineteenth-Century American South* (New York: Oxford University Press, 1984), 192–93.

8. For an overview of the New South ideology, see Paul M. Gaston, *The New South Creed: A Study in Southern Mythmaking* (New York: Alfred Knopf, 1970).

9. Campbell Gibson, "Table 18: Population of the 100 Largest Urban Places: 1950," *Population of the 100 Largest Cities and Other Urban Places in the United States: 1790–1990* (Washington, DC: U.S. Census Bureau, 1998). https://www.census.gov/population/www/documentation/twps0027/twps0027.html

10. For examples of the formal criminal justice system in the South prior to 1920, see Ayers, *Vengeance and Justice;* David M. Oshinsky, *"Worse Than Slavery": Parchman Farm and the Ordeal of Jim Crow Justice* (New York: Free Press, 1997); Alex Lichtenstein, *Twice the Work of Free Labor: The Political Economy of Convict Labor in the New South* (New York: Verso Books, 1997); Talitha L. LeFlouria, *Chained in Silence: Black Women and Convict Labor in the New South* (Chapel Hill: University of North Carolina Press, 2015).

11. Silvan Niedermeier, *The Color of the Third Degree: Racism, Police Torture, and Civil Rights in the American South, 1930–1955,* trans. Paul Cohen (Chapel Hill: University of North Carolina Press, 2019), 21–22.

12. "Enforcement Needed," *Louisiana Weekly,* April 14, 1928.

13. Balto, *Occupied Territory,* 42–48.

14. Roger Lane, *Roots of Violence in Black Philadelphia, 1860–1900* (Cambridge, MA: Harvard University Press, 1986); Jeffrey S. Adler, "Black Violence in the New South: Patterns of Conflict in Late-Nineteenth-Century Tampa," in *The African American Heritage of Florida,* ed. David R. Colburn and Jane L. Landers (Gainesville: University Press of Florida, 1995), 207–39, and *First in Violence, Deepest in Dirt: Homicide in Chicago, 1875–1920* (Cambridge, MA: Harvard University Press, 2006), 120–58.

15. Robin D. G. Kelley found that working-class black southerners often employed strategies

to "receive equitable treatment, they wanted to be personally treated with respect and dignity, they wanted to be heard and possibly understood, they wanted to get to work on time, *and above all, they wanted to exercise power over institutions that controlled them or on which they were* dependent." Kelley, *Race Rebels: Culture Politics, and the Black Working Class* (New York: Free Press, 1994), 74–75.

16. MPD Homicide Report for Sherman Miles, June 1, 1937.

17. For more on the lack of concern for crimes committed against African Americans, see Raymond B. Fosdick, *American Police Systems* (New York: Century Co., 1920), 45; Ayers, *Vengeance and Justice*, 231; Lawrence M. Friedman, *Crime and Punishment in American History* (New York: BasicBooks, 1993), 375; Randall Kennedy, *Race, Crime, and the Law* (New York: Vintage Books, 1997), 3–135.

18. Myrdal, *An American Dilemma*, 540–43; Litwack, *Trouble in Mind*, 263–65; Johnson, *Street Justice*, 57–86, 181–228; Moore, *Black Rage in New Orleans;* Muhammad, *Condemnation of Blackness*, 226–68; Balto, *Occupied Territory.*

19. These numbers and statistics are culled from my own datasets created using the MPD Homicide Reports; NOPD Homicide Reports; NOPD Witness Transcripts; and the NOPD Offense Reports.

20. For more on avoidance or self-help in the black community, see Adler, "Black Violence in the New South," 224–28; H. C. Brearley, "The Pattern of Violence," in *Culture in the South,* ed. W. T. Couch (Chapel Hill: University of North Carolina Press, 1934), 690. For more on aggression toward law enforcement, see William Ivy Hair, *Carnival of Fury: Robert Charles and the New Orleans Race Riot of 1900* (1976; repr., Baton Rouge: Louisiana State University Press, 2008).

21. For examples, see Danielle L. McGuire, *At the Dark End of the Street: Black Women, Rape, and Resistance—A New History of the Civil Rights Movement from Rose Parks to the Rise of Black Power* (New York: Vintage, 2010); Nan Elizabeth Woodruff, *American Congo: The African American Freedom Struggle in the Delta* (Chapel Hill: University of North Carolina Press, 2003); Kidada E. Williams, *The Left Great Marks on Me: African American Testimonies of Racial Violence from Emancipation to World War I* (New York: New York University Press, 2012); Kali N. Gross, *Colored Amazons: Crime, Violence, and Black Women in the City of Brotherly Love, 1880–1910* (Durham, NC: Duke University Press, 2006).

22. Michelle Alexander interviewed by Matthew Pillischer, "The Struggle for Racial Justice Has a Long Way to Go," *International Socialist Review,* no. 84 (June 2012).

23. For more on black intraracial crime causes, see Gilles Vandal, *Rethinking Southern Violence: Homicides in Post–Civil War Louisiana, 1866–1884* (Columbus: Ohio State University Press, 2000); Lane, *Roots of Violence;* Adler, "Black Violence in the New South," 207–39, and *Murder in New Orleans.*

24. I focus on black intraracial homicides, thefts, and assaults. I acknowledge that does not cover sexual assaults. Unfortunately, I am not able to adequately address this issue here, largely due to the paucity of police reports and court cases related to sexual assaults.

25. There is an extensive literature on black responses to Jim Crow; see, for example, Kelley, *Race Rebels;* Steven Hahn, *A Nation under Our Feet: Black Political Struggles in the Rural South from Slavery to the Great Migration* (Cambridge, MA: Belknap Press of Harvard University Press, 2003); Thomas J. Sugrue, *Sweet Land of Liberty: The Forgotten Struggle for Civil Rights in the North* (New York: Random House, 2008); Williams, *They Left Great Marks on Me;* Stephen A.

Berrey, *The Jim Crow Routine: Everyday Performances of Race, Civil Rights, and Segregation in Mississippi* (Chapel Hill: University of North Carolina Press, 2015).

26. Considering that much of the scholarship on African Americans and the police focuses on violence and mistreatment at the hands of criminal justice actors and institutions, African Americans come off as powerless in their encounters with law enforcement agents. When black reactions to policing are discussed, scholarship has focused on black organization struggles against police brutality (for example, Moore, *Black Rage in New Orleans)* or on violent reactions to police brutality (see Hair, *Carnival of Fury).* Yet, most African Americans did not join civil rights organizations or engage in pitched battles with the police. The ways in which African Americans responded to the changes in policing outside of civil rights organizations or violent encounters are lacking. This is a critique similar to that which was leveled against scholars of lynching, who, in their efforts to understand the social structure and cultural context of the practice, overlooked how African Americans responded to the violence outside of major organizational efforts to combat lynching. See, for example, Michael J. Pfeifer, review of *They Left Great Marks on Me: African American Testimonies of Racial Violence from Emancipation to World War I,* by Kidada E. Williams, *American Historical Review* 117, no. 4 (October 2012): 1231.

27. Laurie B. Green, *Battling the Plantation Mentality: Memphis and the Black Freedom Struggle* (Chapel Hill: University of North Carolina Press, 2007), 7.

28. Robert A. Sigafoos, *Cotton Row to Beale Street: A Business History of Memphis* (Memphis, TN: Memphis State University Press, 1979), 142.

29. Michael K. Honey, *Southern Labor and Black Civil Rights: Organizing Memphis Workers* (Urbana: University of Illinois Press, 1993), 21.

30. Sigafoos, *Cotton Row to Beale Street,* 141.

31. Ibid., 65–147.

32. Honey, *Southern Labor and Black Civil Rights,* 22–23.

33. Robin D. G. Kelley, *Hammer and Hoe: Alabama Communists during the Great Depression* (Chapel Hill: University of North Carolina Press, 1990), 1.

34. Ibid.

35. Blaine A. Brownell, "Birmingham, Alabama: New South City in the 1920s," *Journal of Southern History* 38, no. 1 (February 1972): 25; Kelley, *Hammer and Hoe,* 1–10.

36. This nickname was originally coined by James Powell in 1873. See Karen R. Utz, *Sloss Furnaces* (Mount Pleasant, SC: Arcadia Publishing, 2009), 7.

37. Brownell, "Birmingham, Alabama," 22.

38. For a brief overview of the history of New Orleans, dating back to 1718, see Sharlene Sinegal DeCuir, "Attacking Jim Crow: Black Activism in New Orleans, 1925–1941," (PhD diss., Louisiana State University, 2009), 11–44; David R. Goldfield, "The Urban South: A Regional Framework," *American Historical Review* 86, no. 5 (December 1981): 1013–1015.

39. Walter Johnson, *Soul by Soul: Life Inside the Antebellum Slave Market* (Cambridge, MA: Harvard University Press, 1999), 1–2.

40. Elizabeth Fussell, "Constructing New Orleans, Constructing Race: A Population History of New Orleans," *Journal of American History* 94, no. 3 (December 2007): 848; Goldfield, "The Urban South," 1015.

41. Fussell, "Constructing New Orleans," 850; Daniel Rosenberg, *New Orleans Dockworkers: Race, Labor, and Unionism, 1892–1923* (Albany: State University of New York Press, 1988), 10.

42. Rosenberg, *New Orleans Dockworkers*, 16.

43. Ibid.; Moore, *Black Rage in New Orleans*, 10.

44. Louis M. Kyriakoudes, *The Social Origins of the Urban South: Race, Gender, and Migration in Nashville and Middle Tennessee, 1890–1930* (Chapel Hill: University of North Carolina Press, 2003).

45. Sigafoos, *Cotton Row to Beale Street*, 97.

46. "Birmingham's Population, 1880–2000," last modified: 1/23/2014, accessed May 9, 2014, http://www.bplonline.org/resources/government/BirminghamPopulation.aspx; U.S. Census of Population and Housing, 1990: Population and Housing Unit Counts: United States. Washington: U.S. Dept. of Commerce, Bureau of the Census, 1993 [table 46: Population Rank of Incorporated Places of 100,000 Population or More, 1990; Population, 1790 to 1990; Housing Units: 1940 to 1990] (C 3.223/5: 1990 CPH-2-1), 593–94].

47. U.S. Bureau of the Census, "Table 16. Population of the 100 largest Urban Places: 1930," available at *U.S. Census Bureau*, https://www.census.gov/population/www/documentation/twps0027/tab16.txt. For more on the growth of other southern cities, see Woodward, *Origins of the New South*, 107–41, 291–320; Lawrence H. Larsen, *The Rise of the Urban South* (Lexington: University Press of Kentucky, 1985); Goldfield, "The Urban South," 1009–1034; Bernadette Pruitt, *The Other Great Migration: The Movement of Rural African Americans to Houston, 1900–1941* (College Station: Texas A&M University Press, 2013); Robert D. Thomas and Richard W. Murray, *Progrowth Politics: Change and Governance in Houston* (Berkeley: University of California Press, 1991); Sigafoos, *Cotton Row to Beale Street*, 89; Kelley, *Hammer and Hoe*, 1–13; Georgina Hickey, *Hope and Danger in the New South City: Working-Class Women and Urban Development in Atlanta, 1890–1940* (Athens: University of Georgia Press, 2003).

48. Fussell, "Constructing New Orleans," 852.

49. Hahn, *A Nation under Our Feet*, 465; Pruitt, *The Other Great Migration;* Albert S. Broussard, *Black San Francisco: The Struggle for Racial Equality in the West, 1900–1954* (Lawrence: University Press of Kansas, 1993), 11–37.

50. Pruitt, *The Other Great Migration*, 15–54.

51. Carl V. Harris, "Reforms in Government Control of Negroes in Birmingham, Alabama, 1890–1920," *Journal of Southern History* 38, no. 4 (November 1972): 569–70; "Birmingham's Population, 1880–2000," last modified: 1/23/2014, accessed May 9, 2014, http://www.bplonline.org/resources/government/BirminghamPopulation.aspx

52. Fussell, "Constructing New Orleans," 847.

53. New Orleans employed a few black officers until 1909 and three black police officers were employed in Memphis in 1917 for less than a year. On the whole, from 1920 to 1945, there were no black police officers employed by Birmingham, Memphis, or New Orleans. For more on southern cities that employed black police officers prior to the 1950s, see Dulaney, *Black Police*, 30–46; K. Stephen Prince, "The Trials of George Doyle: Race and Policing in Jim Crow New Orleans," in *Crime and Punishment in the Jim Crow South,* ed. Amy Louise Wood and Natalie J. Ring (Urbana: University of Illinois Press, 2019), 17–33.

54. While the available sources offer invaluable evidence of the range of interactions between law enforcement and African Americans, there is one noticeable and significant shortcoming: namely, the limited level of detail in the sources regarding the background of African Americans who reported crimes, acted as witnesses, or were victims/suspects.. There

are numerous divisions that existed within black communities in every city, including recreational, political, personal, and geographic differences, but evidence of those distinctions is not present in most of the available sources. Thus, an extended analysis of how those divisions affected interactions with law enforcement or concerns over criminal activity is limited.

55. NAACP Branch Files; *Memphis World* 1931–1932, 1943–1945; *Birmingham Reporter,* 1923–1933; *Louisiana Weekly,* 1925–1945; MPD Homicide Reports; NOPD Homicide Reports; NOPD Witness Transcripts; NOPD Offense Reports; JCGJIR.

56. The decision to trace trends in three cities instead of focusing on trends in one city was made because the available sources required for an in-depth study of trends in interactions between police and African Americans were not complete in any one city. Instead, multiple sources from multiple cities were required to provide a more complete understanding of the different ways that these interactions unfolded in different areas of interaction.

57. Matthew D. Lassiter and Joseph Crespino, eds., *The Myth of Southern Exceptionalism* (New York: Oxford University Press, 2009).

58. Sally Hadden, *Slave Patrols: Law and Violence in Virginia and the Carolinas* (Cambridge, MA: Harvard University Press, 2000); Dennis C. Rousey, *Policing the Southern City: New Orleans, 1805–1889* (Baton Rouge: Louisiana State University Press, 1996); Robert C. Wadman and William Thomas Allison, *To Protect and to Serve: A History of Police in America* (Upper Saddle River, NJ: Pearson Prentice Hall, 2004), 27–41, 61–106.

59. Elizabeth Dale, *Criminal Justice in the United States, 1789–1939* (New York: Cambridge University Press, 2011), 97–135; Michael J. Pfeifer, *Rough Justice: Lynching and American Society, 1874–1947* (Urbana: University of Illinois Press, 2004), 122–48.

60. Muhammad, *Condemnation of Blackness,* 226–68; Kelly Lytle Hernandez, *City of Inmates: Conquest, Rebellion, and the Rise of Human Caging in Los Angeles, 1771–1965* (Chapel Hill: University of North Carolina Press, 2017), 158–94; Jeffrey S. Adler, "Less Crime, More Punishment: Violence, Race, and Criminal Justice in Early Twentieth-Century America," *Journal of American History* 102, no. 1 (June 2015): 34–46; David R. Johnson, *American Law Enforcement: A History* (Wheeling, IL: Forum Press, 1981), 105–21; Balto, *Occupied Territory,* 26–90; Johnson, *Street Justice,* 57–86, 181–228.

61. The literature on the early development of American police departments is extensive. In addition to previously referenced books, some of the more important works include, Samuel Walker, *A Critical History of Police Reform: The Emergence of Professionalism* (Lexington, MA: Lexington Books, 1977); Eric H. Monkkonen, *Police in Urban America: 1860–1920* (Cambridge, MA: Cambridge University Press, 1981); Sam Mitrani, *The Rise of the Chicago Police Department: Class and Conflict, 1850–1894* (Chicago: University of Illinois Press, 2013).

62. Cheryl D. Hicks, *Talk with You Like a Woman: African American Women, Justice, and Reform in New York, 1890–1935* (Chapel Hill: University of North Carolina Press, 2010), 182–203; Muhammad, *Condemnation of Blackness,* 126; Johnson, *Street Justice,* 182–83; Dulaney, *Black Police,* 45.

63. Hicks, *Talk with You Like a Woman,* 183.

64. Moore, *Black Rage in New Orleans;* Balto, *Occupied Territory;* Max Felker-Kantor, *Policing Los Angeles: Race, Resistance, and the Rise of the LAPD* (Chapel Hill: University of North Carolina Press, 2019).

65. Michael Javen Fortner, *Black Silent Majority: The Rockefeller Drug Laws and the Politics*

of Punishment (Cambridge, MA: Harvard University Press, 2015); James Forman, Jr., *Locking Up Our Own: Crime and Punishment in Black America* (New York: Farrar, Straus & Giroux, 2017).

66. Jennifer Ludden, "In Baltimore, Violent Crime Is Up, And Residents Say Police Presence Is Down," Weekend Edition Sunday, National Public Radio, June 4, 2015.

CHAPTER 1

Crime, Race, and the Development of Police Departments in the Urban South

1. Jack Carley, "Behind the Scenes at Headquarters," in *Memphis Police Department Year Book: 1924* (Memphis, TN: Memphis Police Relief Association, 1924), 57.

2. Dale, *Criminal Justice in the United States,* 103–105; Jeffrey S. Adler, "'The Greatest Thrill I Get is when I Hear a Criminal Say, 'Yes, I did it'': Race and the Third Degree in New Orleans, 1920–1945," *Law and History Review* 34, no. 1 (February 2016): 9–10; Claire Bond Potter, *War on Crime: Bandits, G-Men, and the Politics of Mass Culture* (New Brunswick, NJ: Rutgers University Press, 1998), 66.

3. Pfeifer, *Rough Justice,* 3–4.

4. Walker, *A Critical History of Police Reform,* ix–xi.

5. Fosdick, *American Police Systems,* 160–66, 211–16, 231–33, 246–48, 249–67, 268–325; August Vollmer, *The Police and Modern Society* (Berkeley: University of California Press, 1936), 3, 84, 119, 216–34; Mitrani, *The Rise of the Chicago Police Department,* 112–65; Johnson, *American Law Enforcement,* 64–71; Friedman, *Crime and Punishment in American History,* 152; Samuel Walker, *Popular Justice: A History of American Criminal Justice,* 2nd ed. (New York: Oxford University Press, 1998), 131; Fogelson, *Big-City Police,* 93–192.

6. Carley, "Behind the Scenes," 57.

7. Muhammad, *Condemnation of Blackness;* Adler, "Less Crime, More Punishment, 34–46; Johnson, *American Law Enforcement,* 105–21.

8. George M. Fredrickson, *The Black Image in the White Mind: The Debate on Afro-American Character and Destiny, 1817–1914* (Middletown, CT: Wesleyan University Press, 1971), 256–82; Adler, "Less Crime, More Punishment," 42–46, and *Murder in New Orleans.*

9. Tom R. Tyler, *Why People Obey the Law* (New Haven, CT: Yale University Press, 1990), 4–5.

10. For more on legitimacy, see Gary LaFree, *Losing Legitimacy: Street Crime and the Decline of Social Institutions in America* (Boulder, CO: Westview Press, 1998), 6–7; 91–113.

11. Richard Hofstadter, *The Age of Reform: From Bryan to F.D.R.* (New York: Alfred A. Knopf, 1956); Gabriel Kolko, *The Triumph of Conservatism: A Reinterpretation of American History, 1900–1916* (New York: Macmillan, 1963); Robert H. Wiebe, *The Search for Order, 1877–1920* (New York: Hill & Wang, 1967); Daniel T. Rodgers, *Atlantic Crossings: Social Politics in a Progressive Age* (Cambridge, MA: Belknap Press of Harvard University Press, 1998); Michael McGerr, *A Fierce Discontent: The Rise and Fall of the Progressive Movement in America, 1870–1920* (New York: Free Press, 2003).

12. G. Wayne Dowdy, *A Brief History of Memphis* (Charleston, SC: History Press, 2011), 67.

13. Andrew A. Bruce and Thomas S. Fitzgerald, "A Study of Crime in the City of Memphis, Tennessee," *Journal of the American Institute of Criminal Law and Criminology* 19, no. 2 (August 1928): 8–9.

14. Carrie Nation, 1907, quoted in Gary Krist, *Empire of Sin: A Story of Sex, Jazz, Murder, and the Battle for Modern New Orleans* (New York: Crown Publishers, 2014), 176.

15. Scott S. Ellis, *Madam Vieux Carre: The French Quarter in the Twentieth Century* (Jackson: University of Mississippi Press, 2010), 34–35; Alecia P. Long, *The Great Southern Babylon: Sex, Race, and Respectability in New Orleans, 1865–1920* (Baton Rouge: Louisiana State University Press, 2004), 102–224.

16. Brownell, "Birmingham, Alabama," 31.

17. For some of the best studies on southern violence, see Sheldon Hackney, "Southern Violence," *American Historical Review*, 74, no. 3 (February 1969): 906–25; Bertram Wyatt-Brown, *Southern Honor: Ethics & Behavior in the Old South* (New York: Oxford University Press, 1982); Ayers, *Vengeance and Justice;* Raymond D. Gastil, "Homicide and a Regional Culture of Violence," *American Sociological Review* 36, no. 3 (June 1971): 412–27.

18. For more on the southern honor culture, see Wyatt-Brown, *Southern Honor;* and Ayers, *Vengeance and Justice*. For studies on the weakness of southern legal institutions, see W. Fitzhugh Brundage, *Lynching in the New South: Georgia and Virginia, 1880–1930* (Urbana: University of Illinois Press, 1993); and Christopher Waldrep, *Roots of Disorder: Race and Criminal Justice in the American South, 1817–1880* (Urbana: University of Illinois Press, 1998).

19. According to Frederick Hoffman, the average homicide rate for twenty-eight major American cities for 1900 was 5.1, for 1910 was 8.1, and for 1920 was 8.5. See Hoffman, *The Homicide Problem* (Newark, NJ: Prudential Press, 1925), 96. As a comparison, the homicide rate in New York City from 1900 to 1950 remained under 6/100,000, except for 1931. See Eric H. Monkkonen, *Murder in New York City* (Berkeley: University of California Press, 2001), 21.

20. Adler, "Less Crime, More Punishment," 39.

21. For these rates, see Hoffman, *The Homicide Problem,* 7, 14, 37, 43, 55–56, 68, 75–76, 92, 98.

22. The homicide rates for Boston was 4.8, Chicago was 13.6, New York City was 4.2, Los Angeles was 13.9, and Washington, DC, was 15.4; see Hoffman, *The Homicide Problem,* 75–76.

23. Ibid., 75–76.

24. For more on factors that contributed to high rates of black intraracial violence, see Lane, *Roots of Violence;* Vandal, *Rethinking Southern Violence;* Adler, "Black Violence in the New South," 224–28.

25. The rates of homicide within racial communities came from the Mortality Statistics of 1922; see U.S. Department of Commerce, Department of the Census, *Mortality Statistics 1922: Twenty-Third Annual Report,* 140–43.

26. Green, *Battling the Plantation Mentality,* 16; Hahn, *A Nation under Our Feet.*

27. Adler, "The Killer behind the Badge," 498; Fredrickson, *The Black Image in the White Mind,* 256–82; Muhammad, *Condemnation of Blackness;* Dollard, *Caste and Class,* 287–88.

28. J. J. Durrett and W. G. Stromquist, *A Study of Violent Deaths Registered in Atlanta, Birmingham, Memphis and New Orleans for the Years 1921 and 1922* (Memphis, TN: Department of Health, City of Memphis, 1923), 33.

29. Muhammad, *Condemnation of Blackness,* 8.

30. Frederick L. Hoffman, *Race Traits and Tendencies of the American Negro* (New York: American Economic Association, 1896), 228, 234, 236.

31. Bruce and Fitzgerald, "A Study of Crime in the City of Memphis," 15–16.

32. Ibid., 94.

33. There is debate among scholars regarding the emergence of segregation in the Jim Crow period. C. Vann Woodward argued that widespread racial segregation emerged during the 1890s with the passage of segregation laws across the South; see Woodward, *The Strange Career of Jim Crow* (New York: Oxford University Press, 1955). Other historians, most notably Howard N. Rabinowitz and Joel Williamson, posited that the segregation laws passed in the 1890s simply codified racial segregation that had already existed for much of the late nineteenth century; see Rabinowitz, *Race Relations in the Urban South, 1865–1890* (New York: Oxford University Press, 1978); and Williamson, *The Crucible of Race: Black-White Relations in the American South since Emancipation* (New York: Oxford University Press, 1984).

34. Charles E. Connerly, *"The Most Segregated City in America": City Planning and Civil Rights in Birmingham, 1920–1980* (Charlottesville: University of Virginia Press, 2005), 36–68; Roger L. Rice, "Residential Segregation by Law, 1910–1917," *Journal of Southern History* 34, no. 2 (May 1968): 179–99; Daphne Spain, "Race Relations and Residential Segregation in New Orleans: Two Centuries of Paradox," *Annals of the American Academy of Political and Social Science* 441 (January 1979): 88–90; Gloria Brown Melton, "Black in Memphis, Tennessee, 1920–1955: A Historical Study," (PhD diss., Washington State University, 1982), 1, 13–18.

35. For more on segregation in Memphis, see Melton, "Blacks in Memphis, Tennessee," 10–13.

36. Litwack, *Trouble in Mind*, 218.

37. "Annual Message of the Mayor and Reports of the Officers of the City of Birmingham, Alabama for the Fiscal Year Ending December 31, 1907 (Birmingham: Alabama Paper and Printing Company, 1908), 17.

38. Bruce and Fitzgerald, "A Study of Crime in the City of Memphis," 12.

39. Pfeifer, *Rough Justice,* 2–3.

40. Ibid., 3.

41. In Tennessee mobs lynched fifteen African Americans in Shelby County (of which Memphis is the county seat) between 1890 and 1930; see Margaret Vandiver, *Lethal Punishment: Lynchings and Legal Executions in the South* (New Brunswick, NJ: Rutgers University Press, 2006), 199–200. Mobs in Orleans Parish (of which New Orleans is the parish seat) lynched eleven whites in 1890 and one African American in 1893; see Pfeifer, *Rough Justice,* 161–78. For more on lynchings in southern cities, see Dwight D. Watson, "In the Name of Decency and Progress: The Response of Houston's Civic Leaders to the Lynching of Robert Powell in 1928," *Houston Review* 1, no. 2 (Spring 2013): 26–30.

42. Vandiver, *Lethal Punishment,* 119–40.

43. Pfeifer, *Rough Justice,* 122–48; Dale, *Criminal Justice in the United States,* 2–3, 17, 90–91; Elizabeth Dale, "Getting Away with Murder," *American Historical Review* 111, no. 1 (2006): 102–3; Williams, *They Left Great Marks on Me,* 9, 226 n. 20; Kidada E. Williams, "Resolving the Paradox of Our Lynching Fixation: Reconsidering Racialized Violence in the American South after Slavery," in *Lynching Reconsidered: New Perspectives in the Study of Mob Violence,* ed. William D. Carrigan (New York: Routledge, 2008), 97–124.

44. W. Fitzhugh Brundage, *Lynching in the New South: Georgia and Virginia, 1880–1930* (Urbana: University of Illinois Press, 1993), 162, 171; Claude A. Clegg III, *Troubled Ground: A Tale of Murder, Lynching, and Reckoning in the New South* (Urbana: University of Illinois Press, 2010), 68, 156–57.

45. "Where the Blame Is," *Memphis Commercial-Appeal,* May 26, 1917; for other reactions, see Vandiver, *Lethal Punishment,* 133–35.

46. Pfeifer, *Rough Justice;* Dale, *Criminal Justice in the United States,* 97–139.

47. Pfeifer, *Rough Justice,* 139.

48. The demand for order and fear of violence disrupting economic growth and stability prompted many cities to create police departments in the nineteenth century; see Miller, *Cops and Bobbies,* 5–8; Mitrani, *The Rise of the Chicago Police Department,* 3; Harring, *Policing a Class Society,* 13–20.

49. "Lynching and Law," *Memphis Commercial-Appeal,* May 23, 1917.

50. Pfeifer, *Rough Justice,* 4.

51. For more on the notion of legitimacy, see LaFree, *Losing Legitimacy,* 6–7; 91–113; Tyler, *Why People Obey the Law,* 4–5.

52. Pfeifer, *Rough Justice,* 122–48; Johnson, American Law Enforcement, 105–54.

53. Walker, *A Critical History of Police Reform,* 3.

54. Ibid., 3, 53–55; Jeffrey S. Adler, "Shoot to Kill: The Use of Deadly Force by the Chicago Police, 1875–1920," *Journal of Interdisciplinary History* 38, no. 2 (Autumn 2007): 233–54.

55. Hair, *Carnival of Fury,* 119.

56. K. Stephen Prince, "Remembering Robert Charles: Violence and Memory in Jim Crow New Orleans," *Journal of Southern History* 83, no. 2 (May 2017): 297–328.

57. "Annual Message of Mayor George B. Ward," 1907, 9–10.

58. Wiebe, *The Search for Order,* 160, 165–66.

59. Walker, *A Critical History of Police Reform,* 53, 136–37.

60. Eddie M. Ashmore, "The History of the Memphis Police Department," 25, http://www.memphispolice.org/Memphis%20PD%20History.pdf. (Accessed May 2014.)

61. Ibid., 27.

62. Frank and Gennie Myers, *Memphis Police Department 1827–1975* (Marceline, MO: Walsworth Publishing Company, 1975), 29.

63. Ashmore, "The History of the Memphis Police Department," 31.

64. New Orleans Police Department, *Fifty Years of Progress, 1900–1950* (New Orleans: Franklin Printing Company, 1950), 7.

65. Ibid., 11.

66. Ibid., 39.

67. "167 Men Protect City of 178,273," and "165 Patrolmen Should Be Increased to 600 for Size of Area, Suggestion," BPD Scrapbooks.

68. Fosdick, *American Police,* 188–216.

69. Walker, *A Critical History of Police Reform,* 53–166.

70. New Orleans Police Department, *Fifty Years,* 11.

71. "Annual Reports of Heads of Departments," in *Year Book: City of Birmingham, Alabama, 1924* (Birmingham, AL: City Commission of Birmingham, 1924), 16.

72. "165 Patrolmen Should Be Increased To 600 for Size of Area, Suggestion," BPD Scrapbooks.

73. Fosdick, *American Police Systems,* 307.

74. Ashmore, "The History of the Memphis Police Department," 29; Walker, *A Critical History of Police Reform,* 136.

75. Myers, *Memphis Police Department,* 48.

76. Ibid., 51.

77. Ibid., 53–54.

78. Walker, *A Critical History of Police Reform,* 136.

79. New Orleans Police Department, *Fifty Years,* 11, 19, 33.

80. "Ex-Drive of Horse Patrol Is Now Master of Fast Auto," *Birmingham News,* September 30, 1929, BPD Scrapbooks.

81. Walker, *A Critical History of Police Reform,* 136.

82. Along with police at the local level, the Federal Bureau of Investigation adopted automobiles to help combat high-profile bank robbers in the 1930s; see Elliot J. Gorn, *Dillinger's Wild Ride: The Year That Made America's Public Enemy Number One* (Oxford: Oxford University Press, 2009); Potter, *War on Crime.*

83. New Orleans Police Department, *Fifty Years,* 7.

84. "Annual Message of Mayor George B. Ward," 1907, 36.

85. Ashmore, "The History of the Memphis Police Department," 25.

86. Ibid., 28.

87. Myers, *Memphis Police Department,* 54.

88. "Radio Effective in Breaking Up Crime," *Memphis Commercial-Appeal,* December 25, 1932.

89. Myers, *Memphis Police Department,* 54; Ashmore, "The History of the Memphis Police Department," 31, 33.

90. New Orleans Police Department, *Fifty Years,* 39.

91. "Radio Police System Is Advocated Here," *Birmingham News,* January 15, 1932, BPD Scrapbooks.

92. "Birmingham Citizens and Property Protected by Broadcast Unit," *Birmingham News,* January 30, 1938; "Radio-Equipped Police Patrol to Cut Down Crime Here, Is Opinion," *Birmingham News,* December 16, 1932. All of the above cited articles are to be found in BPD Scrapbooks.

93. Fosdick, *American Police Systems,* 307, 354–78.

94. Miller, *Cops and Bobbies,* 2.

95. Fosdick, *American Police Systems,* 298–305, 337–33.

96. "The Police Training School of the City of Birmingham," *Historical Souvenir: Birmingham Police Department* 1902–1930, BPD Scrapbooks.

97. "Crime School Opens with 25 'Students,'" *Memphis Commercial-Appeal,* April 6, 1937, MPD Clippings File, 1800s–1930s.

98. "25 in Police School Make Good Progress," *Memphis Commercial-Appeal,* April 11, 1937, MPD Clippings File, 1800s–1930s.

99. "New Police Science Is Shown at Theater," *Memphis Commercial-Appeal,* March 12, 1939, MPD Clippings File, 1938–1949.

100. "Tom Smith Wins Arrest Honors," *Memphis Evening Appeal,* January 1, 1929, MPD Clippings File, 1800s–1930s; "Passes 20th Year as Keeper of Peace," *Memphis Commercial-Appeal,* December 13, 1930, MPD Clippings File, 1800s–1930s; "Posts Left Vacant by Sweeping Suspensions To Be Filled Immediately," *Memphis Evening Appeal,* September 23, 1927, MPD Clippings File, 1800s–1930s; "Justice for Policemen," *Memphis Press-Scimitar,* August 7, 1940, MPD Clippings File, 1938–1949.

101. Adler, "The Killer behind the Badge," 504.

102. Lane, *Murder in America*, 214–67; Adler, "Less Crime, More Punishment," 36.

103. Lane, *Murder in America*, 218–20.

104. Ibid., 215.

105. Ibid., 214–48; Adler, "'The Greatest Thrill I Get,'" 9.

106. Adler, "Less Crime, More Punishment," 36.

107. Potter, *War on Crime*, 31–105.

108. Adler, "Less Crime, More Punishment," 41.

109. Adler, "Shoot to Kill," 233–54; Muhammad, *Condemnation of Blackness*, 226–68.

110. "Memphis Free of Drug Evil, Probers Find," *Memphis Evening Appeal*, September 13, 1928, Memphis-Crime Clippings File, Memphis and Shelby County Room, Memphis Public Library, Memphis, Tennessee.

111. "Police Clamp That Lid Again," *Memphis Press-Scimitar*, June 17, 1935, Memphis-Crime Clippings File.

112. Johnson, *Policing the Urban Underworld: The Impact of Crime on the Development of the American Police, 1800–1887* (Philadelphia: Temple University Press, 1979), 179–80.

113. "War on Prostitution Called All-Out Here," *Memphis Commercial-Appeal*, June 9, 1942, MPD Clippings File, 1938–1949.

114. "Entire Police Force Girded for Campaign," *Memphis Commercial-Appeal*, January 9, 1939, MPD Clippings File, 1938–1949; Honey, *Southern Labor and Black Civil Rights*, 3, 17–18, 49–50, 61–63.

115. Miller, *Cops and Bobbies*, 51–54.

116. New Orleans Police Department, *Fifty Years*, 33.

117. Myers, *Memphis Police Department*, 65.

118. "Special Squad Put on Trail of Vandals in the City," *Birmingham News*, January 14, 1938.

119. Adam Fairclough, *Race and Democracy: The Civil Rights Struggle in Louisiana, 1915–1972* (Athens: University of Georgia Press, 1995), 1–105; Adler, "Less Crime, More Punishment," 42–45; Honey, *Southern Labor and Black Civil Rights;* Elizabeth Gritter, *River of Hope: Black Politics and the Memphis Freedom Movement, 1865–1954* (Lexington: University Press of Kentucky, 2014), 51–174; Kelley, *Hammer and Hoe;* Muhammad, *Condemnation of Blackness;* Hernandez, *City of Inmates*, 158–94.

120. Adler, "'The Greatest Thrill I Get,'" 21, and "Less Crime, More Punishment," 42–43.

121. Adler, "Less Crime, More Punishment," 34–46.

122. Adler, *Murder in New Orleans*.

123. For a representation of the "New Negro" mentality and culture, see Locke, *The New Negro*.

124. "Current Comment," *Louisiana Weekly*, October 10, 1925.

125. Connerly, *"The Most Segregated City in America,"* 36–101; McNeil, *Groundwork*, 57–212.

126. *Harmon v. Tyler*, 273 U.S. 668 (1927); Stephen Grant Meyer, *As Long as They Don't Move Next Door: Segregation and Racial Conflict in American Neighborhoods* (New York: Rowman & Littlefield, 2001), 31.

127. *Patterson v. Alabama*, 294 U.S. 600 (1935); *Norris v. Alabama*, 294 U.S. 587 (135).

128. Eugene Stanley, 1935, quoted in Adler, "Less Crime, More Punishment," 42.

129. Adler, "'The Greatest Thrill I Get,'" 20–21.

130. Adler, "Less Crime, More Punishment," 42–45, and *Murder in New Orleans*, 160; Lane, *Murder in America*, 220–28. For an example of the relatively low rates of interracial homicides

compared to intraracial homicides, see Bruce and Fitzgerald, "A Study of Crime in the City of Memphis," 15–20.

131. This number is based on my own reading of the *Birmingham News* from January 1, 1938, to April 20, 1938. There are a total of 119 days in which the paper was published during this time. Black crime stories appeared in 27 percent of issues.

132. "Negro Stomps, Robs Woman," *Birmingham News,* April 24, 1938.

133. Muhammad, *Condemnation of Blackness.*

134. For more on these men, see Adler, *Murder in New Orleans;* Michael K. Honey, *Going Down Jericho Road: The Memphis Strike, Martin Luther King's Last Campaign* (New York: W. W. Norton, 2008), 11; Sharon D. Wright, *Race, Power, and Political Emergence in Memphis* (New York: Routledge, 1999), 33; William A. Nunnelley, *Bull Connor* (Tuscaloosa: University of Alabama Press, 1991), 4–5.

135. Glenn Feldman, *Politics, Society, and the Klan in Alabama: 1915–1949* (Tuscaloosa: University of Alabama Press, 1999), 45, 81, 143, 247, 295; Kenneth T. Jackson, *The Ku Klux Klan in the City, 1915–1930* (New York: Oxford University Press, 1967), 54–55).

136. Feldman, *Politics, Society, and the Klan,* 29–30.

137. Wright, *Race, Power, and Political Emergence in Memphis,* 33.

138. Douglas A. Blackmon, *Slavery by Another Name: The Re-Enslavement of Black Americans from the Civil War to World War II* (New York: First Anchor Books, 2009); Harris, "Reforms in Government," 579.

139. See FBI Uniform Crime Reports, 1931–1945.

140. Adler, *Murder in New Orleans;* Muhammad, *Condemnation of Blackness,* 226–68.

141. Letter from Roy Wilkins to James Gayle, April 6, 1934, Folder 10, "New Orleans, LA, 1934," Box I:G82, NAACP Branch Files.

142. Blackmon, *Slavery by Another Name;* Lichtenstein, *Twice the Work of Free Labor,* 73–195.

143. Adler, "Less Crime, More Punishment," 42–46.

144. Theodore Ray, 1929, quoted in Adler, "Less Crime, More Punishment," 43.

145. Gritter, *River of Hope,* 132; Preston Lauterbach, *Beale Street Dynasty: Sex, Song, and the Struggle for the Soul of Memphis* (New York: W. W. Norton, 2015), 274–77, 282–83.

146. "Shakeup Is Made in Police Assignments," *Memphis Commercial-Appeal,* December 2, 1932.

147. "Police Carry on Drive on Policy Writers," *n-Appeal,* December 8, 1932.

148. Johnson, *Policing the Urban Underworld,* 179–80.

149. Increased police violence, particularly lethal violence, emerged as a result of police professionalization. As officers responded to criticisms that they could not combat crime effectively, departments embraced aggressive crime-fighting strategies that often included "shoot to kill" orders. See Adler, "Shoot to Kill," 243.

150. For examples, see Adler, "Killer behind the Badge"; Watson, *A Change Did Come,* 19–20, 22, 33, 54, 58, 59, 66–67, 72–89, 104–7; Johnson, *Street Justice,* 12–228; Joel Williamson, *A Rage for Order: Black-White Relations in the American South since Emancipation* (New York: Oxford University Press, 1986), 133–41; Howard N. Rabinowitz, "Conflicts between Blacks and Police in the Urban South, 1865–1900," *The Historian* 39, no. 1 (November 1976): 63–76; Myrdal, *American Dilemma,* 540–45.

151. Adler, "Cognitive Bias: Interracial Homicide in New Orleans, 1921–1945," *Journal of Interdisciplinary History* 43, no. 1 (Summer 2012): 43–61.

152. According to the MPD Homicide Reports, African Americans killed eleven police officers from 1917 to 1946, and the majority (eight) of those killings occurred between 1918 and 1922. From 1923 to 1946 three officers died at the hands of African Americans. In New Orleans, nine police officers were killed by African Americans from 1925 to 1945; see Adler, "The Killer behind the Badge," 507. The best-known example of a black southerner killing southern police officers occurred on July 23, 1900, when Robert Charles shot several NOPD officers, which resulted in days of rioting; see Hair, *Carnival of Fury.*

153. MPD Homicide Reports documented this in eighty-four cases out of a total of ninety-three police killings of African Americans.

154. MPD Homicide Report for Levon Carlock, February 25, 1933; "Deposition of Fannie Henderson, Police Brutality in Memphis," 1945, Box 8, Series II, Robert R. Church Family Papers, University of Memphis Special Collections, Memphis, Tennessee; Lauterbach, *Beale Street Dynasty,* 274–76; Michael K. Honey, *Black Workers Remember: An Oral History of Segregation, Unionism, and the Freedom Struggle* (Berkeley: University of California Press, 1999), 20–23.

155. Honey, *Southern Labor and Black Civil Rights,* 3.

156. This number is based on the fourteen years for which complete records have survived between 1925 and 1945; see Adler, "'The Killer behind the Badge,'" 505.

157. Adler, "'The Killer behind the Badge,'" 510–11.

158. "Man Shot by Officer Dies," *Louisiana Weekly,* September 3, 1932.

159. "Woman Killed by Officers Saturday Night," *Birmingham Reporter,* January 7, 1933.

160. "True to Form," *Birmingham Reporter,* January 7, 1933.

161. Kenneth E. Barnhart, "A Study of Homicide in the United States," *Birmingham-Southern College Bulletin* 25, no. 3 (May 1932): 34–35.

162. State of Alabama vs. Willie Lee Anderson, January Term, 1920 case Number 142, JCGJIR.

163. Adler, "Less Crime, More Punishment," 1, 7; Randolph Roth, *American Homicide* (Cambridge, MA: Harvard University Press, 2009), 4, 440–50; Monkkonen, *Murder in New York City,* 22; Lane, *Murder in America,* 215.

164. Niedermeier, *The Color of the Third Degree,* 26. Also see W. Fitzhugh Brundage, *Civilizing Torture: An American Tradition* (Cambridge, MA: Harvard University Press, 2018), 206–48.

165. Friedman, *Crime and Punishment,* 361.

166. Adler, "'The Greatest Thrill I Get,'" 6.

167. Ibid., 5.

168. Ibid., 1–3.

169. For more on law enforcement's use of the third degree, see Wickersham Commission, *Report on Lawlessness in Law Enforcement* (Washington, DC: U.S. Government Printing Office, 1931). For more on the third degree in the South in particular, see Niedermeier, *The Color of the Third Degree.*

170. "Says Police Beat Youth," *Memphis World,* April 5, 1932.

171. "Death Sentence Reversed Because of 'Third Degree,'" *Birmingham Reporter,* February 4, 1933.

172. *Brown v. Mississippi,* 297 U.S. 278 (1936).

173. James Oakes, *Slavery and Freedom: An Interpretation of the Old South* (New York: Alfred A. Knopf, 1990), 6; Kenneth M. Stamp, *The Peculiar Institution: Slavery in the Ante-Bellum South* (New York: Alfred A. Knopf, 1956), 174–77; Williams, *They Left Great Marks on Me," and* "Resolving the Paradox of Our Lynching Fixation"; Stewart E. Tolnay and E. M. Beck, *A Festival of Violence: An Analysis of Southern Lynchings, 1882–1930* (Urbana: University of Illinois Press, 1995); Brundage, *Lynching in the New South,* 17–48.

174. "Posters Cause Arrest of Birmingham N.A.A.C.P. Head, Papers of the NAACP, Folder 2, "Birmingham, ALA, March–May 1933, Box I:G2, NAACP Branch Files.

175. Litwack, *Trouble in Mind,* 59; Watson, *A Change Did Come,* 4.

176. G. Wayne Dowdy, *Mayor Crump Don't Like It: Machine Politics in Memphis* (Oxford: University Press of Mississippi, 2008).

177. Gritter, *River of Hope,* 117.

178. Ibid., 141–42.

179. Lauterbach, *Beale Street Dynasty,* 295–97.

180. Ibid., 299–300.

181. Honey, *Southern Labor and Black Civil Rights,* 8.

182. Ibid., 7; Kelley, *Hammer and Hoe.*

183. Fairclough, *Race and Democracy,* 34.

184. Kelley, *Hammer and Hoe,* xiv, 78–91, 123.

185. "Law Officers Watch I. D. L. Meeting," *Birmingham World,* October 8, 1932.

186. There were a total of 292 members of the BPD in 1932; see "… Birmingham…" in *Historical Souvenir: Birmingham Police Department,* 1902–1930, Compiled and Issued for Benefit of Birmingham Police Relief Association, Manuscripts and Archives Division, Birmingham Public Library, Birmingham, AL.

187. For a good overview on literature relating to police presence and public concerns over crime, see Jihong "Solomon" Zhao, Matthew Scheider, and Quint Thurman, "The Effect of Police Presence on Public Fear Reduction and Satisfaction: A Review of the Literature," *Justice Professional* 15, no. 3 (2002): 273–99.

188. "Caution, Caution!!," *Birmingham Reporter,* October 8, 1932.

189. Honey, *Southern Labor and Black Civil Rights,* 3.

190. Ibid., 2–4.

191. Sgts England, Hutchinson, Thomas, and Johnston to Chief Inspector M. A. Hinds, November 10, 1943, Folder "Negroes-1943," Box 199, Series 4—General Correspondence 1925–1954, E. H. Crump Collection, Memphis/Shelby County Public Library and Information Center, Memphis, TN; Lauterbach, *Beale Street Dynasty,* 149, 164, 275–76, 286, 290.

192. New Orleans Police Department, *Fifty Years,* 10.

193. Quoted in Honey, *Black Workers Remember,* 18.

CHAPTER 2

African American Responses to Crime in the Urban South

1. "Public Safety, Relief from Crime Waves," *Birmingham Reporter,* May 26, 1928.

2. Fredrickson, *Black Image in the White Mind,* 276; Muhammad, *Condemnation of Blackness,* 35–87.

3. For examples of black scholars arguing against the dominant narratives put forth by men like Frederick Hoffman, see W. E. B. Du Bois, "The Negro Criminal," in *The Philadelphia Negro: A Social Study* (Philadelphia: University of Pennsylvania Press, 1899): 235–368, and *Some Notes on Negro Crime, Particularly in Georgia* (Atlanta: Atlanta University Press, 1904); Monroe N. Work, "Crime among the Negroes of Chicago: A Social Study," *American Journal of Sociology* 6, no. 2 (September 1900): 224–37, and "Negro Criminality in the South," *Annals of the American Academy of Political and Social Sciences* 49 (September 1913): 74–80.

4. Muhammad, *Condemnation of Blackness,* 15–87.

5. Adler, *Murder in New Orleans,* 105–6.

6. For all of these articles, see *Louisiana Weekly,* April 23, 1932.

7. For an example of the effect of crime stories on newspaper circulation, see Margaret T. Gordon and Linda Heath, "The News Business, Crime, and Fear," in *Reactions to Crime,* ed. D. Lewis (Beverly Hills, CA: Sage, 1981), 227–50.

8. For more on the idea of a continuum of white-on-black violence during this era, see Brent M. S. Campney, *Hostile Heartland: Racism, Repression, and Resistance in the Midwest* (Urbana: University of Illinois Press, 2019); Williams, *They Left Great Marks on Me.*

9. According to my dataset culled from the MPD and NOPD homicide reports, there were 199 white-on-black homicides in Memphis from 1917 to 1945 and 72 white-on-black homicides in New Orleans for the years 1926–31, 1935, 1938–39, 1941–43, and 1945.

10. MPD Homicide Report for Will Moore, July 4, 1924.

11. For more on lack of punishment for white perpetrators of violence against African Americans, see Kennedy, *Race, Crime, and the Law,* 41–47, 69–75.

12. NOPD Witness Transcripts, "Statement of Emergency Supernumerary Patrolman Charles Guerand, relative to the Shooting and Dangerously Wounding of One Hattie McCray," February 10, 1930; NOPD Homicide Report for Hattie McCray, February 10, 1930; "14-Year-Old Girl Is Murdered," *Louisiana Weekly,* February 15, 1930.

13. According to my dataset culled from the MPD and NOPD homicide reports, there were 1,302 black intraracial homicides in Memphis from 1917 to 1945 and 674 black intraracial homicides in New Orleans for the years 1926–31, 1935, 1938–39, 1941–43, and 1945.

14. NOPD Homicide Report for Clarance Williams, May 12, 1927.

15. Rabinowitz, *Race Relations in the Urban South,* 351; Ayers, *Vengeance and Justice,* 231–33.

16. Lane, *Roots of Violence;* Vandal, *Rethinking Southern Violence,* 157–73; Adler, "Black Violence in the New South," 224–28.

17. As a point of comparison, the black homicide rate in 1922 was 145 in Memphis, 108 in Birmingham, and 57.5 in New Orleans. The most homicidal country in the world in 2012 was Honduras, with a rate of 90.4. For 1922 rates, see U.S. Department of Commerce, Department of the Census, *Mortality Statistics 1922: Twenty-Third Annual Report,* 140–43. The 2012 rates were taken from the United Nations Office of Drugs and Crime, "Global Study on Homicide Report for 2013." https://www.unodc.org/gsh/en/data.html.

18. Ayers, *Vengeance and Justice,* 231–33.

19. Dr. C. Fisher, "Killings Continue," *Louisiana Weekly,* May 19, 1928.

20. "Our Weekly Sermon," *Birmingham Reporter,* January 15, 1927.

21. Myrdal, *American Dilemma,* 551; Kennedy, *Race, Crime, and the Law,* 69–75. Scholars traced a similar concern among black urban dwellers over crime in their own communities in

the second half of the twentieth century; see Fortner, *Black Silent Majority;* Foreman, *Locking Up Our Own.*

22. Ayers, *Vengeance and Justice,* 231–33; Lane, *Roots of Violence;* Kennedy, *Race, Crime, and the Law,* 19–20, 69–72; Vandal, *Rethinking Southern Violence,* 157–73.

23. E. Franklin Frazier, *Black Bourgeoisie* (New York: Free Press, 1957), 20.

24. Williamjames Hull Hoffer, *Plessy v. Ferguson: Race and Inequality in Jim Crow America* (Lawrence: University of Kansas Press, 2012), 9–10, 54, 183–84.

25. Kelley, *Hammer and Hoe,* 3.

26. Du Bois, "The Negro Criminal," 235–368, and *Some Notes on Negro Crime;* Work, "Crime among the Negroes of Chicago," 224–37, and "Negro Criminality in the South," 74–80; Charles S. Johnson, *The Negro in American Civilization: A Study of Negro Life and Race Relations in the Light of Social Research* (New York: Henry Holt, 1930), 299–336, 443–60; Muhammad, *Condemnation of Blackness,* 146–91; Oshinsky, *Worse than Slavery,* 98–99.

27. "Bad Examples," *Louisiana Weekly,* November 7, 1931.

28. Johnson, *The Negro in American Civilization,* 214–19; Litwack, *Trouble in Mind,* 336–38.

29. "Crime Wave: Cause and Cure," *Louisiana Weekly,* July 26, 1941.

30. Muhammad, *Condemnation of Blackness,* 146–91.

31. For more on the politics of respectability, see Evelyn Brooks Higginbotham, *Righteous Discontent: The Women's Movement in the Black Baptist Church, 1880–1920* (Cambridge, MA: Harvard University Press, 1993), 185–230.

32. Hicks, *Talk with You Like a Woman,* 182–203.

33. For examples, see Allison Davis and John Dollard, *Children of Bondage: The Personality Development of Negro Youth in the Urban South* (New York: Harper & Row, 1940), 49–50, 78, 258, 266, 270–71; Johnson, *The Negro in American Civilization,* 330–36.

34. Carol W. Hayes, "Some Remedies for Juvenile Delinquency," *Birmingham Reporter,* December 22, 1923.

35. "The Negro in Court, *Birmingham Reporter,* August 9, 1924.

36. "No Place to Go," *Louisiana Weekly,* June 25, 1932; "Juvenile Delinquency," *Louisiana Weekly,* October 14, 1939.

37. "The Crime Wave Goes On," *Louisiana Weekly,* January 21, 1928.

38. "Bad News," *Birmingham Reporter,* March 5, 1932.

39. "The Law Is Supreme," *Birmingham Reporter,* March 7, 1925.

40. For more on due process, see Pfeifer, *Rough Justice;* Dale, *Criminal Justice in the United States,* 97–135.

41. Raper, *The Tragedy of Lynching,* 13; James Campbell, *Crime and Punishment in African American History* (New York: Palgrave Macmillan, 2013), 119.

42. Ida B. Wells-Barnett, "Red Record," in *Southern Horrors and Other Writings: The Anti-Lynching Campaign of Ida B. Wells, 1892–1900,* ed. Jacqueline Jones Royster (New York: Bedford/St. Martin's, 1997), 148.

43. "Law and Order," *Louisiana Weekly,* July 27, 1929.

44. "Judge Lynch Again," *Louisiana Weekly,* July 19, 1930.

45. Pfeifer, *Rough Justice,* 122–48.

46. "Mass Meeting to Favor Law and Order," *Birmingham Reporter,* March 19, 1927.

47. "A Thought for the Week," *Birmingham Reporter,* June 4, 1927.

48. For examples of the dual system of justice, see Fosdick, *American Police Systems,* 45; Ayers, *Vengeance and Justice,* 179. In terms of intraracial homicide convictions, black killers were convicted at half the rate of white killers in New Orleans in the early 1920s. Jeffrey S. Adler, "'Spineless Judges and Shyster Lawyers': Criminal Justice in New Orleans, 1920–1945," *Journal of Social History* 49, no. 4 (Summer 2016): 918.

49. This idea is based on the theory of deterrence, whereby the certainty of punishment will reduce the likelihood that a potential criminal will commit a criminal act. For a good overview of deterrence theory, see Ronald L. Akers and Christin S. Sellers, *Criminological Theories: Introduction, Evaluation, and Application,* 5th ed. (New York: Oxford University Press, 2009), 17–45; Daniel S. Nagin, "Deterrence in the Twenty-First Century," *Crime and Justice* 42, no. 1 (August 2013): 199–263.

50. "The Way of the Transgressor," *Louisiana Weekly,* April 10, 1926.

51. "Check the Criminal," *Louisiana Weekly,* June 2, 1928.

52. Kennedy, *Race, Crime, and the Law,* 29–135; Oshinsky, *"Worse than Slavery,"* 87–161.

53. "Murder Outs—But Gets Away," *Louisiana Weekly,* May 7, 1932.

54. "Louisiana Justice," *Louisiana Weekly,* July 30, 1932.

55. Black southerners fought for black jurors throughout the Jim Crow era; see Christopher Waldrep, *Jury Discrimination: The Supreme Court, Public Opinion, and a Grassroots Fight for Racial Equality in Mississippi* (Athens: University of Georgia Press, 2010).

56. "The Red Bird Is Protected," *Louisiana Weekly,* May 13, 1933.

57. "No True Bill," *Louisiana Weekly,* June 10, 1933.

58. "We Need Jurors," *Memphis World,* September 18, 1931.

59. Waldrep, *Jury Discrimination.*

60. Fosdick, *American Police Systems,* 45; Ayers, *Vengeance and Justice,* 231; Friedman, *Crime and Punishment in American History,* 375; Kennedy, *Race, Crime, and the Law,* 3–135.

61. "Enforcement Needed," *Louisiana Weekly,* April 14, 1928.

62. "Murders Must Stop!" *Louisiana Weekly,* April 15, 1939.

63. "Strict Enforcement Needed," *Louisiana Weekly,* April 22, 1939.

64. "A Need for Better Treatment," *Louisiana Weekly,* March 10, 1928.

65. Police brutality covered a broad range of actions, including police killings, unlawful arrests, assaults, abusive language, sexual exploitation of women, beating prisoners and suspects in custody, among others; see Moore, *Black Rage in New Orleans,* 1–2.

66. For examples, see Kelley, *Hammer and Hoe,* 57–91; Watson, *A Change Did Come,* 13–36; Adler, "The Killer behind the Badge," 495–531; Niedermeier, *The Color of the Third Degree.*

67. Adler, "Less Crime, More Punishment," 42–46.

68. Formally known as the National Commission on Law Observance and Enforcement and commissioned by President Herbert Hoover in 1929 to investigate the causes of crime and problems within the criminal justice system, the Wickersham Commission published the *Report on Lawlessness in Law Enforcement* in 1931. This report brought the problem of aggressive and abusive policing to the fore of the public consciousness and prompted some changes in local criminal justice practices; see Walker, *Popular Justice,* 154–57.

69. For more on Tureaud, see Rachel L. Emanuel and Alexander P. Tureaud, Jr., *A More Noble Cause: A. P. Tureaud and the Struggle for Civil Rights in Louisiana: A Personal Biography* (Baton Rouge: Louisiana State University Press, 2011).

70. "Tureaud Studies Police Brutalities," *Louisiana Weekly,* August 2, 1930.

71. "Not Guilty," *Louisiana Weekly,* May 30, 1931.

72. Adler, *Murder in New Orleans,* 156–58.

73. The leadership's decision to make police brutality a central component of their organizational efforts occurred in response to the growth of the Communist Party (CPUSA) in the city. In the early 1930s, the CPUSA moved into several southern cities, but much of its activism centered in and around Birmingham. As the CPUSA sought to attract a sizeable base of support among the black working class, this challenged the traditional local African American leadership and also re-ignited the NAACP's efforts to solidify its place as the main civil rights organization in southern cities. See Kelley, *Hammer and Hoe,* 80; Dorothy Autrey, "The National Association for the Advancement of Colored People in Alabama, 1913–1952" (PhD diss, University of Notre Dame, 1985), 122.

74. "Negro Is Killed Resisting Arrest," *Birmingham Age-Herald,* January 1, 1933; "Petition to the Birmingham City Commission," undated, NAACP Branch Files Microfilm, Reel 1, Slide 755.

75. "Petition to the Birmingham City Commission," undated, NAACP Branch Files Microfilm, Reel 1, Slides 753–757.

76. McPherson to White, February 7, 1933, NAACP Branch Files Microfilm, Reel 1, Slides 745–746.

77. Fairclough, *Race and Democracy,* 50.

78. Shortridge to E. Frederic Morrow, September 20, 1938, Folder 3, "Birmingham, ALA., 1939," Box I:G3, NAACP Branch Files.

79. "Court House Lynching in Birmingham," *Daily Worker,* May 13, 1938; "Negro Youth, Convicted and Sentenced, Is Shot in Courthouse Corridor," *Birmingham News,* May 12, 1938.

80. Helen Shores Lee and Barbara S. Shores, *The Gentle Giant of Dynamite Hill: The Untold Story of Arthur Shores and His Family's Fight for Civil Rights* (Grand Rapids, MI: Zondervan, 2012), 16.

81. Kelley, *Hammer and Hoe,* 181.

82. "Annual Report," March 31, 1939, Folder 4, "Birmingham, ALA., 1939," Box I:G3, NAACP Branch Files.

83. Petition for the Civil Service Board, June 24, 1939, Folder 1, Box I:C279, NAACP Administrative File.

84. "In the Matter of Will Hall vs. George Williams, Patrolman," July 27, 1939, Folder 1, Box I:C279, NAACP Administrative File.

85. "Birmingham Cop Placed on Probation for Year in Beating of Negro," Folder 1, Box I:C279, NAACP Administrative File.

86. "Advancement" Booklet, undated, Folder 9, "Birmingham, Alabama, 1940–1944," Box II:C1, NAACP Branch Files 1940–1955.

87. "NAACP Enters Jackson Case; Probe Urged," *Birmingham World,* May 6, 1941.

88. Autrey, "NAACP in Alabama," 204; "Jackson Case to be Aired," *Birmingham World,* May 9, 1941.

89. "Birmingham Gets Prize for Best NAACP Branch," June 20, 1941, Folder 9, "Birmingham, Alabama, 1940–1944," Box II:C1, NAACP Branch Files 1940–1955.

90. Autrey, "NAACP in Alabama," 203.

91. For more on the larger effort of the NAACP to fight police brutality, see Niedermeier, *The Color of the Third Degree;* Fairclough, *Race and Democracy,* 21–105.

92. Barnhart, "Study of Homicide in the United States," 34–35. Sociologist H. C. Brearley came to a similar conclusion in his study of homicide in the United States. Brearley claimed, "the number of persons slain by officers of the law is, consequently, by no means insignificant." See Brearley, *Homicide in the United States* (Chapel Hill: University of North Carolina Press, 1932), 67.

93. "The Unidentified Criminal," *Birmingham Reporter,* August 13, 1931. Black residents in New Orleans expressed similar concerns over the lack of cooperation between African Americans and police officers. For an example, see "Check the Criminal," *Louisiana Weekly,* April 13, 1929.

94. "Colored Civic League Passes Resolution," *Louisiana Weekly,* January 23, 1926. For more on early efforts of black police in these cities, see Dulaney, *Black Police in America,* 30–46; Prince, "The Trials of George Doyle," 17–33.

95. Dulaney, *Black Police in America,* 32.

96. "Negro Police Are Suggested to Curb Project Vandalism," *Louisiana Weekly,* August 9, 1941.

97. Ibid.

98. "Negro Policemen and Law and Order," *Louisiana Weekly,* August 23, 1941.

99. "Participation in the Protection," *Birmingham World,* September 7, 1943.

100. "Negro Policemen Now," *Birmingham World,* April 24, 1945.

101. "Negro Agency Voices Plea for Race Policemen," *Memphis World,* October 17, 1944.

102. Dulaney, *Black Police in America,* 44–45.

CHAPTER 3
Police Investigations of African American Homicides

1. NOPD Witness Transcripts, Statement of Alma Cain, January 21, 1930.

2. NOPD Witness Transcripts, Statement of Isaac Morris, January 21, 1930.

3. For more on the shift to rule of law, see Dale, *Criminal Justice in the United States,* 97–135; Pfeifer, *Rough Justice,* 122–48.

4. For more on self-policing or self-help in black communities, see Dollard, *Caste and Class,* 267–86; Adler, "Black Violence in the New South," 207–39.

5. For more on the lack of concern for crimes committed against African Americans, see Fosdick, *American Police Systems,* 45; Ayers, *Vengeance and Justice,* 231; Friedman, *Crime and Punishment in American History,* 375; Kennedy, *Race, Crime, and the Law,* 3–135.

6. For more on the laxity of gun laws in these cities and the lack of enforcement of those laws, see Robert J. Spitzer, *Guns across America: Reconciling Gun Rules and Rights* (New York: Oxford University Press, 2015).

7. A key component of any officer's job during an investigation is "gathering, sorting, compiling, and evaluating information." Most of the information available to officers comes from interviews with people. For more on the centrality of individuals to police investigations, see Charles R. Swanson, Neil C. Chamelin, Leonard Territo, and Robert W. Taylor, *Criminal Investigation,* 10th ed. (New York: McGraw-Hill, 2009), 142–81.

8. Two theoretical approaches shape this chapter as well as the next two. First, my discussion of why black residents used the police is loosely based on the theory of "interest convergence." According to Derick A. Bell, Jr., the "principle of 'interest convergence' provides: The interest of blacks in achieving racial equality will be accommodated only when it converges with the interests of whites"; Bell, "Brown v. Board of Education and the Interest-Convergence Dilemma," *Harvard Law Review* 93 (1979–1980): 523. In the case of black southerners using law enforcement in investigations of crimes in black communities, I am suggesting that African Americans' interest in removing violent individuals, retrieving stolen property, or altering the balance of power in confrontations with each other converged with white police officers' and city officials' effort to impose greater control over the black population via the formal criminal justice system. My examination of the ways African Americans exerted influence in their interactions with police officers on the beat is influenced by James C. Scott's theory of everyday resistance of subaltern people, taken largely from his book *Weapons of the Weak: Everyday Forms of Peasant Resistance and Domination and the Arts of Resistance* (New Haven, CT: Yale University Press, 1985). Scott argues that oppressed groups challenge people and institutions in power through their "hidden transcript," or the ways short of large-scale collective defiance that challenge existing power structures. Scott emphasizes foot dragging, feigned ignorance, slander, arson, sabotage, and dissimulation, desertion, false compliance, and other forms of resistance that might not readily be identified by the powerful groups as defiant acts. I will examine the ways that African Americans, largely a group devoid of formal political power, carved out spaces of influence over police officers in a variety of interactions.

9. For a good examination of homicide rates for several major cities in the United States throughout the early twentieth century, see Hoffman, *The Homicide Problem;* Brearley, *Homicide in the United States.* For more on homicides in Memphis, New Orleans, and Birmingham, see Memphis Department of Health, *A Study of Violent Deaths Registered in Atlanta, Birmingham, Memphis and New Orleans for the Years 1921 and 1922* (Memphis, TN: Davis Printing Co., 1923); Barnhardt, "A Study of Homicide in the United States."

10. For national headlines relating to Memphis's homicide rate, see Hoffman, *The Homicide Problem;* "Memphis Leads All in Homicide Cases, "*New York Times,* November 18, 1920; "1,910 Murders Done in 28 Cities in 1921," *New York Times,* December 7, 1922; "Our 12,000 Killings in 1926," *Literary Digest,* July 2, 1927. For more on the way the law enforcement officials turned to the criminal justice system to bring more African Americans under the control of the state, see Muhammad, *Condemnation of Blackness,* 226–68; Hernandez, *City of Inmates,* 158–94.

11. According to police homicide reports, police made arrests in 924 cases out of a total of 1,221 black intraracial homicides from 1920 to 1945. This data came from the MPD Homicide Reports.

12. New Orleans Police Department homicide reports are missing for the years 1932, 1933, 1934, 1936, 1937, 1940, and 1944.

13. From 1920 to 1931 there were 1,425 total homicides in Birmingham; see Barnhart, "A Study of Homicides," 19. For the number of homicides brought before a grand jury, see JCGJIR.

14. While the clearance rate may have remained above 60 percent for most of the period, suspects routinely escaped punishment or received light sentences as their cases moved forward through the court system; see *Memphis Police Department Yearbook* (Memphis, TN: Memphis Police Relief Association, 1924), 62.

15. African American intraracial homicides made up 69.78 percent of all homicides in Memphis between 1920 and 1945, and comprised 62.47 percent of all homicides in New Orleans between 1926 and 1945. See MPD Homicide Reports and NOPD Homicide Reports.

16. The records for 1920 to 1924 do not consistently list arrests, so I began in 1925. The number of arrests that occurred in less than one week throughout the period totaled 556. This information comes from my own dataset culled from the MPD Homicide Reports.

17. MPD Homicide Report for Willie Ray Haynes, February 20, 1937.

18. MPD Homicide Report for Leroy Robinson, July 18, 1920.

19. The FBI promoted a centralized fingerprint database throughout the 1920s and 1930s, and they often offered their fingerprinting services and training to local police departments; see Walker, *Popular Justice*, 159–63; Johnson, *American Law Enforcement*, 116.

20. Johnson, *American Law Enforcement*, 105–17.

21. The Chicago Police Department arrested suspects accused of murder in Memphis on ten occasions, and the St. Louis Police Department arrested Memphis homicide suspects on thirteen occasions. This information came from my own datasets based on the MPD Homicide Reports.

22. Police departments' interest in the black community grew out of a desire to impose institutional control over massive black populations in the cities across the United States; see Muhammad, *Condemnation of Blackness*, 226–68; Adler, "Less Crime, More Punishment," 34–46; Hernandez, *City of Inmates*, 158–94.

23. There were 1,215 black intraracial homicides in Memphis from 1920 to 1945.

24. There were 674 black intraacial homicides in New Orleans from 1926 to 1945 (not including 1932, 1933, 1934, 1936, 1937, 1940, and 1944).

25. This also occurred in northern cities, such as Chicago, where African American communities faced high rates of intraracial violence. For examples, see Adler, *First in Violence, Deepest in Dirt;* and Chicago Police Department, "Homicides and Important Events, 1870–1920," Illinois State Archives, Springfield, IL.

26. For more on the notion of black intraracial violence as a self-help method of dispute resolution among African Americans, see Adler, "Black Violence in the New South," 224–28; Brearley, "The Pattern of Violence," 690.

27. State of Alabama vs. Perry Henry, alias Perry Carter, case no. 4432, January Term 1924, JCGJIR.

28. NOPD Homicide Report for Ella Davis, July 13, 1942.

29. State of Alabama vs. Pearl Harris, case 1138, January Term 1921, JCGJIR.

30. MPD Homicide Report for Early Alexander, April 14, 1929.

31. MPD Homicide Report for Quintell Smith, March 5, 1942.

32. NOPD Homicide Report for Charles Brooks, October 15, 1941.

33. MPD Homicide Report for Jerry Robinson, November 5, 1926.

34. MPD Homicide Report for George Duncan, December 29, 1934.

35. NOPD Homicide Report for Thodile Jacobs, April 28, 1939.

36. Marcus Gleisser, *Juries and Justice* (New York: A. S. Barnes and Company, 1968), 121–22.

37. Adler, "Spineless Judges and Shyster Lawyers," 904–27.

38. For a discussion of the importance of eyewitness testimony to criminal prosecutions, see Elizabeth F. Loftus, *Eye Witness Testimony* (Cambridge, MA: Harvard University Press,

1979); William Carrol and Michael Seng, *Eyewitness Testimony: Strategies and Tactics,* 2nd ed. (Eagan, MN: West Publishing, 2003), 1–5.

39. Honey, *Southern Labor and Black Civil Rights,* 16; "Birmingham's Population, 1880–2000," last modified: 1/23/2014, accessed May 9, 2014, http://www.bplonline.org/resources/government/BirminghamPopulation.aspx; U.S. Census of Population and Housing, 1990: Population and Housing Unit Counts: United States. Washington: U.S. Dept. of Commerce, Bureau of the Census, 1993. [Table 46: Population Rank of Incorporated Places of 100,000 Population or More, 1990; Population, 1790 to 1990; Housing Units: 1940 to 1990] (C 3.223/5: 1990 CPH-2-1), 593–594; Fussell, "Constructing New Orleans," 847.

40. The Memphis and New Orleans rates are culled from my own dataset utilizing the MPD and NOPD Homicide Reports. The Birmingham rate was calculated using Barnhart, "A Study of Homicide in the United States," 28; U.S. Department of Commerce, *Mortality Statistics 1931 and 1932* (Washington, DC: U.S. Government Printing Office), 26–27, 48–49; *Mortality Statistics 1933,* 78–79; *Mortality Statistics 1934,* 58–59; *Mortality Statistics 1935,* 102–3; *Mortality Statistics 1936,* 100–101.

41. The proportion for African American intraracial street homicide rose from 3.8 percent during the early 1920s to 28.2 percent during the early 1930s; see Adler, "'Spineless Judges and Shyster Lawyers,'" 904–27. According to my own dataset for Memphis, the number of black intraracial homicides occurring on the streets rose from roughly 30 percent to 35 percent in the early 1920s to 60 to 70 percent in the late 1930s.

42. Connerly, *"The Most Segregated City in America,"* 36–68; Rice, "Residential Segregation by Law," 179–99; Spain, "Race Relations and Residential Segregation in New Orleans," 88–90; Melton, "Black in Memphis," 1, 13–18.

43. Melton, "Blacks in Memphis," 1, 10–14; Spain, "Race Relations and Residential Segregation in New Orleans," 89–90.

44. This excludes 1941 because the MPD listed witnesses differently for that year, making it difficult to reliably identify the corpus delicti witness. See MPD Homicide Reports.

45. MPD Homicide Report for Costie Louis Brown, August 22, 1926.

46. NOPD Homicide Report for Oscar Hardin, November 26, 1939.

47. MPD Homicide Report for Rayfield Bullock, July 2, 1927.

48. NOPD Witnesses Transcripts, Statement of Joseph Harris, April 7, 1930.

49. NOPD Witnesses Transcripts, Statement of Leona Charles and Eddie Bell, April 7, 1930.

50. NOPD Homicide Report for Louis Mitchell, April 7, 1930.

51. State of Alabama vs. Clayton Snow, case no. 9136, January Term 1928, JCGJIR.

52. State of Alabama vs. Dan Twety, alias Dan Tweedy, case no. 8766, July Term 1927, JCGJIR.

53. Robert L. Snow, *Murder 101: Homicide and Its Investigation* (Westport, CT: Praeger Publishers, 2005), 88.

54. MPD Homicide Report for Will Ross, April 23, 1932.

55. State of Alabama vs. Jessie Albert, case no. 10321, January Term 1929, JCGJIR.

56. MPD Homicide Report for William "Peacie" Graham, October 9, 1933.

57. NOPD Homicide Report for Elvira Peters, July 23, 1939.

58. Dollard, *Caste and Class,* 71; Muhammad, *Condemnation of Blackness,* 251.

59. MPD Homicide Report for Ike McKinney, September 17, 1922.

60. State of Alabama vs. Will Redfor, alias Duncan Redford, alias Rutherford., case no. 14333, July Term 1931, JCGJIR.

61. NOPD Homicide Report for Beverly Frank, January 9, 1926.

62. MPD Homicide Report for Moses Hart, March 26, 1933.

63. MPD Homicide Report for Arcarrie Hudson, May 9, 1936.

64. NOPD Witness Transcripts, Statement of Tom Webbs, February 3, 1931.

65. MPD Homicide Report for Charlie Williams, March 10, 1934.

66. NOPD Homicide Report for Solomon Sanders, June 9, 1941.

67. This number comprises all of the instances where the homicide reports explicitly stated that someone surrendered to police. Occasions where someone was arrested at the scene were not included unless it was noted that they surrendered. See MPD Homicide Reports.

68. MPD Homicide Report for Charles Jackson, June 29, 1937.

69. MPD Homicide Report for Joe Ellis, May 26, 1934.

70. MPD Homicide Report for Walter Brown, May 29, 1928.

71. NOPD Homicide Report for Wills Lendsy, February 2, 1926.

72. MPD Homicide Report for Jerry Robinson, November 5, 1926.

73. Section 334–335: "Rules and Regulations of the Police Department of the City of Memphis, Tennessee," 95–96, Memphis and Shelby County Room, Memphis Public Library, Memphis, Tennessee; Adler, "The Killer behind the Badge," 501–2.

74. Adler, "The Killer behind the Badge," 495–531.

75. "In What Will This Slaughtering End," *Birmingham Reporter*, April 7, 1928.

76. "Not Guilty," *Louisiana Weekly*, May 30, 1931, 6.

77. "The Killer behind the Badge," *Louisiana Weekly*, October 3, 1942, 10.

78. Quoted in Honey, *Southern Labor and Black Civil Rights*, 49–50.

79. For more on police killings in New Orleans, see Adler, "The Killer behind the Badge," 495–531, and "Cognitive Bias," 43–61.

80. Adler, "The Greatest Thrill I Get," 1–44.

81. Wickersham Commission, *Report on Lawlessness in Law Enforcement.*

82. Police records indicate twenty-five black Memphians and one black New Orleanian surrendered with an attorney present. Jefferson County records did not indicate anyone who surrendered with an attorney present; however, based on the records of Memphis and the NOPD, it is likely that African Americans in the county did. This seems not to have been something that the prosecutor brought up during the grand jury proceedings. While these numbers are small, they do not necessarily represent all of the cases when African Americans surrendered with attorneys present, just the ones recorded and preserved in official records. They are most likely indicative of much larger trends that occurred in numerous cities across the country.

83. For examples of legal counsel being denied to defendants, see *Powell v. Alabama*, 287 U.S. 45 (1932), and *Gideon v. Wainwright*, 372 U.S. 335 (1963).

84. NOPD Homicide Report for Victoria Young, November 30, 1941.

85. MPD Homicide Report for Mason Washington, March 5, 1929.

86. Niedermeier, *The Color of the Third Degree;* Wickersham Commission, *Report on Lawlessness in Law Enforcement.*

87. "Negro 'Posse' Kills Race Man, Who Shoots His Wife," *Memphis World*, August 8, 1944.

88. For more on extralegal violence within the black community, see Karlos Hill, "Black

Vigilantism: The Rise and Decline of African American Lynch Mob Activity in the Mississippi and Arkansas Deltas, 1883–1923," *Journal of African American History* 95, no. 1 (Winter 2010): 26–43; Adler, "Black Violence in the New South," 225–28; E. M. Beck and Stewart E. Tolnay, "When Race Didn't Matter: Black and White Mob Violence against Their Own Color," in *Under Sentence of Death: Lynching in the South,* ed. W. Fitzhugh Brundage (Chapel Hill: University of North Carolina Press, 1997), 137–43.

89. State of Alabama vs. Clarence Reese, Case no. 5234, October Term 1924, JCGJIR.

90. For an examination on life as a fugitive, see Alice Goffman, *On the Run: Fugitive Life in an American City* (Chicago: University of Chicago Press, 2014).

CHAPTER 4

African Americans and the Police in Black Stolen-Property Cases

1. NOPD Offense Report for Emerly West, February 4, 1920.

2. Thefts refer to the taking of property without violence or the threat of violence. Burglary is entering of a building or residence with the intention to commit a theft or any felonious crime. Burglary does not require that property be stolen or that person-to-person interaction occur. However, in this chapter all burglaries involved the theft of property. Throughout the chapter these types of crimes will be referred to individually or collectively as "stolen-property cases" or "property loss cases."

3. African Americans using state institutions to shape the behavior of black residents in urban areas was not unique to southern cities. See, for example, Hicks, *Talk with You Like a Woman,* 182–203.

4. Dale, *Criminal Justice in the United States,* 97–135; Pfeifer, *Rough Justice,* 122–48.

5. "Bad Examples," *Louisiana Weekly,* November 7, 1931.

6. This was not just a problem in the South, however. The FBI's Uniform Crime Reports document the scope of thefts on a national level. For example, from January to March of 1932, the FBI counted 42,463 burglaries, 72,855 larceny cases, and 40,834 automobile thefts. See Federal Bureau of Investigation, "Offenses Known to the Police, First Quarter, 1932, 1,253 Miscellaneous Cities; Number and Rates per 100,000," in *Uniform Crime Reports* 3, no. 1 (1932): 6.

7. This number comes from my own dataset culled from the Offense Reports of the New Orleans Police Department. For all of the statistics in this chapter, I have relied on NOPD Offense Reports for the years 1920, 1925, 1930, 1935, 1940, and 1945. Due to the sheer number of cases, I pulled data from every fifth year. Although I only used data from every fifth year, I will refer to the period as a whole from 1920 to 1945 throughout the chapter.

8. This rise in the 1920s and decline in the 1930s mirrors a similar rise and subsequent decline in homicide rates in New Orleans, and across the country. See Adler, "Less Crime, More Punishment," 34–46.

9. This is according to my dataset using the JCGJIR. The numbers for New Orleans and Birmingham are so different because the New Orleans numbers come from complaints received by the NOPD, while the Jefferson County numbers come from the grand jury records. A large number of cases were (are still are) dropped from the time a complaint is made to the moment a case is brought before a grand jury. Moreover, grand jury cases cover only thefts in which an

arrest was made by law enforcement. Thus, the number of cases that went unsolved were not accounted for.

10. The totals for 1925 are omitted because of the lack of consistency in reporting for this year.

11. For national rates, see Federal Bureau of Investigation, "Annual Trends, Offenses Known to the Police, 1931–1938," in *Uniform Crime Reports* 9, no. 4 (1938): 132.

12. Problems of theft in the black community frequently made the pages of the black press. For examples, see "Three Men Face Theft Charge," *Birmingham Reporter*, December 26, 1925; "Three Charged with Drug Store Theft," *Birmingham World*, May 13, 1941; "3 Women Arrested in Connection with Theft Here," *Birmingham World*, July 21, 1944; "Robbery by Violence," *Memphis World*, September 20, 1932; "Negro Agency Voices Plea for Race Policemen," *Memphis World*, October 17, 1944; "Algiers Youth Arrested for Theft," *Louisiana Weekly*, March 2, 1929; "Lad Shoots Uncle for Abuse, Theft," *Louisiana Weekly*, November 9, 1935; "Arrest Woman for Alleged Money Theft," *Louisiana Weekly*, May 14, 1938.

13. This is often referred to as the "dark figure" that "represent[s] crimes that go unreported and contacts between the criminal justice system and the citizenry that go unrecorded." For more on the "dark figure,'" see Albert D. Biderman and Albert J. Reiss, Jr., "On Exploring the 'Dark Figure' of Crime," *Annals of the American Academy of Political and Social Science* 374, no. 1 (November 1967): 1–15; Clive Coleman and Jenny Moynihan, *Understanding Crime Data: Haunted by the Dark Figure* (Philadelphia: Open University Press, 1996); Wesley G. Skogan, "Dimensions of the Dark Figure of Unreported Crime," *Crime & Delinquency* 23, no. 1 (January 1977): 41–50; Allen Steinberg, *The Transformation of Criminal Justice: Philadelphia, 1800–1880* (Chapel Hill: University of North Carolina Press, 1989), 26.

14. Fosdick, *American Police Systems*, 45; Dollard, *Caste and Class*, 279–80; Ayers, *Vengeance and Justice*, 231; Friedman, *Crime and Punishment*, 375; Litwack, *Trouble in Mind*, 264–65.

15. "Police Brutality," *Louisiana Weekly*, February 3, 1940.

16. Muhammad, *Condemnation of Blackness*, 226–68.

17. NOPD Offense Report for Benjimen Watson, January 25, 1925.

18. For more on criminalizing of various behaviors and the effects on African Americans, see, Myrdal, *American Dilemma*, 535–41; Kennedy, *Race, Crime, and the Law*, 86–92; Muhammad, *Condemnation of Blackness*, 4, 232–33.

19. For more on self-help practices among black urban residents, see Dollard, *Caste and Class*, 279; Raper, *The Tragedy of Lynching*, 34–35; Adler, "Black Violence in the New South," 224–28.

20. "Young Burglar Slain by Matron," *Memphis World*, July 16, 1945. This trend was not unique to southern cities in the early twentieth century. Roger Lane found a similar trend among Philadelphia's black community in the late nineteenth and early twentieth centuries. See Lane, *Roots of Violence in Black Philadelphia*, 164–65. Sociologist Donald Black has argued that self-help strategies still exist in the United States, but the behaviors are often defined as crimes. See Black, "Crime as Social Control," *American Sociological Review* 48, no. 1 (February 1983): 34–45.

21. State of Alabama vs. Ben Cleveland, case no. 4481, January Term, 1924, JCGJIR.

22. While the records are far from comprehensive, I found twenty-three instances where African American theft victims informed the grand jury that their items were returned. This represented just 3.3 percent of the 704 black theft cases listed in the JCGJIR. This low number is probably the result of a lack of consistency in reporting. In the twenty-three instances I found,

the prosecutor or one of the grand jurors usually asked the victim if the items were returned, but this did not happen, or at least was not recorded as having happened, with any regularity.

23. State of Alabama vs. Charlie Maryland, case no. 151, January Term, 1920, JCGJIR.

24. State of Alabama vs. Will Davis, case no. 15630, July Term, 1932, JCGJIR.

25. While this was not a robbery (which involves violence or the threat of violence), law enforcement and victims often used the term robbery to refer to thefts or burglaries.

26. State of Alabama vs. Walter White and John Grayson, case no. 8108, January Term, 1927, JCGJIR.

27. For more on the growing reliance on formal criminal justice institutions at the expense of extralegal forms of social control, see Dale, *Criminal Justice in the United States*, 97–135; Pfeifer, *Rough Justice*, 122–48.

28. The NOPD became much more interested in crimes in black communities, even intraracial crimes, during the late 1920s and 1930s as part of a broader effort to control the swelling black urban population. This was part of a national trend as police departments across the country assumed the responsibility of policing black communities. See Adler, "Less Crime, More Punishment," 42–46; Muhammad, *Condemnation of Blackness*, 226–68.

29. Adler, "Less Crime, More Punishment," 42–46; Muhammad, *Condemnation of Blackness*, 226–68.

30. Potter, *War on Crime*, 31–105; Adler, "Less Crime, More Punishment," 34–46.

31. W. E. B. Du Bois spoke to the increase in property among black residents in Georgia. He found that African Americans' total property holdings increased significantly throughout the late nineteenth and early twentieth centuries. Moreover, he found that the per capita value of black property also increased during the same period. This suggested that black residents in general acquired more property over time. He stated "that there is a growing class of thrifty, saving Negroes [which] is the central fact of post-bellum history, and this class cannot be ignored." Du Bois, *Notes on Negro Crime*, 62–64. While African Americas remained some of the poorest residents in the Jim Crow South, even poor blacks acquired property of some sort, including jewelry, clothing, tobacco, and money.

32. For more on the black employment in southern cities during Jim Crow, see Myrdal, *American Dilemma*, 205, 279- 332; Loren Schweninger, *Black Property Owners in the South, 1790–1915* (Urbana: University of Illinois Press, 1990), 216.

33. NOPD Offense Report for Alfred Pierce, January 8, 1930.

34. NOPD Offense Report for Louis Gelestin, July 15, 1935.

35. The late-1930s averages are below the national averages as recorded in the FBI Uniform Crime Reports. The average value of stolen property in the late 1930s totaled 87 dollars. See Federal Bureau of Investigation, "Value of Property Stolen, by Type of Crime, January to December, Inclusive, 1938; 40 Cities over 100,000," in *Uniform Crime Reports* 7, no. 4 (1936):149; Federal Bureau of Investigation, "Value of Property Stolen," in *Uniform Crime Reports* 8, no. 4 (1937): 208; Federal Bureau of Investigation, "Value of Property Stolen, by Type of Crime," in *Uniform Crime Reports* 9, no 4 (1938): 151; Federal Bureau of Investigation, "Value of Property Stolen, by Type of Crime," in *Uniform Crime Reports* 10, no. 4(1939): 197. For more on the plight of black southerners during the Great Depression, see Myrdal, *American Dilemma*, 397–408.

36. For black employment opportunities during WWII, see Myrdal, *American Dilemma*, 409–26.

37. U.S. Department of Commerce, Bureau of the Census, "Sixteenth Census of the United

States—1940, Population and Housing Families" (Washington, DC: U.S. Government Printing Office, 1943), 291.

38. For population statistics, see Fourteenth Census of the United States Taken in the Year 1920, Population, Volume 1 (Washington, DC: Government Printing Office, 1921), 122; Fifteenth Census of the United States: 1930, Population, Volume III, Part 1 (Washington, DC: Government Printing Office, 1932), 990; Sixteenth Census of the United States: 1940, Population, Volume II (Washington, DC: U.S. Government Printing Office, 1943), 426.

39. This is according to reported cases in the NOPD Offense Reports. This trend is similar to current statistics that show men are victims of robbery at much higher rates than women, see Callie Marie Rennison, *Criminal Victimization 2000* (Washington, DC: U.S. Department of Justice, Office of Justice Programs, 2001), 6, 8. For more on the idea of black patriarchy, see Hicks, *Talk with You Like a Woman*, 56–59.

40. In terms of clearance rates, the NOPD cleared cases of stolen property reported by men in roughly the same percentage as men filed complaints. Moreover, the percentage of cleared female cases rises and falls in ways that mirror the gender breakdown in reported cases in figure 4.6. Thus, there seemed to be little difference in the eyes of police officers regarding who made complaints as far as gender is concerned.

41. This represented just 9.6 percent of the 594 black stolen-property cases in the JCGJIR and is undoubtedly much lower than the actual number of thefts reported by black victims. The JCGJIR testimony mostly focused on the crime and not on who contacted law enforcement.

42. For more on abuse of African Americans, see Adler, "'The Greatest Thrill I Get,'" 1–44.

43. NOPD Offense Report for Cornelious B. Washington, April 26, 1925.

44. State of Alabama vs. Jerome Mack and Frank Patterson, case no. 10758, January Term, 1929, JCGJIR.

45. NOPD Offense Report for John Simpson, May 12, 1920.

46. State of Alabama vs. Charles Estes, case no. 12467, January Term, 1930, JCGJIR.

47. NOPD Offense Report for Georgia Douglas. October 7, 1920.

48. State of Alabama vs. Harrison Jackson and Chaffie Burris, case no. 6225, October Term, 1925, JCGJIR.

49. NOPD Offense Report for Stacy Bracken, November 15, 1945.

50. Dollard, *Caste and Class*, 282.

51. African Americans and law enforcement officers often used the term robbery when they actually described a theft, such is the case here.

52. NOPD Offense Report for Lucien Pleasant, October 16, 1920.

53. This is not the same as arrests made by police officers that occurred following a complaint by a black victim.

54. Police-initiated arrests also proved very uncommon in white cases and occurred just 7 percent of the time. This number comes from my own dataset culled from the NOPD Offense Reports.

55. NOPD Offense Report for Gilbert Guilyot, September 20, 1930.

56. Federal Bureau of Investigation, "Percentage of Offenses Cleared by Arrest, 1931 and 1932," in *Uniform Crime Reports* 4, no. 1 (1933): 15.

57. Federal Bureau of Investigation, "Percentage of Offenses Cleared by Arrest, 1934–1938," in *Uniform Crime Reports* 10, no. 1 (1939): 30.

58. The numbers for New Orleans is culled from my own dataset based on the NOPD Offense Reports for 1920, 1925, 1930, 1935, 1940, and 1945.

59. New Orleans Police Department, *Fifty Years of Progress,* 39. As a point of comparison, in 1915 the force totaled just 520; see New Orleans Police Department, *Fifty Years,* 11.

60. Policing manpower decreased and roles diversified across the country during the 1940s as the United States geared up for and fought in World War II; see Wadman and Allison, *To Protect and to Serve,* 103–4. For more on black militancy and the police response in New Orleans, see Fairclough, *Race and Democracy,* 79–80.

61. White complaints made up 91 percent of all complaints in New Orleans while black complaints made up just 9 percent for the years 1920, 1925, 1930, 1935, 1940, and 1945. This disparity suggested that African Americans did not report every theft or burglary that occurred. Scholars of the criminal justice system refer to the number of crimes that are unknown to authorities as the "dark figure."

62. White southerners appeared to be more likely to report thefts and burglaries to the police even if they did not have any information regarding suspects because their interactions with law enforcement were not as fraught with distrust and potentials for abuse.

63. NOPD Offense Report for Menola Stuart, April 23, 1945.

64. In white cases that ended in arrest, white victims and witnesses provided law enforcement with information in 65.7 percent of cases.

65. For more on the rise of racially segregated living spaces in early twentieth-century New Orleans, see Spain, "Race Relations and Residential Segregation in New Orleans," 88–90.

66. For more on this idea, see Kelley, *Race Rebels,* 74–75.

67. For more on segregation in Birmingham, see, Connerly, *"The Most Segregated City in America."*

68. This occurred in 63.1 percent of all black stolen-property cases in which African Americans supplied the police with information vital to the arrest of a suspect, but only in 36.0 percent of white cases that ended in an arrest.

69. NOPD Offense Report for Clara Syous, November 24, 1925.

70. State of Alabama vs. Willie Allen, case no. 7653, January Term, 1927, JCGJIR.

71. NOPD Offense Report for Joseph Toulme, December 26, 1935.

72. NOPD Offense Report for F. S. Lambert, June 5, 1925.

73. NOPD Offense Report for Ida Jones, February 15, 1920.

74. This occurred in 29.7 percent of white cases that ended in an arrest.

75. This occurred in 19.5 percent of white cases that ended in an arrest.

76. This occurred in 10.2 percent of white cases that ended in an arrest.

77. In their study on legal cynicism in Chicago, Robert J. Sampson and Dawn Jeglum Bartusch found that African Americans were less tolerant of deviance in their own communities than whites. However, African Americans also distrusted law enforcement more than white Chicagoans. Thus, in the cases where African American theft victims and witnesses identified or apprehended suspects, they illustrated their discontent with deviance (theft and burglary) and their concern that white police officers would not succeed in tracking down suspects. See Sampson and Bartusch, "Legal Cynicism and (Subcultural?) Tolerance of Deviance: The Neighborhood Context of Racial Differences," *Law and Society Review* 32, no. 4 (1998): 777–804.

78. NOPD Offense Report for Richard Brown, May 14, 1920.

79. NOPD Offense Report for Cornelius Mosely, December 27, 1920.

80. According to my dataset, black women captured suspects in 22.5 percent of apprehension cases involving black victims in the city.

81. NOPD Offense Report for Mary Lewis, January 12, 1930.

82. This occurred in eleven cases.

83. Black women were victims in five of the eleven cases listed in the NOPD Offense Reports.

84. The protection of black women was often central to black men's understanding of their own masculinity. See Hicks, *Talk with You Like a Woman,* 54–58.

85. NOPD Offense Report for Laverich Smith, January 19, 1935.

86. Myrdal, *American Dilemma,* 541–42; Allison Davis, Burleigh B. Gardner, and Mary R. Gardner, *Deep South: A Social Anthropological Study of Caste and Class* (Chicago: University of Chicago Press, 1941), 500–503; Johnson, *Patterns of Negro Segregation,* 299; Dollard, *Caste and Class,* 285, 333.

87. NOPD Offense Report for Percy Bickham, March 10, 1940.

88. This occurred in less than 1 percent of all cases in which African Americans helped police secure an arrest.

89. NOPD Offense Report for Cleo Smith, November 20, 1945.

90. NOPD officers made arrests with no information provided by white victims or witnesses in 31.8 percent of cases with white victims and 19.5 percent of black cases.

CHAPTER 5
African Americans and the Police in Assault Cases, 1920-1945

1. State of Alabama vs. Ada Deampers, case no. 10606, January Term, 1929, JCGJIR.

2. For more on conflict in the black community during the Jim Crow era, see Dollard, *Caste and Class,* 267–87; Davis and Dollard, *Children of Bondage;* Powdermaker, *After Freedom,* 143–221; Grace Elizabeth Hale, *Making Whiteness: The Culture of Segregation in the South, 1890–1940* (New York: Pantheon Books, 1998), 24–31. These types of violent altercations might also have been a form of social control within the black community of the Jim Crow South. As sociologist Donald Black suggested, actions defined as criminal behavior in modern society are often forms of self-help strategies, or "the expression of a grievance by unilateral aggression such as personal violence or property destruction." See Black, "Crime as Social Control," 34–45.

3. Adler, "Black Violence in the New South," 225–28; Jeffrey S. Adler, "'I Wouldn't Be No Woman If I Wouldn't Hit Him': Race, Patriarchy, and Spousal Homicide in New Orleans," *Journal of Women's History* 27, no. 3 (Fall 2015): 27.

4. For more on the broader shift away from extralegal justice to the rule of law, see Dale, *Criminal Justice in the United States,* 97–135; Pfeifer, *Rough Justice.*

5. In his observational study of the Jim Crow South, anthropologist Allison Davis found African Americans using the police in intraracial assault cases as well; see Davis, Gardner, and Gardner, *Deep South,* 506. Although my examination focuses on interactions between the police and African Americans, I am not suggesting that these types of interactions only occurred between black residents and the police. During the same time period, white southerners also used law enforcement in similar ways. For an example, see Adler, "'I Wouldn't Be No Woman If I Wouldn't Hit Him,'" 27–28.

6. While it is difficult to know the number of times African Americans did not report altercations to the police, qualitative evidence suggests this occurred quite often. Louis Armstrong provides several examples in his autobiography; see Louis Armstrong, *Satchmo: My Life in New Orleans* (New York: Prentice Hall, 1954).

7. This idea comes from the notion of a "sanctioning threshold" for law enforcement, which suggests that police officers' decision to respond to a call or arrest a suspect is shaped by their understanding of what types of violence are acceptable and unacceptable. See Henry P. Lundsgaarde, *Murder in Space City: A Cultural Analysis of Houston Homicide Patterns* (New York: Oxford University Press, 1977), 187. I am proposing something slightly different, which emphasizes that what shapes the victims' or witnesses' decision to call the police is also shaped by a larger cultural understanding of acceptable and unacceptable forms of violence. Criminologists have argued similarly, stating that one's decision to notify the police of an assault is largely the result of the victim weighing the actual assault, and the potential positive and negative effects of calling the police and reporting the assault. See Richard Block, "Why Notify the Police: The Victim's Decision to Notify the Police of an Assault," *Criminology* 11, no. 4 (February 1974): 555–69; Richard B. Felson, Steven F. Messner, Anthony W. Hoskin, and Glenn Deane, "Reasons for Reporting and Not Reporting Domestic Violence to the Police," *Criminology* 40, no. 3 (August 2002): 617–47; Felson, Messner, and Hoskin, "The Victim-Offender Relationship and Calling the Police in Assaults," *Criminology* 37, no. 4 (November 1999): 931–48.

8. The numbers for Birmingham are from 1920 to 1932, Memphis from 1931 and 1932, and New Orleans from 1925 to 1945.

9. "Public Safety in Self Respect," *Birmingham Reporter*, January 14, 1926.

10. "Curb Crime!" *Louisiana Weekly*, January 18, 1941.

11. Scholars have identified minor issues as a motivating factor in a large number of cases of violence, especially homicide. Marvin Wolfgang, for example, found similar trends in his study of homicides in Philadelphia between 1948 and 1952; see Marvin E. Wolfgang, *Patterns in Criminal Homicide* (Philadelphia: University of Pennsylvania Press, 1958), 188–99. Several decades later, Roger V. Gould reaffirmed the centrality of minor issues as a precipitating factor in a large number of homicides: see Gould, *Collision of Wills: How Ambiguity about Social Rank Breeds Conflict* (Chicago: University of Chicago Press, 2003). Elijah Anderson commented on the prevalence of minor issues leading to violent confrontations in black neighborhoods in late twentieth-century Philadelphia: see Anderson, *Code of the Street: Decency, Violence, and the Moral Life of the Inner City* (New York: W. W. Norton, 1999), 50. In his study of Indianola, Mississippi, in the 1930s, social scientist John Dollard found similar trends: see Dollard, *Caste and Class*, 272–75. Allison Davis also found similar trends; see Davis, *Deep South*, 506–8.

12. Gould, *Collision of Wills*, 2.

13. Out of the thirty-one assault cases identified in the *Memphis World* between September 1931 and August 1932, miscellaneous assaults comprised 64.53 percent of all identified assaults.

14. Black males assaulting black males accounted for 58.11 percent of miscellaneous assaults in the JCGJIR, 75 percent of miscellaneous assaults in the *Memphis World*, and 75.74 percent of assaults reported in the *Louisiana Weekly*.

15. State of Alabama vs. Green Davis, case no. 5098, October Term, 1924, JCGJIR.

16. All of these statistics are taken from my assessment of the JCGJIR, the *Memphis World*, and the *Louisiana Weekly*. Unfortunately, the sources do not indicate ages or class backgrounds

or ages of combatants, nor is there consistent reporting of information regarding the time of day these altercations occurred.

17. The available evidence does not consistently report who initiated the separation in each case. However, out of the forty-six intimate disputes with identifiable causes, twenty-five occurred as a result of a female-initiated separation. For more on violence and domestic issues in the Jim Crow South, see Jeffrey S. Adler, "'Bessie Done Cut Her Old Man': Race, Common-Law Marriage, and Homicide in New Orleans, 1925–1945," *Journal of Social History* 44, no. 1 (Fall 2010): 123–43.

18. State of Alabama vs. Manuel Gray, case no. 2555, January Term (April Division), 1922, JCGJIR.

19. Most of the evidence for this chapter is based on the JCGJIR from 1920 to 1932. These records proved to be the most complete and had ample testimony from witnesses, victims, and the accused. As such, they provided the most detailed account of assaults that could be found for the three cities. When possible, evidence from Memphis and New Orleans is incorporated to solidify the claims that this was a broad, regional trend.

20. For more on the economic hardships faced by African Americans during the Great Depression, see Thomas J. Sugrue, *Sweet Land of Liberty*, 32–58. Adler noticed similar trends in Chicago in the late nineteenth and early twentieth centuries as violence between men on the streets declined and domestic homicide increased. He argued that this was a result of increasing pressures on male heads of household defining masculinity in terms of domestic tranquility. When marital stability collapsed around things like financial problems, domestic violence rose. See Adler, *First in Violence, Deepest in Dirt*, 45–84. Adler also found that women in Chicago were more willing to challenge their husband's authority, especially when he failed to live up to their expectations. See Adler, *First in Violence, Deepest in Dirt*, 85–119. Adler also found that the Great Depression altered peoples' lifestyles "in ways that reduce myriad forms of premature death, including homicide." He found that alcohol consumption declined, "raucous leisure activities" were discouraged, and argued that all of these changes "affected the way that [people] resolved conflict." See Jeffrey S. Adler, "Homicide Rates and Mortality Trends: Perspectives from Public-Health Scholarship," *Crime, Histoire et Sociétés / Crime, History and Societies* 21, no. 2 (2017): 343–50.

21. Criminologist Richard Block has argued that the decision by an assault victim to notify the police rests on the notion that the police will do something. Block stated, "Integrated into the victim's decision to notify the police . . . is a belief that the police can do something." Block, "Why Notify the Police," 559. Similarly, criminologists Felson, Messner, Hoskin, and Deane suggested that if victims of assaults "believe that the police will not make an arrest—they may see no reason to report the incident"; Felson et al., "Reasons for Reporting and Not Reporting Domestic Violence to the Police," 624. These ideas were echoed by Tom R. Tyler in his examination of Chicago. He suggested that the legitimacy people grant to legal authorities, such as the police, comes from their experiences with those authorities. When people feel they are treated fairly by legal institutions, he argued, they are more likely to view the criminal justice system favorably. See Tyler, *Why People Obey the Law*, 71–84.

22. Although the available data on assaults does not allow for the same kind of analysis of trends in reporting over time as homicides or thefts, the evidence suggested that the trajectory of black-reported assault cases mirrored that of black-reported homicide cases. Criminologists

suggest that rates and trends of homicides and aggravated assaults are closely correlated. Assaults are often viewed as "a failed homicide and it is very unlikely that a given area would have high rates of one type of serious violence without the other." For more on this relationship, see Keith D. Harries, *Serious Violence: Patterns of Homicide and Assault in America* (Springfield, IL: Charles C. Thomas, 1990), 16–20, 47–61.

23. For more on the prevalence of black intraracial violence in the Jim Crow era, see Hoffman, *The Homicide Problem*, 80; Dollard, *Caste and Class*, 267–86; Adler, "Black Violence in the New South," 225–28; Brandon Jett, "'The Most Murderous Civilized City in the World': Patterns of Homicide in Jim Crow Memphis, 1917–1926," *Tennessee Historical Quarterly* (Summer 2015): 104–127.

24. For national trends in assaults, see FBI Uniform Crime Reports.

25. Harries, *Serious Violence*, 16–20, 47–61.

26. Adler, "Less Crime, More Punishment," 42–46; Muhammad, *Condemnation of Blackness*, 226–68.

27. Unfortunately, the JCGJIR did not indicate who initially reported crimes in every case; however, in some instances this information appeared in the statements given by witnesses. In twenty cases, African Americans stated they informed the police that an assault had occurred. In seven of these cases, the victims summoned the police. This represents only 6.6 percent of all cases, but African Americans undoubtedly reported many more of assault cases to police or law enforcement officers; however, they did not indicate so in the testimony given before the grand jury.

28. State of Alabama vs. Cora Barnes, case no. 6931, April Term, 1926, JCGJIR.

29. Miller, *Cops and Bobbies*, 32–37; Balto, *Occupied Territory*, 7.

30. State of Alabama vs. Henry Holmes, case no. 12802, January Term, 1930, JCGJIR.

31. "Stabbing," *Louisiana Weekly*, June 24, 1933. At the time the story came out in the *Louisiana Weekly*, McGee had not been apprehended by the police.

32. Myrdal, *American Dilemma*, 535–46; Dollard, *Caste and Class*, 279–81.

33. For more on segregation in Birmingham, see Connerly, *"The Most Segregated City in America,"* 36–68.

34. The number of witnesses listed in the JCGJIR did not necessarily account for every African American interviewed by police.

35. Harries, *Serious Violence*, 16–20, 47–61.

36. State of Alabama vs. Lucile Blount, case no. 4401, January Term, 1924, JCGJIR.

37. State of Alabama vs. Robert Griffin, case no. 6644, January Term, 1926, JCGJIR.

38. State of Alabama vs. Jesse Hillman, case no. 5204, October Term, 1924, JCGJIR.

39. State of Alabama vs. Sam Ardis, case no. 8615, July Term, 1927, JCGJIR.

40. State of Alabama vs. John Culpepper, case no. 1798, July Term (September Division), 1921, JCGJIR.

41. State of Alabama vs. Carrie Roden, case no. 4470, January Term, 1924, JCGJIR.

42. "WPA Worker Rams Scissors through Wife's Neck," *Louisiana Weekly*, January 27, 1940.

43. State of Alabama vs. Luree Williams, case no. 6901, April Term, 1926, JCGJIR.

44. State of Alabama vs. John Fifer, case no. 4896, July Term, 1924, JCGJIR.

45. State of Alabama vs. Paul DeJarnett, case no. 12903, January Term, 1930, JCGJIR.

46. This represents 2.3 percent of the 221 assault cases identified between 1929 and 1944 in the *Louisiana Weekly*.

47. "Stabbed in the Abdomen," *Louisiana Weekly*, July 16, 1938.

48. Alexander, *The Law of Arrest*, 362.

49. In order for a case to come before the grand jury, a law enforcement officer must have arrested the defendant and the magistrate then needed to decide that there was sufficient evidence that a crime occurred. See Clinton M. McGee, *Criminal Procedure in Alabama* (Tuscaloosa: University of Alabama Press, 1954), 10, 41, 46; Joel Prentiss Bishop, *New Criminal Procedure or New Commentaries on the Law of Pleading and Evidence and the Practice in Criminal Cases* 2nd ed., vol. 1 (Chicago: T. H. Flood & Company, 1913), 13–16.

50. Because these cases are not an exhaustive list of all assaults made in Birmingham, Memphis, or New Orleans between 1920 and 1945, it is difficult to trace the changes in arrest trends throughout the period.

51. Dollard, *Caste and Class*, 279–81.

52. Arrests did not necessarily lead to convictions or incarceration. Dollard suggested that the southern criminal justice system treated African Americans more leniently when they were accused of crimes against other black southerners. Although he suggested southern law enforcement condoned black intraracial violence, he also indicated that blacks accused of crimes could face some form of punishment. See Dollard, *Caste and Class*, 279–81.

53. It was difficult to determine whether victims or witnesses reported assaults to the police in most cases.

54. Criminologists have demonstrated that when people decide to call the police, they are making a rational choice. As these criminologists argue, the decision to call the police is based on perceived incentives and costs. Incentives for calling the police include protection from violence, a desire for retribution or justice, and a motivation to protect other people. Reasons why a black resident might not call the police often include embarrassment, a desire to protect the offender from criminal prosecution, or fear of reprisals; victims might refrain from calling the police if they, too, engaged in illegal activities or if they sought to avoid the time lost in going through the legal process to secure a conviction. For more on why assault victims and witnesses notified the police, see Felson et al., "Reasons for Reporting and Not Reporting Domestic Violence to the Police," 619. For more on the rational choice framework in criminology, see Michael R. Gottfredson and Denise M. Gottfredson, *Decision Making in Criminal Justice: Toward the Rational Exercise of Discretion* 2nd ed. (New York: Plenum Press, 1987).

55. Felson et al., "Calling the Police in Assaults," 941–42, 944, and "Reasons for Reporting and Not Reporting Domestic Violence to the Police," 633, 640.

56. Lundsgaarde, *Murder in Space City*, 187.

57. While there might be a class dimension to the decision to notify the police, the available sources do not provide information regarding class backgrounds and employment for the individuals involved in these cases. It is highly likely that most of the assaults used in this chapter occurred between African Americans of a working-class background. Social scientists working in the Jim Crow South consistently found that the physical altercations largely occurred among members of the working-class community. Moreover, they found that middle-class African Americans often touted the lack of violence among their class as one of the distinguishing

characteristics of middle-class status. See Dollard, *Caste and Class*, 267–87; Davis and Dollard, *Children of Bondage*.

58. Out of 148 total miscellaneous AIM cases, in 109 of the cases there were no identifiable previous altercations between the victim and the assailant.

59. State of Alabama vs. Will Green, case no. 2960, July Term, 1922, JCGJIR.

60. According to observers of the time, fights were common in black neighborhoods, but many black residents remained concerned about violence, especially the use of guns. For examples, see Davis and Dollard, *Children of Bondage*, 45, 258.

61. State of Alabama vs. Vonnell Barron, case no. 1031, January Term, 1921, JCGJIR.

62. Richard Block suggested that victims' and witnesses' decision to call the police is often related to the seriousness of the assault; see Block, "Why Notify the Police," 561.

63. State of Alabama vs. Randall Baker, case no. 5495, January Term, 1925, JCGJIR.

64. Criminologist Richard Block argued, "The greater the individual's injury, the greater the attacker's threat and the more likely the police will be notified; see Block, "Why Notify the Police," 561.

65. Not all African Americans utilized the criminal justice system to resolve or intervene in intraracial disputes. There is evidence that some African Americans lynched black victims in the South, but this became increasingly rare by the early twentieth century. For more on this issue, see Hill, "Black Vigilantism," 26–43; Adler, "Black Violence in the New South," 225–28; Beck and Tolnay, "When Race Didn't Matter," 137–43.

66. For examples of domestic violence outside of the South, see Jeffrey S. Adler, "'We've Got a Right to Fight; We're Married': Domestic Homicide in Chicago, 1875–1920," *Journal of Interdisciplinary History* 34, no 1 (Summer 2003): 27–48.

67. Dollard, *Caste and Class*, 272–75; Litwack, *Trouble in Mind*, 350. In his study of Philadelphia in the late twentieth century, Elijah Anderson also noted, "the seeming intractability of their [poor African Americans] situation, caused in large part by the lack of well-paying jobs and the persistence of racial discrimination, has engendered deep-seated bitterness and anger in many of the most desperate and poorest blacks." He suggested that this bitterness and anger "shorten[ed] the fuse" in these residents and increased the likelihood of violent confrontations. See Anderson, *Code of the Street*, 46.

68. Adler, "'I Wouldn't Be No Woman,'" 18–19.

69. Litwack, *Trouble in Mind*, 350; Hale, *Making Whiteness*, 32; Anderson, *Code of the Street*, 46.

70. The JCGJIR listed female victims and male assailants in 74.29 percent of cases, the *Memphis World* noted this trend in 75 percent of cases, and the *Louisiana Weekly* documented these instances in 60.71 percent of cases. See also Dollard, *Caste and Class*, 272–75. There is an extensive literature on domestic violence. For studies on policy and legal responses to domestic and family violence, see Elizabeth Pleck, *Domestic Tyranny: The Making of American Social Policy against Family Violence from Colonial Times to the Present* (New York: Oxford University Press, 1987). For scholarship regarding the trends and changing causes of domestic homicide, see Roth, *American Homicide*, 255–78; and Adler, *First in Violence, Deepest in Dirt*, 45–84. For more on race and the South as they relate to domestic violence, see Adler, "Bessie Done Cut Her Old Man," 123–43; and Adler, "I Wouldn't Be No Woman," 14–36.

71. M. P. Baumgartner suggested that the techniques women used to manage their conflicts with men included, "insults and criticisms, voiced either privately or publicly; expressions of

distress such as sulking or moping; acts of avoidance, either temporary or permanent; efforts to inflict deprivation, such as when wives refuse to cook for their husbands or to sleep with them; the invocation of third parties, whether to mediate or adjudicate; and violent self-help, or the handling of a grievance by unilateral aggression." See Baumgartner, "Violent Networks: The Origins and Management of Domestic Conflict," in *Aggression and Violence: Social Interactionist Perspectives*, ed. Richard B. Felson and James T. Tedeschi (Washington, DC: American Psychological Association, 1993), 213–14.

72. Adler, "'I Wouldn't Be No Woman,'" 22, 26–29.

73. This was not confined to the South. African American women in Chicago, for example, often turned to law enforcement and the courts to sever abusive relationships. See Adler, "'We've Got a Right to Fight,'" 43.

74. Adler, "'I Wouldn't Be No Woman," 14–36. Black women who called the police during or after a violent domestic argument acted in ways that mirror battered women who used the private prosecutorial process to punish abusive husbands in nineteenth-century Philadelphia. By calling the police, these women illustrated their ability to "use the law as a tool in their struggle to define the power dynamic of the family, to challenge the legitimacy of violence as an element of that dynamic." See Steinberg, *The Transformation of Criminal Justice*, 47.

75. Criminologists have argued that domestic violence victims' decision to call the police often rests on the severity of the assault. According to Felson et al., "Victims should be more likely to report incidents in which the offender uses a weapon, has superior strength and size, or causes injury to the victim." See Felson et al., "Reasons for Reporting and Not Reporting Domestic Violence to the Police," 620.

76. State of Alabama vs. Nathaniel Carter, case no. 1825, July Term (September Division), 1921, JCGJIR.

77. Black women explicitly stated that they wanted their husbands prosecuted in eleven total domestic dispute cases; however, the statements did not always indicate whether or not victims wanted the defendants prosecuted. As a result, this relatively low number is probably much lower than the actual number of victims who wanted their abusive spouses prosecuted.

78. State of Alabama vs. Sylvester Parker, alias James Parker, case no. 3446, January Term, 1923, JCGJIR.

79. State of Alabama vs. Ernest Hawkins, case no. 15787, July Term, 1932, JCGJIR.

80. MPD Homicide Report for Minnie Gilliam, August 25, 1936.

81. A white police officer speaking to John Dollard in Indianola, Mississippi, in the 1930s made a similar observation. He stated, "A Negro man and woman will have a fight or cutting party, the woman will get her husband thrown into jail, but the very next day she will be down begging to have him out." While the officer viewed this as evidence of black women's "capricious and temperamental character," perhaps this act was indicative of black women's efforts to use the police to mediate conflicts. See Dollard, *Caste and Class*, 275.

82. I identified three cases of black intraracial domestic dispute AIM cases in which the victims specifically testified that they did not want their attackers prosecuted.

83. State of Alabama v. Jack Ward, case no. 2213, January Term, 1922, JCGJIR.

84. I identified two cases in which black women decided not to prosecute their husbands because their husbands paid their medical bills.

85. State of Alabama vs. Will Patterson, case no. 86, January Term, 1920, JCGJIR.

86. In her study of a black community in Philadelphia in the early twenty-first century, sociologist Alice Goffman found black women also used the legal system in their social relations with men in their lives. Goffman argued, "A man's legal precariousness can come in handy as a weapon against him. In anger and frustration at men's bad behavior, women at times harness a man's warrant or probation sentence as a tool of social control, to dictate his behavior or to punish him for various wrongs." Goffman, *On the Run,* 99. It appears that black women in Jim Crow Birmingham engaged in a similar fashion, using the legal system as a negotiating tool in their relationship with men.

87. Litwack, *Trouble in Mind,* 252.

88. State of Alabama vs. Louis Jones, case no. 6596, January Term, 1926, JCGJIR.

89. Joseph Cantrell, Annette Watters, Ahmad Ijaz, Carolyn Trent, and Carl Ferguson, "Alabama's Changing Economy through the Twentieth Century," *Alabama Business & Economic Indicators* 68, no. 12 (December 1999): 2.

90. McGee, *Criminal Procedure in Alabama,* 53.

91. Scholars have argued that beginning in the 1920s, city officials and police departments used the formal criminal justice system to control and monitor African Americans; see Adler, "Less Crime, More Punishment," 40–46; Muhammad, *Condemnation of Blackness,* 226–68.

92. State of Alabama v. Lee Cook, alias Roy Cook, case no. 14155, July Term, 1931, JCGJIR.

93. MPD Homicide Report for Wesley Johnson, May 6, 1929.

94. MPD Homicide Report for Lilly Gage, October 21, 1934.

95. Fear of reprisals is often cited as a reason that victims of domestic violence do not report incidents; see Felson et al., "Reasons for Reporting and Not Reporting Domestic Violence to the Police," 621.

96. State of Alabama vs. Floyd Wallace, case no. 14571, January Term, 1932, JCGJIR.

97. Powdermaker, *After Bondage,* 143, 145–49; Hale, *Making Whiteness,* 31–35.

98. Dollard, *Caste and Class,* 153; Powdermaker, *After Bondage,* 143; Martin Summers, *Manliness and Its Discontents: The Black Middle Class and the Transformation of Masculinity, 1900–1930* (Chapel Hill: University of North Carolina Press, 2004), 3; Leslie Brown and Anne Valk, *Living with Jim Crow: African American Women and Memories of the Segregated South* (New York: Palgrave Macmillan, 2009), 55–78.

99. Charles S. Johnson, *Shadow of the Plantation* (Chicago: University Press of Chicago, 1934), 51–55, 77; Hale, *Making Whiteness,* 31–35.

100. Dollard, *Caste and Class,* 269–71; Davis and Dollard, *Children of Bondage,* 48–49, 266.

Conclusion

1. W. E. B. Du Bois, *The Souls of Black Folk* (1903; repr., New York: Pocket Books, 2005), 3.

2. For more on racial etiquette, see Johnson, *Patterns of Negro Segregation,* 117–55; Myrdal, *American Dilemma,* 606–18; Davis, Gardner, and Gardner, *Deep South,* 22–24; Dollard, *Caste and Class,* 174–86; Hale, *Making Whiteness;* Berrey, *The Jim Crow Routine;* Jennifer Ritterhouse, *Growing Up Jim Crow: How Black and White Southern Children Learned Race* (Chapel Hill: University of North Carolina Press, 2006).

3. The literature on black resistance to white supremacy in the late nineteenth and early

twentieth century is robust. A book that highlights the breadth of the kinds of resistance is Hahn, *A Nation under our Feet*.

4. There is an extensive literature on lynching in the American South. For examples, see George C. Wright, *Racial Violence in Kentucky, 1865–1940: Lynchings, Mob Rule, and "Legal Lynchings"* (Baton Rouge: Louisiana State University Press, 1990); Brundage, *Lynching in the New South;* Tolnay and Beck, *A Festival of Violence;* Pfeifer, *Rough Justice;* William D. Carrigan, *The Making of a Lynching Culture: Violence and Vigilantism in Central Texas, 1836–1916* (Urbana: University of Illinois Press, 2004); Amy Louise Wood, *Lynching and Spectacle: Witnessing Racial Violence in America, 1890–1940* (Chapel Hill: University of North Carolina Press, 2009).

5. Brundage, *Lynching in the New South*, 161–244; Tolnay and Beck, *Festival of Violence*, 202–38.

6. This was part of a larger trend in American history whereby the "rule of law" supplanted "rough justice." For more on this shift, see Pfeifer, *Rough Justice;* Dale, *Criminal Justice in the United States.*

7. Myrdal, *American Dilemma*, 535; Litwack, *Trouble in Mind*, 263; Watson, *A Change Did Come*, 4; Moore, *Black Rage in New Orleans*, 1, 19; Dulaney, *Black Police in America*, xi, 39; Escobar, *Race, Police, and the Making of a Political Identity*, 12.

8. Myrdal, *American Dilemma*, 538.

9. Johnson, *Patterns of Negro Segregation*, 244–315.

10. Ibid., 267.

11. Ibid., 294.

12. Ibid., 244.

13. Avoidance could also be described as self-help in the Jim Crow black community; see, for example, Adler, "Black Violence in the New South," 224–28; Brearley, "The Pattern of Violence," 690.

14. Myrdal, *American Dilemma*, 540–69.

15. For more on this, see Black, "Crime as Social Control," 34–45.

16. Charles S. Johnson described these resisters as black men who "disregard[ed] the racial etiquette defining his sphere and role. He will fight and take no thought of consequences." Johnson, *Patterns of Negro Segregation*, 299.

17. Prince, "Remembering Robert Charles," 297–328.

18. Ida B. Wells-Barnett, "Mob Rule in New Orleans," in *Southern Horrors and Other Writings: The Anti-Lynching Campaign of Ida B. Wells, 1892–1900*, ed. Jacqueline Jones Royster (New York: Bedford/St. Martin's, 1997), 158–208.

19. Johnson, *Patterns of Negro Segregation*, 299; Prince, "Remembering Robert Charles," 297–328.

20. Johnson, *Patterns of Negro Segregation*, 313–15.

21. For more on how cooperation with the police is related to police legitimacy, see Tyler, "Enhancing Police Legitimacy," *Annals of the American Academy of Political and Social Science* 593 (May 2004): 84–99; Tyler, *Why People Obey the Law.*

22. All quotations from Myrdal, *American Dilemma*, 540.

23. For more on racial etiquette, see Johnson, *Patterns of Negro Segregation*, 117–55; Myrdal,

American Dilemma, 606–18; Davis, *Deep South,* 22–24; Dollard, *Caste and Class,* 174–86; Hale, *Making Whiteness;* Berrey, *Jim Crow Routine;* Ritterhouse, *Growing Up Jim Crow.*

24. This distinction was repeated by a number of sociologists and anthropologists from the time, including Powdermaker, *After Freedom,* 40; Davis, *Deep South,* 24, 48, 403, 525; Myrdal, *American Dilemma,* 1363 fn. 13; Davis and Dollard, *Children of Bondage,* 169; Dollard, *Caste and Class,* 335; Johnson, *Patterns of Negro Segregation,* 210–13.

25. Davis, *Deep South,* 503.

26. Powdermaker, *After Freedom,* 40.

27. Dulaney, *Black Police in America,* 19–29; Thoma J. Sugrue, *Sweet Land of Liberty,* 1–129.

28. This is not to suggest that black residents in northern cities did not face similar problems related to the white supremacist nature of police officers. Nor am I suggesting that black police officers or electoral politics offered a panacea to the problems of policing in black communities. As Simon Balto has demonstrated, policing in northern cities such as Chicago still unfolded in racially discriminatory and problematic ways for black communities. See Balto, *Occupied Territory.*

29. Ritterhouse, *Growing Up Jim Crow,* 22–54; Berrey, *Jim Crow Routine,* 19–60.

30. The rituals examined are in no way meant to be an exhaustive list, but are instead just examples of some of the rituals offered by black southerners. For more on racial etiquette, see Ritterhouse, *Growing Up Jim Crow,* 48–49; Berrey, *Jim Crow Routine,* 2, 9–10.

31. Tyler, "Enhancing Police Legitimacy," 85.

32. Ibid., 85.

33. For more on black informants during the antebellum period, see Andrea L. Dennis, "A Snitch in Time: An Historical Sketch of Black Informing during Slavery," *Marquette Law Review* 97, no. 2 (2013): 279–334. Jim Crow police officers also relied on black informants to help track down black suspects. These informants, or "stool pigeons," often worked in exchange for immunity from arrest. They were, according to Myrdal, held in low opinion in the black community and seen as pawns of white police officers. For more on black informants during Jim Crow, see Myrdal, *American Dilemma,* 541.

34. Myrdal, *American Dilemma,* 540–41.

35. Tyler, "Enhancing Police Legitimacy," 84–90.

36. NOPD Witness Transcripts, Statement of Granville Magnard, March 29, 1931.

37. African Americans typically sat in the rear of buses and railcars; see Berrey, *Jim Crow Routine,* 45–46. I am assuming that similar rules applied in a police car. For an example of the status conveyed when police placed a nonsuspect in the back of their car while looking for a stolen vehicle, see Anderson, *Streetwise: Race, Class, and Change in an Urban Community* (Chicago: University of Chicago Press, 1990), 190–94.

38. For more on the physical and mental intimidation exerted on suspects who are brought in to police precincts and headquarters, see *Miranda v. Arizona,* 384 U.S. 436 (1966).

39. For more on police brutality during interrogations, see Wickersham Commission, *Report on Lawlessness in Law Enforcement;* Adler, "The Greatest Thrill I Get," 1–44. For more on law enforcement inability or unwillingness to protect blacks in custody from lynch mobs, see Raper, *The Tragedy of Lynching,* 44–45.

40. While arrests for black intraracial crimes occurred, legal institutions still did not treat black intraracial crime the same way they did crimes committed against whites; see Myrdal,

American Dilemma, 523–74; Kennedy, *Race, Crime, and the Law,* 40–75; Litwack, *Trouble in Mind,* 252–70.

41. For more on the structural causes that led to crime in black communities, see Lane, *Roots of Violence;* Adler, "Black Violence in the New South," 207–39; Adler, *First in Violence, Deepest in Dirt,* 120–58; Balto, *Occupied Territory.*

42. Du Bois, *The Souls of Black Folk,* 7.

43. Hair, *Carnival of Fury,* 137–200; Sullivan, *Lift Every Voice,* 85–88.

44. For an example of how black southerners relied on racial etiquette to manipulate whites, see Johnson, *Patterns of Negro Segregation,* 257.

45. Charles S. Johnson argued that "avoidance" was "the most common type of response to the personal implications of the race system"; see Johnson, *Patterns of Negro Segregation,* 267. For more on self-help in the Jim Crow black community, see Adler, "Black Violence in the New South, 224–28; Brearley, "The Pattern of Violence," 690.

46. Johnson identified hostility and aggression as another form of response to Jim Crow. While violent encounters between whites and African Americans occurred, Johnson also argued that "organized aggression" also occurred as "the more aggressive Negroes have directed their resentment of personal and group discrimination through these organizations which have more power to effect changes or to punish" (Johnson, *Patterns of Negro Segregation,* 313).

47. Shirley A. Hill, *Inequality and African-American Health: How Racial Disparities Create Sickness* (Bristol: Policy Press, 2016); Angela M. Odoms-Young and Bruce A. Marino, "Examining the Impact of Structural Racism on Food Insecurity: Implications for Addressing Racial/Ethnic Disparities," *Family and Community Health* 41, no 2 (April/June 2018): S3-S6; Alexander, *The New Jim Crow;* Eduardo Bonilla-Silva, *Racism Without Racists: Color-Blind Racism and the Persistence of Racial Inequality in America,* 5th ed. (New York: Rowman & Littlefield, 2017); William Julius Wilson, *The Truly Disadvantaged: The Inner City, the Underclass, and Public Policy,* 2nd ed. (Chicago: University of Chicago Press, 2012); Fred Harris and Alan Curtis, eds., *Healing Our Divided Society: Investing in America Fifty Years after the Kerner Report* (Philadelphia: Temple University Press, 2018).

48. Alexander, *The New Jim Crow.*

49. Watson, *A Change Did Come;* Moore, *Black Rage in New Orleans;* Forman, *Locking Up Our Own;* Fortner, *Black Silent Majority.*

50. Mariame Kaba, "Yes, We Mean Literally Abolish the Police," *New York Times,* June 12, 2020.

A NOTE ON SOURCES

To trace the moments of interaction between law enforcement officers and African Americans documented in this book, I have relied on various sources and qualitative and quantitative methodologies from all three cities to complement each other. The bulk of my preliminary research comes from reports generated from local police departments, local court records, and branch files of the NAACP. The information from these sources is supplemented by black newspapers, clippings files in local archives, and yearbooks and annual reports published by the police departments. Taken together, these sources offer a variety of perspectives from which it is possible to glean an in-depth understanding of the interactions between the police and African Americans.

My examination of street-level interactions between law enforcement and black urban dwellers is based on over 21,000 police homicide reports, police offense reports, and grand jury indictment records. The police reports provided extraordinarily rich detail regarding the demographic information of people involved in homicides, thefts, and assaults, the location of the incidents, the date and time of investigations, the number and race of witnesses, and arrests. From the Memphis Police Department and New Orleans Police Department homicide reports, I traced the number of African Americans who reported crimes, as well as black witnesses and victims for each year between 1920 and 1945 (the NOPD Homicide Reports are nearly complete for these years. They run from 1926 to 1931, 1935, 1938–1939, 1941–1943, and 1945.). Due to the sheer number of theft reports listed in the NOPD records, my databases detail every theft reported to NOPD only for the years 1920, 1925, 1930, 1935, 1940, and 1945. Similar to my plotting of the homicide databases, I outlined the changes in black- and white-reported cases, along with black victims and witnesses. For my examination of interactions between law enforcement and African Americans in Birmingham, I relied largely on the Jefferson County Grand Jury Indictment Records (JCGJIR). These sources are more problematic than the police records because cases brought before the grand jury are not necessarily an indication of every crime perpetrated against black residents, or each offense reported by African Americans.

Nonetheless, I created databases that charted the number of black homicides, assaults, and thefts recorded between 1920 and 1932. Each case also listed the names, races, and detailed testimony of all witnesses brought before the grand jury. The trends in reported crimes and witnesses identified in the JCGJIR mirrored the changes found in the police reports from Memphis and New Orleans. In addition to numbers, each report recorded lengthy witness testimony that allowed me to illustrate the actions of African American victims and witnesses before and after crimes, how and why these black residents notified law enforcement, and the variety of interactions that occurred once the police arrived on the scene. When used in conjunction with the police records for other cities, these sources provided an extensive trove of data related to police/minority encounters.

This material formed the basis of several databases I compiled. I generated cross-tabulations by year of factors related to homicides, assaults, and thefts. For each type of crime, I identified the number of black-reported and white-reported offenses, the method of lodging complaints with law enforcement, arrest rates, the number of witnesses in each case, and the type of information or evidence provided by each witness. I then traced the changes in frequency of each factor for each year from 1920 to 1945. The compiled statistics allowed me to compare shifts in the types of interactions that occurred between black southerners and the police.

To supplement the police reports, court records, and NAACP files, I relied largely on black newspapers that survive in each of the cities. The black newspapers I utilized were the *Memphis World* (1931–1932, 1943–1945); *Birmingham Reporter* (1923–1933); *Birmingham World* (1940–1945); and *Louisiana Weekly* (1925–1945). On the whole, these newspapers provided confirmation of black intraracial homicides and police killings, listed examples of thefts and assaults, and offered narratives on the actions of victims, witnesses, and police officers in the wake of crimes. Due to the fact that police reports often gave the perspective of the white officers involved in generating the documents, black newspapers provided African American perspective that could be lost in the legal records. Moreover, these sources also followed some of the cases in more depth than the police reports or grand jury records. Newspaper editorials frequently shed light as well on black views of law enforcement and crime in the African American community that place the interactions documented in this study in appropriate context.

Race, Crime, and Policing in the Jim Crow South combines quantitative data culled from official reports with qualitative sources to explore the nature of interactions between law enforcement and blacks living in southern cities. This type of balanced approach has allowed me to trace changes in the behavior of police and African Americans over time based on statistics, while elaborating on those behaviors through rich narratives surrounding crimes, police investigations, and arrests. Consequently, the various sources work together and balance out the weakness of each to form a more complete picture of police/civilian interactions in the Jim Crow South.

BIBLIOGRAPHY

Primary Sources
Archival Collections

Birmingham Police Department Scrapbooks, 1910–1969, Archives and Manuscripts, Birmingham Public Library, Birmingham, Alabama.

Robert R. Church Family Papers, University of Memphis Special Collections,
Memphis, Tennessee.

E. H. Crump Collection, Memphis/Shelby County Public Library and Information
Center, Memphis, Tennessee.

Memphis-Crime Clippings File, Memphis and Shelby County Room, Memphis
Public Library, Memphis, Tennessee.

Memphis Police Department Clippings Files, 1800s–1930s and 1938–1949,
Memphis and Shelby County Room, Memphis Public Library, Memphis,
Tennessee.

Papers of the National Association for the Advancement of Colored People, Manuscript Division, Library of Congress, Washington, DC.

Police and Court Records

City of New Orleans Police Department Offense Reports, 1920–1945, New Orleans
Police Department, City of New Orleans, Louisiana Division/City Archives,
New Orleans Public Library, New Orleans, Louisiana.

Jefferson County Grand Jury Indictment Records, 1920–1932, Archives and
Manuscripts Department, Birmingham Public Library, Birmingham, Alabama.

Memphis Police Department Homicide Reports, 1917–1946, Shelby County
Archives, Memphis, Tennessee.

New Orleans Police Department Homicide Reports, 1925–1945, New Orleans
Police Department, City of New Orleans, Louisiana Division/City Archives,
New Orleans Public Library, New Orleans, Louisiana.

Transcripts of Statements of Witnesses to Homicides, New Orleans Police Department, City of New Orleans, Louisiana Division/City Archives, New Orleans
Public Library, New Orleans, Louisiana.

Newspapers

Birmingham Reporter
Birmingham World
Louisiana Weekly
Memphis World

Secondary Sources

Adler, Jeffrey S. "'Bessie Done Cut Her Old Man': Race, Common-Law Marriage, and Homicide in New Orleans, 1925–1945." *Journal of Social History* 44, no. 1 (Fall 2010): 123–43.

———. "Black Violence in the New South: Patterns of Conflict in Late-Nineteenth-Century Tampa." In *The African American Heritage of Florida*, ed. David R. Colburn and Jane L. Landers, 207–39. Gainesville: University Press of Florida, 1995.

———. "Cognitive Bias: Interracial Homicide in New Orleans, 1921–1945." *Journal of Interdisciplinary History* 43, no. 1 (Summer 2012): 43–61.

———. *"First in Violence, Deepest in Dirt": Homicide in Chicago, 1875–1920.* Cambridge, MA: Harvard University Press, 2006.

———. "'The Greatest Thrill I Get Is When I Hear a Criminal Say, "Yes, I did it"': Race and the Third Degree in New Orleans, 1920–1945." *Law and History Review* 34, no. 1 (February 2016): 1–44.

———. "Homicide Rates and Mortality Trends: Perspectives from Public-Health Scholarship." *Crime, Histoire &Sociétés/Crime, History & Societies* 21, no. 2 (2017): 343–50.

———. "'I Wouldn't Be No Woman If I Wouldn't Hit Him': Race, Patriarchy, and Spousal Homicide in New Orleans." *Journal of Women's History* 27, no. 3 (Fall 2015): 14–36.

———. "'The Killer behind the Badge,': Race and Police Homicide in New Orleans, 1925–1945." *Law and History Review* 30, no. 2 (May 2012): 495–531.

———. "Less Crime, More Punishment: Violence, Race, and Criminal Justice in Early Twentieth-Century America." *Journal of American History* 102, no. 1 (June 2015): 34–46.

———. *Murder in New Orleans: The Creation of Jim Crow Policing.* Chicago: University of Chicago Press, 2019.

———. "Shoot to Kill: The Use of Deadly Force by the Chicago Police, 1875–1920." *Journal of Interdisciplinary History* 38, no. 2 (Autumn 2007): 233–54.

———. "'Spineless Judges and Shyster Lawyers': Criminal Justice in New Orleans, 1920–1945." *Journal of Social History* 49, no. 4 (Summer 2016): 904–27.

———. "'We've Got a Right to Fight; We're Married': Domestic Homicide in Chicago, 1875–1920." *Journal of Interdisciplinary History* 34, no 1 (Summer 2003): 27–48.

Akers, Ronald L., and Christin S. Sellers. *Criminological Theories: Introduction, Evaluation, and Application.* 5th ed. New York: Oxford University Press, 2009.

Alexander, Michelle. *The New Jim Crow: Mass Incarceration in the Age of Colorblindness.* New York: New Press, 2010.

Anderson, Elijah. *Code of the Street: Decency, Violence, and the Moral Life of the Inner City.* New York: W. W. Norton, 1999.

———. *Streetwise: Race, Class, and Change in an Urban Community.* Chicago: University of Chicago Press, 1990.

Armstrong, Louis. *Satchmo: My Life in New Orleans.* New York: Prentice Hall, 1954.

Ashmore, Eddie M. "The History of the Memphis Police Department." http://www. memphispolice.org/Memphis%20PD%20History.pdf. (Accessed May 2014.)

Autrey, Dorothy. "The National Association for the Advancement of Colored People in Alabama, 1913–1952." PhD diss., University of Notre Dame, 1985.

Ayers, Edward L. *Vengeance and Justice: Crime and Punishment in the Nineteenth-Century American South.* New York: Oxford University Press, 1984.

Balto, Simon. *Occupied Territory: Policing Black Chicago from Red Summer to Black Power.* Chapel Hill: University of North Carolina Press, 2019.

Barnhart, Kenneth E. "Study of Homicide in the United States." *Birmingham-Southern College Bulletin* 25, no. 3 (May 1932): 7–38.

Baumgartner, M. P. "Violent Networks: The Origins and Management of Domestic Conflict." In *Aggression and Violence: Social Interactionist Perspectives.* ed. Richard B. Felson and James T. Tedeschi, 209–32. Washington, DC: American Psychological Association, 1993.

Beck, E. M., and Stewart E. Tolnay, "When Race Didn't Matter: Black and White Mob Violence against Their Own Color." In *Under Sentence of Death: Lynching in the South,* ed. W. Fitzhugh Brundage, 132–54. Chapel Hill: University of North Carolina Press, 1997.

Bell, Derick A., Jr. "Brown v. Board of Education and the Interest-Convergence Dilemma." *Harvard Law Review* 93 (1979–1980): 518–33.

Berrey, Stephen A. *The Jim Crow Routine: Everyday Performances of Race, Civil Rights, and Segregation in Mississippi.* Chapel Hill: University of North Carolina Press, 2015.

Biderman, Albert D., and Albert J. Reiss, Jr. "On Exploring the 'Dark Figure' of Crime." *Annals of the American Academy of Political and Social Science* 374, no. 1 (November 1967): 1–15.

Bishop, Joel Prentiss. *New Criminal Procedure or New Commentaries on the Law of Pleading and Evidence and the Practice in Criminal Cases.* 2nd ed., vol. 1. Chicago: T. H. Flood & Company, 1913.

Black, Donald. "Crime as Social Control." *American Sociological Review* 48, no. 1 (February 1983): 34–45.

Blackmon, Douglas A. *Slavery by Another Name: The Re-Enslavement of Black Americans from the Civil War to World War II.* New York: First Anchor Books, 2009.

Block, Richard. "Why Notify the Police: The Victim's Decision to Notify the Police of an Assault." *Criminology* 11, no. 4 (February 1974): 555–69.

Bonilla-Silva, Eduardo. *Racism without Racists: Color-Blind Racism and the Persistence of Racial Inequality in America.* 5th ed. New York: Rowman & Littlefield, 2017.

Brearley, H. C. *Homicide in the United States.* Chapel Hill: University of North Carolina Press, 1932.

———. "The Pattern of Violence." In *Culture in the South,* ed. W. T. Couch, 678–92. Chapel Hill: University of North Carolina Press, 1934.

Broussard, Albert S. *Black San Francisco: The Struggle for Racial Equality in the West, 1900–1954.* Lawrence: University Press of Kansas, 1993.

Brown, Leslie, and Anne Valk. *Living with Jim Crow: African American Women and Memories of the Segregated South.* New York: Palgrave Macmillan, 2009.

Brownell, Blaine A. "Birmingham, Alabama: New South City in the 1920s." *Journal of Southern History* 38, no. 1 (February 1972): 21–48.

Bruce, Andrew A., and Thomas S. Fitzgerald. "A Study of Crime in the City of Memphis, Tennessee." *Journal of the American Institute of Criminal Law and Criminology* 19, no. 2 (August 1928): 3–124.

Brundage, W. Fitzhugh. *Civilizing Torture: An American Tradition.* Cambridge, MA: Harvard University Press, 2018.

———. *Lynching in the New South: Georgia and Virginia, 1880–1930.* Urbana: University of Illinois Press, 1993.

Campbell, James. *Crime and Punishment in African American History.* New York: Palgrave Macmillan, 2013.

Campney, Brent M. S. *Hostile Heartland: Racism, Repression, and Resistance in the Midwest.* Urbana: University of Illinois Press, 2019.

Cantrell, Joseph, Annette Watters, Ahmad Ijaz, Carolyn Trent, and Carl Ferguson. "Alabama's Changing Economy through the Twentieth Century." *Alabama Business and Economic Indicators* 68, no. 12 (December 1999): 1–4.

Carrigan, William D. *The Making of a Lynching Culture: Violence and Vigilantism in Central Texas, 1836–1916.* Urbana: University of Illinois Press, 2004.

Carrol, William, and Michael Seng. *Eyewitness Testimony: Strategies and Tactics.* 2nd ed. Eagan, MN: West Publishing, 2003.

Clegg, Claude A., III. *Troubled Ground: A Tale of Murder, Lynching, and Reckoning in the New South*. Urbana: University of Illinois Press, 2010.

Coleman, Clive, and Jenny Moynihan. *Understanding Crime Data: Haunted by the Dark Figure* Philadelphia: Open University Press, 1996.

Connerly, Charles E. *"The Most Segregated City in America": City Planning and Civil Rights in Birmingham, 1920–1980*. Charlottesville: University of Virginia Press, 2005.

Curriden, Mark, and Leroy Phillips, Jr. *Contempt of Court: The Turn-of-the-Century Lynching That Launched 100 Years of Federalism*. New York: Anchor Books, 1999.

Dale, Elizabeth. *Criminal Justice in the United States, 1879–1939*. New York: Cambridge University Press, 2011.

———. "Getting Away with Murder." *American Historical Review* 111, no. 1 (2006): 95–103.

Davis, Allison, Burleigh B. Gardner, and Mary R. Gardner. *Deep South: A Social Anthropological Study of Caste and Class*. Chicago: University of Chicago Press, 1941.

Davis, Allison, and John Dollard. *Children of Bondage: The Personality Development of Negro Youth in the Urban South*. 1940; repr., New York: Harper & Row, 1964.

DeCuir, Sharlene Sinegal. "Attacking Jim Crow: Black Activism in New Orleans, 1925–1941." PhD diss., Louisiana State University, 2009.

del Mar, David Peterson. *What Trouble I Have Seen: A History of Violence against Wives*. Cambridge, MA: Harvard University Press, 1996.

Dennis, Andrea L. "A Snitch in Time: An Historical Sketch of Black Informing during Slavery." *Marquette Law Review* 97, no. 2 (2013): 279–334.

Dollard, John. *Caste and Class in a Southern Town*. 3rd ed. Garden City, NY: Doubleday & Company, 1957.

Dowdy, G. Wayne. *A Brief History of Memphis*. Charleston, SC: History Press, 2011.

———. *Mayor Crump Don't Like It: Machine Politics in Memphis*. Oxford: University Press of Mississippi, 2008.

Du Bois, W. E. B. "The Negro Criminal." In *The Philadelphia Negro: A Social Study*. Philadelphia: University of Pennsylvania Press, 1899.

———. *Some Notes on Negro Crime, Particularly in Georgia*. Atlanta: Atlanta University Press, 1904.

———. *The Souls of Black Folk*. 1903; repr., New York: Pocket Books, 2005.

Dulaney, W. Marvin. *Black Police in America*. Bloomington: Indiana University Press, 1996.

Durrett, J. J., and W. G. Stromquist. *A Study of Violent Deaths Registered in Atlanta, Birmingham, Memphis and New Orleans for the Years 1921 and 1922*. Memphis, TN: Department of Health, City of Memphis, 1923.

Ellis, Scott S. *Madam Vieux Carre: The French Quarter in the Twentieth Century.* Jackson: University of Mississippi Press, 2010.

Emanuel, Rachel L., and Alexander P. Tureaud, Jr. *A More Noble Cause: A. P. Tureaud and the Struggle for Civil Rights in Louisiana: A Personal Biography.* Baton Rouge: Louisiana State University Press, 2011.

Escobar, Edward J. *Race, Police, and the Making of a Political Identity: Mexican Americans and the Los Angeles Police Department, 1900–1945.* Los Angeles: University of California Press, 1999.

Fairclough, Adam. *Race and Democracy: The Civil Rights Struggle in Louisiana, 1915–1972.* Athens: University of Georgia Press, 1995.

Feldman, Glenn. *Politics, Society, and the Klan in Alabama, 1915–1949.* Tuscaloosa: University of Alabama Press, 1999.

Felker-Kantor, Max. *Policing Los Angeles: Race, Resistance, and the Rise of the LAPD.* Chapel Hill: University of North Carolina Press, 2019.

Felson, Richard B., Steven F. Messner, and Anthony W. Hoskin. "The Victim-Offender Relationship and Calling the Police in Assaults." *Criminology* 37, no. 4 (November 1999): 931–48.

Felson, Richard B., Steven F. Messner, Anthony W. Hoskin, and Glenn Deane. "Reasons for Reporting and Not Reporting Domestic Violence to the Police." *Criminology* 40, no. 3 (August 2002): 617–47.

Fogelson, Robert M. *Big-City Police.* Cambridge, MA: Harvard University Press, 1977.

Forman, James, Jr. *Locking Up Our Own: Crime and Punishment in Black America.* New York: Farrar, Straus & Giroux, 2017.

Forret, Jeff. *Slave against Slave: Plantation Violence in the Old South.* Baton Rouge: Louisiana State University Press, 2015.

Fortner, Michael Javen. *Black Silent Majority: The Rockefeller Drug Laws and the Politics of Punishment.* Cambridge, MA: Harvard University Press, 2015.

Fosdick, Raymond B. *American Police Systems.* New York: Century Co., 1920.

Fredrickson, George M. *The Black Image in the White Mind: The Debate on Afro-American Character and Destiny, 1817–1914.* Middletown, CT: Wesleyan University Press, 1971.

Friedman, Lawrence M. *Crime and Punishment in American History.* New York: BasicBooks, 1993.

Fussell, Elizabeth. "Constructing New Orleans, Constructing Race: A Population History of New Orleans." *Journal of American History* 94, no. 3 (December 2007): 846–55.

Gastil, Raymond D. "Homicide and a Regional Culture of Violence." *American Sociological Review* 36, no. 3 (June 1971): 412–27.

Gaston, Paul M. *The New South Creed: A Study in Southern Mythmaking.* New York: Alfred Knopf, 1970.

Gleisser, Marcus. *Juries and Justice*. New York: A. S. Barnes & Company, 1968.

Goffman, Alice. *On the Run: Fugitive Life in an American City*. Chicago: University of Chicago Press, 2014.

Goldfield, David R. "The Urban South: A Regional Framework." *American Historical Review* 86, no. 5 (December 1981): 1009–1034.

Gordon, Linda. *Heroes of Their Own Lives: The Politics and History of Family Violence*. New York: Penguin, 1988.

Gordon, Margaret T., and Linda Heath. "The News Business, Crime, and Fear." In *Reactions to Crime*, ed. D. Lewis, 227–50. Beverly Hills, CA: Sage, 1981.

Gorn, Elliot J. *Dillinger's Wild Ride: The Year That Made America's Public Enemy Number One*. Oxford: Oxford University Press, 2009.

Gottfredson, Michael R., and Denise M. Gottfredson. *Decision Making in Criminal Justice: Toward the Rational Exercise of Discretion*. 2nd ed. New York: Plenum Press, 1987.

Gould, Roger V. *Collision of Wills: How Ambiguity about Social Rank Breeds Conflict*. Chicago: University of Chicago Press, 2003.

Green, Laurie B. *Battling the Plantation Mentality: Memphis and the Black Freedom Struggle*. Chapel Hill: University of North Carolina Press, 2007.

Gritter, Elizabeth. *River of Hope: Black Politics and the Memphis Freedom Movement, 1865–1954*. Lexington: University Press of Kentucky, 2014.

Gross, Kali N. *Colored Amazons: Crime, Violence, and Black Women in the City of Brotherly Love, 1880–1910*. Durham, NC: Duke University Press, 2006.

Hackney, Sheldon. "Southern Violence." *American Historical Review* 74, no. 3 (February 1969): 906–25.

Hahn, Steven. *A Nation under Our Feet: Black Political Struggles in the Rural South from Slavery to the Great Migration*. Cambridge, MA: Belknap Press of Harvard University Press, 2003.

Hair, William Ivy. *Carnival of Fury: Robert Charles and the New Orleans Race Riot of 1900*. Baton Rouge: Louisiana State University Press, 1976.

Hale, Grace Elizabeth. *Making Whiteness: The Culture of Segregation in the South, 1890–1940*. New York: Pantheon Books, 1998.

Harries, Keith D. *Serious Violence: Patterns of Homicide and Assault in America*. Springfield, IL: Charles C. Thomas, 1990.

Harring, Sidney L. *Policing a Class Society: The Experience of American Cities, 1865–1915*. New Brunswick, NJ: Rutgers University Press, 1983.

Harris, Carl V. "Reforms in Government Control of Negroes in Birmingham, Alabama, 1890–1920." *Journal of Southern History* 38, no. 4 (November 1972): 567–600.

Harris, Fred, and Alan Curtis, eds. *Healing Our Divided Society: Investing in America Fifty Years after the Kerner Report*. Philadelphia: Temple University Press, 2018.

Hernandez, Kelly Lytle. *City of Inmates: Conquest, Rebellion, and the Rise of Human Caging in Los Angeles, 1771–1965.* Chapel Hill: University of North Carolina Press, 2017.

Hickey, Georgina. *Hope and Danger in the New South City: Working-Class Women and Urban Development in Atlanta, 1890–1940.* Athens: University of Georgia Press, 2003.

Hicks, Cheryl D. *Talk with You Like a Woman: African American Women, Justice, and Reform in New York, 1890–1935.* Chapel Hill: University of North Carolina Press, 2010.

Higginbotham, Evelyn Brooks. *Righteous Discontent: The Women's Movement in the Black Baptist Church, 1880–1920.* Cambridge, MA: Harvard University Press, 1993.

Hill, Karlos. "Black Vigilantism: The Rise and Decline of African American Lynch Mob Activity in the Mississippi and Arkansas Deltas, 1883–1923." *Journal of African American History* 95, no. 1 (Winter 2010): 26–43.

Hill, Shirley A. *Inequality and African-American Health: How Racial Disparities Create Sickness.* Bristol: Policy Press, 2016.

Hobbs, Tameka Bradley. *Democracy Abroad, Lynching at Home: Racial Violence in Florida.* Gainesville: University Press of Florida, 2015.

Hoffman, Frederick. *The Homicide Problem.* Newark, NJ: Prudential Press, 1925.

——. *Race Traits and Tendencies of the American Negro.* New York: American Economic Association, 1896.

Hofstadter, Richard. *The Age of Reform: From Bryan to F.D.R.* New York: Alfred A. Knopf, 1956.

Holt, Thomas. *Black over White: Negro Political Leadership in South Carolina during Reconstruction.* Urbana: University of Illinois Press, 1977.

Honey, Michael K. *Black Workers Remember: An Oral History of Segregation, Unionism, and the Freedom Struggle.* Berkeley: University of California Press, 1999.

——. *Going Down Jericho Road: The Memphis Strike, Martin Luther King's Last Campaign.* New York: W. W. Norton, 2008.

——. *Southern Labor and Black Civil Rights: Organizing Memphis Workers.* Urbana: University of Illinois Press, 1993.

Jackson, Kenneth T. *The Ku Klux Klan in the City, 1915–1930.* New York: Oxford University Press, 1967.

Jett, Brandon T. "'The Most Murderous Civilized City in the World': Patterns of Homicide in Jim Crow Memphis, 1917–1926." *Tennessee Historical Quarterly* (Summer 2015): 104–27.

Johnson, Charles S. *The Negro in American Civilization: A Study of Negro Life and Race Relations in the Light of Social Research.* New York: Henry Holt & Company, 1930.

———. *Patterns of Negro Segregation*. New York: Harper & Brothers, 1943.

———. *Shadow of the Plantation*. Chicago: University Press of Chicago, 1934.

Johnson, David R. *American Law Enforcement: A History*. Wheeling, IL: Forum Press, 1981.

———. *Policing the Urban Underworld: The Impact of Crime on the Development of the American Police, 1800–1887*. Philadelphia: Temple University Press, 1979.

Johnson, Marilynn S. *Street Justice: A History of Police Violence in New York City*. Boston: Beacon Press, 2003.

Johnson, Walter. *Soul by Soul: Life inside the Antebellum Slave Market*. Cambridge, MA: Harvard University Press, 1999.

Kelley, Robin D. G. *Hammer and Hoe: Alabama Communists during the Great Depression*. Chapel Hill: University of North Carolina Press, 1990.

———. *Race Rebels: Culture, Politics, and the Black Working Class*. New York: Free Press, 1994.

Kennedy, Randall. *Race, Crime, and the Law*. New York: Vintage Books, 1997.

Kolko, Gabriel. *The Triumph of Conservatism: A Reinterpretation of American History, 1900–1916*. New York: Macmillan, 1963.

Krist, Gary. *Empire of Sin: A Story of Sex, Jazz, Murder, and the Battle for Modern New Orleans*. New York: Crown Publishers, 2014.

Kyriakoudes, Louis M. *The Social Origins of the Urban South: Race, Gender, and Migration in Nashville and Middle Tennessee, 1890–1930*. Chapel Hill: University of North Carolina Press, 2003.

LaFree, Gary. *Losing Legitimacy: Street Crime and the Decline of Social Institutions in America*. Boulder, CO: Westview Press, 1998.

Lane, Roger. *Murder in America: A History*. Columbus: Ohio State University Press, 1997.

———. *Policing the City: Boston, 1822–1885*. Cambridge, MA: Harvard University Press, 1967.

———. *Roots of Violence in Black Philadelphia, 1860–1900*. Cambridge, MA: Harvard University Press, 1986.

Larsen, Lawrence H. *The Rise of the Urban South*. Lexington: University Press of Kentucky, 1985.

Lassiter, Matthew D., and Joseph Crespino, eds. *The Myth of Southern Exceptionalism*. New York: Oxford University Press, 2009.

Lauterbach, Preston. *Beale Street Dynasty: Sex, Song, and the Struggle for the Soul of Memphis*. New York: W. W. Norton, 2015.

Lee, Helen Shores, and Barbara S. Shores. *The Gentle Giant of Dynamite Hill: The Untold Story of Arthur Shores and His Family's Fight for Civil Rights*. Grand Rapids, MI: Zondervan, 2012.

LeFlouria, Talitha L. *Chained in Silence: Black Women and Convict Labor in the New South*. Chapel Hill: University of North Carolina Press, 2015.

Lichtenstein, Alex. *Twice the Work of Free Labor: The Political Economy of Convict Labor in the New South*. New York: Verso, 1996.

Litwack, Leon F. *Trouble in Mind: Black Southerners in the Age of Jim Crow*. New York: Vintage Books, 1998.

Locke, Alain, ed. *The New Negro: Voices of the Harlem Renaissance*. New York: Albert & Charles Boni, Inc., 1925.

Loftus, Elizabeth F. *Eye Witness Testimony*. Cambridge, MA: Harvard University Press, 1979.

Long, Alecia P. *The Great Southern Babylon: Sex, Race, and Respectability in New Orleans, 1865–1920*. Baton Rouge: Louisiana State University Press, 2004.

Lundsgaarde, Henry P. *Murder in Space City: A Cultural Analysis of Houston Homicide Patterns*. New York: Oxford University Press, 1977.

McGee, M. Clinton. *Criminal Procedure in Alabama*. Tuscaloosa: University of Alabama Press, 1954.

McGerr, Michael. *A Fierce Discontent: The Rise and Fall of the Progressive Movement in America, 1870–1920*. New York: Free Press, 2003.

McGuire, Danielle L. *At the Dark End of the Street: Black Women, Rape, and Resistance—a New History of the Civil Rights Movement from Rose Parks to the Rise of Black Power*. New York: Vintage Books, 2010.

McNeil, Genna Rae. *Groundwork: Charles Hamilton Houston and the Struggle for Civil Rights*. Philadelphia: University of Pennsylvania Press, 1983.

Melton, Gloria Brown. "Black in Memphis, Tennessee, 1920–1955: A Historical Study." PhD diss., Washington State University, 1982.

Meyer, Stephen Grant. *As Long as They Don't Move Next Door: Segregation and Racial Conflict in American Neighborhoods*. New York: Rowman & Littlefield, 2001.

Miller, Wilbur R. *Cops and Bobbies: Police Authority in New York and London, 1830–1870*. 2nd ed. Columbus: Ohio State University Press, 1999.

Mitrani, Sam. *The Rise of the Chicago Police Department: Class and Conflict, 1850–1894*. Urbana: University of Illinois Press, 2013.

Monkkonen, Eric H. *Murder in New York City*. Berkeley: University of California Press, 2001.

———. *Police in Urban America: 1860–1920*. Cambridge: Cambridge University Press, 1981.

Montell, William Lynwood. *Killings: Folk Justice in the Upper South*. Lexington: University Press of Kentucky, 1986.

Moore, Jacqueline M. *Booker T. Washington, W. E. B. DuBois, and the Struggle for Racial Uplift*. New York: Rowman & Littlefield, 2003.

Moore, Leonard N. *Black Rage in New Orleans: Police Brutality and African American Activism from World War II to Hurricane Katrina*. Baton Rouge: Louisiana State University Press, 2010.

Morris, Aldon D. *The Origins of the Civil Rights Movement: Black Communities Organizing for Change.* New York: Free Press, 1984.

Muhammad, Khalil Gibran. *The Condemnation of Blackness: Race, Crime, and the Making of Modern Urban America.* Cambridge, MA: Harvard University Press, 2010.

Myers, Frank, and Gennie Myers. *Memphis Police Department 1827–1975.* Marceline, MO: Walsworth, 1975.

Myrdal, Gunnar. *An American Dilemma: The Negro Problem and Modern Democracy.* New York: Harper & Brothers, 1944.

Nagin, Daniel S. "Deterrence in the Twenty-First Century." *Crime and Justice* 42, no. 1 (August 2013): 199–263.

New Orleans Police Department. *Fifty Years of Progress, 1900–1950.* New Orleans: Franklin Printing Company, 1950.

Niedermeier, Silvan. *The Color of the Third Degree: Racism, Police Torture, and Civil Rights in the American South, 1930–1955.* Translated by Paul Cohen. Chapel Hill: University of North Carolina Press, 2019.

Nunnelley, William A. *Bull Connor.* Tuscaloosa: University of Alabama Press, 1991.

Oakes, James. *Slavery and Freedom: An Interpretation of the Old South.* New York: Alfred A. Knopf, 1990.

Odoms-Young, Angela M., and Bruce A. Marino. "Examining the Impact of Structural Racism on Food Insecurity: Implications for Addressing Racial/Ethnic Disparities." *Family & Community Health* 41, no 2 (April/June 2018): S3-S6.

Oshinsky, David M. *Worse Than Slavery: Parchman Farm and the Ordeal of Jim Crow Justice.* New York: Free Press, 1997.

Payne, Charles M. *I've Got the Light of Freedom: The Organizing Tradition and the Mississippi Freedom Struggle.* Berkeley: University of California Press, 1995.

Pfeifer, Michael J. *Rough Justice: Lynching and American Society, 1874–1947.* Urbana: University of Illinois Press, 2004.

Pleck, Elizabeth. *Domestic Tyranny: The Making of American Social Policy against Family Violence from Colonial Times to the Present.* New York: Oxford University Press, 1987.

Potter, Claire Bond. *War on Crime: Bandits, G-Men, and the Politics of Mass Culture.* New Brunswick, NJ: Rutgers University Press, 1998.

Powdermaker, Hortense. *After Freedom: A Cultural Study in the Deep South.* New York: Atheneum, 1939; repr. Madison: University of Wisconsin Press, 1993.

Prince, K. Stephen. "Remembering Robert Charles: Violence and Memory in Jim Crow New Orleans." *Journal of Southern History* 83, no. 2 (May 2017): 297–328.

———. "The Trials of George Doyle: Race and Policing in Jim Crow New Orleans." In *Crime & Punishment in the Jim Crow South,* ed. Amy Louise Wood and Natalie J. Ring, 17–33. Urbana: University of Illinois Press, 2019.

Pruitt, Bernadette. *The Other Great Migration: The Movement of Rural African*

Americans to Houston, 1900–1941. College Station: Texas A&M University Press, 2013.

Rabinowitz, Howard N. "Conflicts between Blacks and Police in the Urban South, 1865–1900." *The Historian* 39, no. 1 (November 1976): 62–75.

———. *Race Relations in the Urban South, 1865–1900.* New York: Oxford University Press, 1978; repr. Urbana: University of Illinois Press, 1980.

Raper, Arthur F. *The Tragedy of Lynching.* Chapel Hill: University of North Carolina Press, 1933.

Rennison, Callie Marie. *Criminal Victimization 2000.* Washington, DC: U.S. Department of Justice, Office of Justice Programs, 2001.

Rice, Roger L. "Residential Segregation by Law, 1910–1917." *Journal of Southern History* 34, no. 2 (May 1968): 179–99.

Richardson, James F. *The New York Police: Colonial Times to 1901.* New York: Oxford University Press, 1970.

Ritterhouse, Jennifer. *Growing Up Jim Crow: How Black and White Southern Children Learned Race.* Chapel Hill: University of North Carolina Press, 2006.

Rodgers, Daniel T. *Atlantic Crossings: Social Politics in a Progressive Age.* Cambridge, MA: Belknap Press of Harvard University Press, 1998.

Rosenberg, Daniel. *New Orleans Dockworkers: Race, Labor, and Unionism, 1892–1923.* Albany: State University of New York Press, 1988.

Roth, Randolph. *American Homicide.* Cambridge, MA: Harvard University Press, 2009.

Rousey, Dennis C. *Policing the Southern City: New Orleans, 1805–1889.* Baton Rouge: Louisiana State University Press, 1996.

Royster, Jacqueline Jones, ed. *Southern Horrors and Other Writings: The Anti-Lynching Campaign of Ida B. Wells, 1892–1900.* New York: Bedford/St. Martin's, 1997.

Sampson, Robert J. *Great American City: Chicago and the Enduring Neighborhood Effect.* Chicago: University of Chicago Press, 2012.

Sampson, Robert J., and Dawn Jeglum Bartusch. "Legal Cynicism and (Subcultural?) Tolerance of Deviance: The Neighborhood Context of Racial Differences." *Law and Society Review* 32, no. 4 (1998): 777–804.

Schweninger, Loren. *Black Property Owners in the South, 1790–1915.* Urbana: University of Illinois Press, 1990.

Scott, James C. *Weapons of the Weak: Everyday Forms of Peasant Resistance and Domination and the Arts of Resistance.* New Haven, CT: Yale University Press, 1985.

Sigafoos, Robert A. *Cotton Row to Beale Street: A Business History of Memphis.* Memphis, TN: Memphis State University Press, 1979.

Skogan, Wesley G. "Dimensions of the Dark Figure of Unreported Crime." *Crime and Delinquency* 23, no. 1 (January 1977): 41–50.

Snow, Robert L. *Murder 101: Homicide and Its Investigation.* Westport, CT: Praeger, 2005.

Spain, Daphne. "Race Relations and Residential Segregation in New Orleans: Two Centuries of Paradox." *Annals of the American Academy of Political and Social Science* 441 (January 1979): 82–96.

Spitzer, Robert J. *Guns across America: Reconciling Gun Rules and Rights.* New York: Oxford University Press, 2015.

Stamp, Kenneth M. *The Peculiar Institution: Slavery in the Ante-Bellum South.* New York: Alfred A. Knopf, 1956.

Steinberg, Allen. *The Transformation of Criminal Justice: Philadelphia, 1800–1880.* Chapel Hill: University of North Carolina Press, 1989.

Sugrue, Thomas J. *Sweet Land of Liberty: The Forgotten Struggle for Civil Rights in the North.* New York: Random House, 2008.

Sullivan, Patricia. *Lift Every Voice: The NAACP and the Making of the Civil Rights Movement.* New York: New Press, 2009.

Summers, Martin. *Manliness and Its Discontents: The Black Middle Class and the Transformation of Masculinity, 1900–1930.* Chapel Hill: University of North Carolina Press, 2004.

Swanson, Charles R., Neil C. Chamelin, Leonard Territo, and Robert W. Taylor. *Criminal Investigation.* 10th ed. New York: McGraw-Hill, 2009.

Thomas, Robert D., and Richard W. Murray. *Progrowth Politics: Change and Governance in Houston.* Berkeley: University of California Press, 1991.

Tindall, George Brown. *The Emergence of the New South, 1913–1945.* Baton Rouge: Louisiana State University Press, 1967.

Tolnay, Stewart E., and E. M. Beck. *A Festival of Violence: An Analysis of Southern Lynchings, 1882–1930.* Urbana: University of Illinois Press, 1995.

Tyler, Tom R. "Enhancing Police Legitimacy." *Annals of the American Academy of Political and Social Science* 593 (May 2004): 84–99.

———. *Why People Obey the Law.* New Haven, CT: Yale University Press, 1990.

Utz, Karen R. *Sloss Furnaces.* Mount Pleasant, SC: Arcadia, 2009.

Vandal, Gilles. *Rethinking Southern Violence: Homicides in Post–Civil War Louisiana, 1866–1884.* Columbus: Ohio State University Press, 2000.

Vandiver, Margaret. *Lethal Punishment: Lynchings and Legal Executions in the South.* New Brunswick, NJ: Rutgers University Press, 2006.

Vollmer, August. *The Police and Modern Society.* Berkeley: University of California Press, 1936.

Wadman, Robert C., and William Thomas Allison. *To Protect and to Serve: A History of Police in America.* Upper Saddle River, NJ: Pearson Prentice Hall, 2004.

Waldrep, Christopher. *African Americans Confront Lynching: Strategies of Resistance from the Civil War to the Civil Rights Era.* New York: Rowman & Littlefield, 2009.

———. *Jury Discrimination: The Supreme Court, Public Opinion, and a Grassroots Fight for Racial Equality in Mississippi*. Athens: University of Georgia Press, 2010.

———. *Roots of Disorder: Race and Criminal Justice in the American South, 1817–1880*. Urbana: University of Illinois Press, 1998.

Walker, Samuel. *A Critical History of Police Reform: The Emergence of Professionalism*. Lexington, MA: Lexington Books, 1977.

———. *Popular Justice: A History of American Criminal Justice*. 2nd ed. New York: Oxford University Press, 1998.

Watson, Dwight D. *A Change Did Come: Race and the Houston Police Department, 1930–1990*. College Station: Texas A&M University Press, 2005.

———. "In the Name of Decency and Progress: The Response of Houston's Civic Leaders to the Lynching of Robert Powell in 1928." *Houston Review* 1, no. 2 (Spring 2013): 26–30.

Wiebe, Robert H. *The Search for Order, 1877–1920*. New York: Hill & Wang, 1967.

Wickersham Commission, U.S. *Report on Lawlessness in Law Enforcement*. Washington, DC: U.S. Government Printing Office, 1931.

Williams, Kidada E. "Resolving the Paradox of Our Lynching Fixation: Reconsidering Racialized Violence in the American South after Slavery." In *Lynching Reconsidered: New Perspectives in the Study of Mob Violence*, ed. William D. Carrigan, 97–124. New York: Routledge, 2008.

———. *They Left Great Marks on Me: African American Testimonies of Racial Violence from Emancipation to World War I*. New York: New York University Press, 2012.

Williamson, Joel. *The Crucible of Race: Black-White Relations in the American South since Emancipation*. New York: Oxford University Press, 1984.

———. *A Rage for Order: Black-White Relations in the American South since Emancipation*. New York: Oxford University Press, 1986.

Wilson, William Julius. *The Truly Disadvantaged: The Inner City, the Underclass, and Public Policy*. 2nd ed. Chicago: University of Chicago Press, 2012.

Wolfgang, Marvin E. *Patterns in Criminal Homicide*. Philadelphia: University of Pennsylvania Press, 1958.

Wood, Amy L. *Lynching and Spectacle: Witnessing Racial Violence in America, 1890–1940*. Chapel Hill: University of North Carolina Press, 2011.

Woodruff, Nan Elizabeth. *American Congo: The African American Freedom Struggle in the Delta*. Chapel Hill: University of North Carolina Press, 2003.

Woodward, C. Vann. *Origins of the New South, 1877–1913*. Baton Rouge: Louisiana State University Press, 1951.

———. *The Strange Career of Jim Crow*. New York: Oxford University Press, 1955.

Work, Monroe N. "Crime among the Negroes of Chicago: A Social Study." *American Journal of Sociology* 6, no. 2 (September 1900): 224–37.

————. "Negro Criminality in the South." *Annals of the American Academy of Political and Social Sciences* 49 (September 1913): 74–80.

Wright, George C. *Racial Violence in Kentucky, 1865–1940: Lynchings, Mob Rule, and "Legal Lynchings."* Baton Rouge: Louisiana State University Press, 1990.

Wright, Sharon D. *Race, Power, and Political Emergence in Memphis.* New York: Garland, 2000.

Wyatt-Brown, Bertram. *Southern Honor: Ethics and Behavior in the Old South.* New York: Oxford University Press, 1982.

Zhao, Jihong "Solomon," Matthew Scheider, and Quint Thurman. "The Effect of Police Presence on Public Fear Reduction and Satisfaction: A Review of the Literature." *Justice Professional* 15, no. 3 (2002): 273–99.

INDEX

African Americans: as victims of police violence, 1–2, 15–16, 18, 35, 37–45, 64–70, 95, 98–101, 114, 128; attempts to reform police, 3, 62–73, 161; calls for black jurors, 60–61; calls for black police officers, 62, 70–73; calls to defund or abolish police, 168; criminal justice system used to control, 3, 18, 33–46, 138; critique of criminal justice system, 4, 56–62; critique of policing, 4, 63–73; distrust of police, 70, 94, 120, 128 129–30, 133, 151; embrace of rule of law by, 104, 107–8, 111–12, 133 138; gender dynamics in relationships between, 157; interactions with police during assault investigations, 132–58; interactions with police during homicide investigations, 74–102; interactions with police during stolen-property investigations, 103–31; middle class, 4, 14, 52–53, 74, 76, 111–12; middle-class responses to crime, 47–73; migration to cities by, 12–14, 18, 52; and "politics of respectability," 55; reliance on self-help by, 74, 75, 80, 94, 100 104, 107, 109–10, 142, 150, 160–61, 165, 166; using police to regulate community norms, 133–34, 147–49; using police in intimate disputes, 149–58; working-class, 5, 43, 53, 55–56, 67, 73, 74, 80, 111–12, 150, 157. *See also* assaults; Birmingham, Alabama; Birmingham Police Department (BPD); crime; criminal justice system; fair-administration advocates; homicides; Jefferson County, Alabama; Jim Crow; Memphis, Tennessee; Memphis Police Department (MPD); National Association for the Advancement of Colored People (NAACP); New Orleans, Louisiana; New Orleans Police Department (NOPD); police; police brutality

Alexander, Michelle, 8

assaults, 6, 8, 13, 35, 37, 41, 70, 90, 131, 158, 161, 165; African Americans reporting, 138–41; African Americans' interactions with police after, 133, 136–47; African American reports of, 138–39; recorded witnesses to, 142; stemming from intimate-partner disputes, 133, 149–58; stemming from minor disputes, 133–36, 147–49

Birmingham, Alabama, 7, 9, 17, 19, 20, 22, 23, 25, 29, 30, 35, 42, 43, 44, 47, 55, 56, 58, 64, 66, 67, 68, 69, 71, 72, 76, 83, 93, 100, 103, 106, 108, 109, 114, 115, 124, 132, 134, 135, 141, 148, 151, 152, 155, 156, 163, 211; assault trends in, 134–38, 141–42, 147–49; black middle class in, 52–53; crime in, 19; economic growth in, 10–11; homicides in, 19–20, 39, 76, 86; population growth in, 12–13; segregation in, 12, 22, 88; stolen-property complaints in, 106. *See also* Birmingham Police Department (BPD); Jefferson County, Alabama

Birmingham News, 35

Birmingham Police Department (BPD), 43, 66, 68, 79, 92, 93, 108, 115, 124, 132, 139, 140, 142, 143, 144, 145, 148, 149, 153, 155; abuse of African Americans, 41; African American critiques of, 66–70; development of, 26–33; harassment of African Americans, 43–44; investigation of African American assaults by, 132–58; killing of African Americans, 38–40;

CPSIA information can be obtained
at www.ICGtesting.com
Printed in the USA
LVHW090145120222
710916LV00002B/39